THE INTERNATIONAL DESIGN YEARBOOK

THE INTERNATIONAL DESIGN YEARBOOK

1990 / 91

EDITOR
MARIO BELLINI

GENERAL EDITOR
NONIE NIESEWAND

THAMES AND HUDSON

This book was produced by **John
Calmann and King Ltd**, London
Based on an original idea by
Stuart Durant

Designed by Peter Bridgewater
Typeset by CST (Hove) Ltd
Origination by Toppan, Singapore
Printed in Italy

Mario Bellini would like to thank the
architect Marco Romanelli; Elena Bellini,
and Nonie Niesewand for her
enthusiasm, energy and professional
patience while supporting the very hard
selection work.

The publishers and both editors would
like to thank the designers and
manufacturers who submitted work for
inclusion in this book; Peter and Junko
Popham for their help in collecting
Japanese contributions; Kenneth M. Butti
in Tokyo; Patricia Carruthers, and the
following photographers and copyright
holders for use of their material:
ACA/Homer 4.26;
Gil Alkin 5.47;
Aurelio Amendola 1.46;
Studio Angerer 2.7;
Satoshi Asakawa 1.3, 5.65;
Claudio Baini 4.4;
Aldo Ballo 1.83, 113, 2.16;
Barzaghi 2.41;
G. Basilico 1.4;
Mogens Bech 5.42;
Bella & Ruggeri 2.18;
Bitetto & Chimenti 1.71, 2.8, 10;
Rory Carnegie 2.22;
Mario Carrieri 1.42, 146;
Lluis Casals 2.11, 29;
Vincenzo Castella 1.5;
Celnick Studios 1.32;
Coccoli 2.28;
David Cripps 3.28, 29, 30;
Jeff Curtus 5.24;
Richard Davies 1.47;
Giorgio De Vecchi 5.35, 55, 64;
Hans Döring 1.103;
Yves Duronsoy 4.24;
Rick English 5.25;
Fredrik Eriksson 2.25;
Facchinetti 2.50;
Ferrari 1.92;
Studio Forma 3 1.125;
Mitsumasa Fujizuka 1.56;
Michael Ganss 5.32;
Nicolas Georghiou 5.23, 43;
Nick Georgio 5.21;
Ken Gilliam 1.58;
Decio Grassi 1.107;
Jochen Grün 3.50;
Léon Gulikers 3.3, 5;
Alfred Hablübel 1.145;
Hablützel 2.26;
Poul Henriksen 4.20, 21, 5.27;
Hiroyuki Hirai 1.127, 3.51;
Kari Holopainen 1.41;
Impuls 1.10, 18, 72;
Tim Imrie 1.82, 4.62;
Thomas Jeansson 3.15;
Björn Keller 4.32;
Miles Keller 5.40;
Kazayoki Kido 5.66;
Margherita Krischanitz 1.121;
Antti Kylänpää 3.16;
Jennifer Lee 3.18, 19;
Bernie Leroux 1.33;
John Lonczak 5.37;
Ross Lovegrove 5.53;
John McCarthy 4.29;
Guy Manguin 4.14, 16;
Cesare Medri 4.27;
Hasaru Mera 3.32-35, 5.49;
Masaaki Miyazawa 1.38;
Mike Murless 1.140;
T. Nacasa & Partners 1.67, 5.12;
Josh Nefsky 4.18;
W.V. Nueten 2.38;
Nicolas Peron 5.59;
Genunzio Cesare Pordenone 1.28;
Renai 1.9;
Peter Rose 5.26, 31, 36;
Rowenta Fotostudio 5.39;
Benvenuto Saba 3.11, 14, 37, 40;
Santi Caleca 3.26;
Phil Sayer 1.59;
Schnakenburg 1.55;
Schnackenburg & Brahl 1.1;
Heini Schneebli 5.33;
Brian Seaward 3.36, 38, 39;
Roberto Sellitto 1.15, 66, 79, 126;
Kishin Shinoyama 1.52, 53;
Luciano Soave 1.131;
Vic Stannard 3.20;
Keiichi Tahara 4.3, 5;
Yoshio Takase 1.6, 2.6, 5.3;
Frank Thurston 1.172;
Emilio Tremolada 1.51, 87, 88, 150-152,
3.4, 8, 9;
Masahiko Uchiyama 5.11;
Tom Vack 1.96, 3.13, 46;
Tom Vack/Corinne Pfister 1.116,
2.48, 49;
Raven T.C. Warman
2.3-5;
Lynn Werner 1.23;
Heiner Wessel 1.16;
Bill Whitehurst 4.15, 17;
Simon Yan 5.38;
Mizukoshi Yoshimasa 3.52;
Tetsuo Yuasa 1.37;
Miro Zagnoli 1.2;
Andrea Zani 2.37;
Gerald Zugmann 1.89.

CONTENTS

FOREWORD

For over thirty years I have written and argued against the jargonistic abuse of the word "design", against its use as a euphemism for a hypothetical, specialist, autonomous art, supposedly formed, during modernism, as a consequence of the industrial revolution. Now, a trifle paradoxically, here I am engaged in selecting from many thousands of illustrations some five hundred or so to represent prototypes, products and works for this sixth international "design" yearbook.

Mario Bellini

Fortunately, these yearbooks do not pose particular problems of terminology or discipline. With British pragmatism, the editors have always gathered (under the tolerant and slightly leaky umbrella of "design") a balanced mix of furniture, lighting, tableware and textiles, with a small group of industrial products, all limited to domestic use. Furthermore, despite the different kinds of commitment from the various Guest Editors and their diverse personal viewpoints, at first glance the result is surprisingly homogeneous. The books therefore constitute an extraordinary document of comparison and knowledge of their respective periods and of the complex trends of continuity, evolution, decline and innovation usually seen only over a long period of time.

The five categories in this book wisely ignore any concern about the existence and nature of "design" itself, and therefore root themselves in the domestic scene, in the dimension of home living. Here, they study and interpret the objects' forms, independent of any improbable and abstract methodological unity, and any classification by type or production process. This may be interpreted as an implicit and healthy refusal to acknowledge design as an autonomous art, specifically and historically connoted. But I believe it is of interest – at least in the context of this Foreword – to analyse more critically the disquieting questions raised by this premise, even if we arrive at the same conclusion. This applies even if it is still the banner (or perhaps the limp flag) of many schools, associations, congresses and confused avowals of faith. These disturbing but illuminating questions concern the relationship and conflict between design and industrial design, craftsmanship and industry, design as an art and the art of design, the design of furniture and the design of machines, and between decoration and production.

Four years ago, when I became the editor of *Domus*, I wrote my first editorial in which – encouraged by a long and wide experience as a designer and an architect and guided by an intuition of which I am ever more convinced – I placed in a non-academic perspective those themes which, since its foundation, have always been the difficult and intriguing components of that glorious publication: "The house of man – that is, architecture and more than just architecture alone

— is encompassed in this risky subtitle of that early postwar *Domus* (edited by Ernesto Rogers in 1946). This will be the unifying dimension of the new review. Gone is the naive hypothesis that industrial design will overtake architecture. Our objective will be to combine furniture design with the culture of interiors and to return interior design to its architectural context. We will try to show industrial design as part of the materialistic culture of which it is the expression, in the context of the environmental and anthropological scheme to which it belongs, just as architecture belongs in the context of the city or the area where it was born and in which it breathes..."

I must confess that it has not been easy, and sometimes even embarrassing, to follow up those words with selections and facts. Nevertheless, they have reinforced my obsessive and continual questioning of the crucial relationship between architecture, furniture, machines, art, technology, tradition, the modern and the contemporary.

In the effort to make objects suitable for the manufacturing processes, industrial design is still liable to lose contact with its main reference point. This is the place of living, the central point around which the culture of the inhabitant is expressed and measured by his furnishings, objects and machines. In its turn, the domestic product, because of its tendency to isolation, risks mistaking the construction of the place for the design of a myth. In other words, it betrays its purpose, being incapable of evaluating and meeting the inevitable challenges of the industrial era, a civilization perhaps still barbaric but which exudes an irreversible vitality.

The industrial revolution began only two centuries ago and is still in progress, although we ought already to consider ourselves to be in the post-industrial era. In the field of architecture and design, the so-called Modern Movement has been only a partial earthquake, the recording of an initial tremor, a still hopeful and ambitious reaction to that revolution. But it was of great poetic value, producing mainly linguistic experiments and metaphorical contributions of the highest order.

In fact, industrial technologies, at least in architecture and furniture, are not only not yet fully developed, but have not yet shown their superiority. Frequently, they are an obvious hindrance, and even foreign to the consolidated semantic systems of our culture of home living. Technologico-functional considerations by themselves have proved to be insufficient to support an effective and meaningful design for interiors and furniture. This is substantially true also of machines, despite the vast differences which distinguish them from pieces of furniture.

Machines have a short history and often often shaken by continual technological evolutions and revolutions. Their more ephemeral image is often liable to be juxtaposed with their functional value. Furniture, on the other hand, and with it tools and non-mechanical equipment, has a thousand-year-old history. Its image, though subject to continual stylistic revision, cannot be ambiguously split into mechanism and exterior form, and is therefore much more

MARIO BELLINI
Imago office chair for Vitra, 1984

MARIO BELLINI
Cupola coffee service for Rosenthal, 1987

sharply defined and proven. It is profoundly connected with semantic values that have left their traces in it – values of the sacred, of body shape, of rites and meanings bound up with function.

It is here that one can recognize the ineluctable difference of the machine – the "mechanism" as original sin, and the "casing" as the pathetic mask of an industrial civilization which does not yet appear to have found its own authentic form of expression. Only old tools, and furniture in general, have the privilege of integrity, of being entirely and solely that which can be seen, touched and understood.

Think how simple and even commonplace is the design of a whisking machine or a household appliance – by this I mean the external casing.

This popular student exercise can be compared with the design of cutlery or of chairs, which is so direct, so ancient and so difficult – authentic *pièces de résistance* reserved for the great masters of design.

I myself have always liked to think that the most difficult thing in the world to design is the chair. In fact, we can say that the chair has descended from another chair, and another chair before that . . . from a slow process of definition through time, of infinite experiences of living and of building. The chair predates even the cultural choice of sitting above, rather than on, the level of the ground, or on one's heels. But no designer invented "the chair", just as no architect invented "the house".

Machines, furnishings and buildings belong to design groups which originated in remote eras, each far apart from the other, whether thousands or hundreds of years, or just decades, ago. They evolve at different speeds – cars have changed more in the last fifty years than houses have in the last two thousand. This produces goods which differ greatly in durability and usefulness. It is no coincidence that there are no major industrial manufacturers of furniture comparable to those of cars, and yet there is no real technological reason why there should not be, except for a few thousand years of history. If the needs of the motorist can be satisfied with a few models divided according to class, speed, capacity, prestige, cost, etc., the needs of the home dweller are too complex. They defy any classification, following laws and criteria of a different dimension. Against this mighty barrier, the self-assured illusions of standardization and mass production have been shattered. The mass-produced item has conquered the office, and attacked the kitchen, but left the bedroom and the sitting room undefiled.

As travellers, we first sacrificed the fascination of the old carriages, and then the vintage cars, forfeiting plush materials, décor and typologies in order to reap the advantages of price, popularity and performance brought by extreme industrialization. But as home dwellers we have put up a stiffer resistance. We have not been so ready to renounce the pleasures of fine, natural and traditional

MARIO BELLINI
Le Bambole armchair for
B & B, 1972

MARIO BELLINI
Area lamps for Artemide,
1974

materials. We have not given up the infinite variety of designs and decoration. We have remained relatively indifferent to the temptations of new performance levels and to the logic of "progress" in general.

The recent history of modern furniture, which began less than a hundred years ago, ought to have signalled an irreversible turning-point, the expression of an age of rapid transformation under the impetus of mass production and mass culture. But the myth of giving form to the industrial product dissolved before mass production could have any decisive or lasting effect on furniture design. In this respect, the metaphorical theories advanced by the heroic avant gardes of the Twenties and Thirties were never developed or verified. Contrary to the principles which generated them, they have been reabsorbed into the mainstream of history and have become cult objects or models that can be reproduced regardless of their historical and technical roots – the significant expression of the style of their time, the "modern style".

In pre-industrial times "knowledge", and in this case the knowledge of how to create and to build, was passed down by a continuity of tradition, nourished and renewed by the unstoppable flow and corroboration of experience. The Modern Movement suddenly interrupted all this by dogmatically presuming to establish a new idiom, severing links with tradition and theorizing on new technologies which did not meet the industrial reality. But it also had visions of a new culture of living, unmatched by a correspondingly new society, and of a new city which was abstract compared to its organic growth capacities. Thus it dragged architects and builders into a hazardous, though exhilarating, leap into the dark.

The theory and practice of architecture and interior design still suffer from that wrench right up to this day. The separation of the organic correspondence between a common syntax and reciprocal, proven methods of construction and production has left the architect and designer to stand alone against the undefined and independent systems of all possible languages and techniques. Perhaps this lack of what would in any case still be a very difficult beginning of a decisive industrial breakthrough in the architectural and "domestic" scene is actually responsible for the extraordinary vitality of architects and designers today. While it explains the frequent loss of quality and reliability, it prolongs the expectation of infinite possibilities.

Bramante and Borromini never designed any chairs, and did not feel the need to do so. A host of craftsmen-creators continued to supply grand houses and palaces with the right chairs, Renaissance or Baroque, according to the requirements of the time. This lasted until less than a hundred years ago, when the architects felt they could no longer count on the craftsmen class which was weakened and disoriented. The architects themselves, with their new ideas, together with the advent of new industries, had contributed to this problem, but they then decided almost unanimously to deal with the matter directly themselves.

MARIO BELLINI
Break dining chair for Cassina, 1976

Since then, nearly every single architect of note has continued to design "his" chairs, lavishing on this activity the same talent he would dedicate to his architecture, and in some cases attaining extraordinary results destined to bear witness to an epoch. But the scarcity of such successes, compared with the relatively larger number of major architectural achievements by any one architect, reveals the mounting difficulty encountered in this practice, especially since decoration has offered less of a pretext for variations or linguistic digressions.

The limits, liabilities and values of aesthetics such as those of Ungers, Botta, Meier, Venturi and Rossi are today a little more understandable, perhaps thanks to the chairs which, generously, they have begun to design again. Architects have turned their attention once more to this formidably daunting art, taking on a challenging task that in the past has brought more than one master to his knees, and throwing into crisis the optimistic prospect of self-sufficiency for industrial design. Suffice it to say that whereas for centuries it has been considered normal to base the teaching of architecture partially on its history, design schools (including, alas, the architectural schools from which the best furniture designers have come) have not generally felt the need to teach the extremely rich history of furniture. This unjustifiable sense of ideological superiority (or should it be inferiority?) has led to a notable impoverishment of the design panorama in this sector.

MARIO BELLINI
ET 111 electronic
typewriter for Olivetti, 1983

The society we live in must be very disturbed if there are still producers of "real" chairs – made to be used, to sit on – who may be unaware of the irreversible transformation that has succeeded the extinction of a thousand-year-old craft tradition. They passively continue with their products, ignoring the crucial contribution made by a constant design analysis. And more and more designers, maybe unconsciously, are driven by the need to atone, and go on hyper-designing "unreal" chairs with the complicity of manufacturers who are prepared to pay the tribute of a few pieces, lavishly got up, which have no logic of use or of manufacture. This is a disturbed society, mirrored in an industrial culture at times coarse and aggressive, often cynical and fragmentary.

MARIO BELLINI
Divisumma 18 electronic
calculator for Olivetti,
1972

I have already affirmed that, to all effects, "design" can be a form of art in the sense that, like architecture, it is at its best the profound testimony of a civilization. But between a chair by Le Corbusier and a chair by Oldenburg there is a fundamental difference. The chair by Oldenburg is a sculpture that represents a chair; the chair by Le Corbusier *is* a chair, and to cease to be one it would have to be signed by Duchamp and put on a pedestal like the celebrated Bottle-rack.

Naturally, there is nothing to prevent someone from sitting on a sculpture, or a designer playing the artist from having a chair-work put into "production". To try to establish frontiers as to what is or is not art can be risky, but it is even more risky to try to extend "resistance to purpose" (as in the design of a chair, for example) beyond breaking point. This would precipitate us into a waste land of "linguistic research" or autobiographical rhetoric.

In an era when already too much is said about "design" and there is too much nonchalant toying with such an equivocal term, it is still worth remembering that it has no meaning if it is isolated from its natural context, the wide-ranging culture of making, manufacturing, using and living. (Recently, an interviewer asked me how one distinguished between a designer coffee-pot and a normal one.) Far from representing a discipline, design cannot even aspire to represent the style of our times; to do so, it would sadly have to be reduced to just one of many possible styles (as indeed is suggested by the revealing question about the coffee-pot).

It would be interesting to understand what drives designers, manufacturers and others to indulge in these sterile dissipations. Often modest, they mortify both art and technology without enriching our undoubted desire to dream and to fantasize. One suspects they just conceal boredom, cynicism and contempt: boredom with the lengthy task entailed in tenacious and scrupulous research; cynicism about our creative potential which can be enriched by today's technologies, and contempt for the intelligence of all of us, consumers and home dwellers.

Where furniture is concerned (but this is also true of household goods, utensils and the new field of machines), the conversion from handcraft to industrial techniques brought important, traumatic changes. The creator-builder, who for centuries built up a craft knowledge with which he nourished the incessant changes in style and typology (and vice versa), began to die out. Construction techniques became manufacturing techniques and a new character, the industrial designer, came to the fore. He was not allowed to practise the new techniques, which became increasingly foreign to him, but from this time on he was expected to control them through the meta-technical aspects of the project. He had to work out a new technique, that of "design", because he needed to find a way in which he could be creative while being separated from the making process.

Freed from the slavery of traditional technique, but also from the fertile dialectic clash sustained with it for thousands of years, the architect and the designer see their creative principles put to a severe test. They have already been shaken by technicalist and functionalist misunderstandings with which in vain they attempted to shirk the responsibility of a language which, now more than ever, architects, designers and artists are called upon to assume. It must be remembered that the strengthening of new production, or rather reproduction, techniques has not necessarily widened the creative horizons. One need only

MARIO BELLINI
Robot rotating aerial for Brionvega, 1980

MARIO BELLINI
Mindeca thermos flask for Zojirushi, 1983

compare the infinite wealth of typologies and idiomatic variations of pre-industrial chairs with the lean, at times dull, panorama of post-craft "modern". Even in some of its better examples, such as the tubular metal models of the Twenties, it had to make do with metaphoric depictions of a new technique which it did not yet in reality possess, or had only imagined. And then it had to construct them in a substantially artisan way. This is without considering the disorientation provoked by the reverse possibility – organizing on an industrial scale the production of models originally conceived in artisan conditions – which has proved to be increasingly and perversely practicable.

MARIO BELLINI
ETP 55 electronic typewriter for Olivetti, 1985-6

The industrial revolution was also a great market revolution. It substantially upset the delicate balance that had existed between individuals and furnishings, household goods, implements, even homes and cities, by abruptly inundating our environment with machines and electronic equipment. A new concept of goods and forced consumerism overturned the old structure of buying as need dictated. But on top of all this the industrial revolution was also a large-scale revolution in design, not only because design had to be brought to machines and a form had to be given to electronic phantoms, but above all because since then, a time when designing was still considered creating, the conditions surrounding the design of products with an ancient history and a tradition have completely changed.

The rapid modernization of production methods has interrupted the continuity between making and thinking. The artisan-creator had to give way to the new class of pure designers, who found themselves confronted by a blank sheet of paper, just as their older colleagues the architects did some thousands of years ago when they took over from the builders of huts. They discovered, as many have yet to do, that it is more difficult to take the place of a jeweller, a potter, a cabinet-maker, an upholsterer or a tailor (crafts which have not yet quite vanished) than it is to give form and decoration (and unfortunately only rarely any meaning) to machines, which are the newcomers of our industrial civilization. This is the drama of the modern designer: liberated from the necessity of producing, he can feel like God. But in the depths of his reasoning, when deprived of the light and the experience of actually making, he can generate monsters.

MARIO BELLINI
Cab chair for Cassina, 1976

His pencil – swifter and more powerful than chisel, saw, pickaxe, graver's tool, scissors, needle, trowel or any machine – can design anything, and thus transform the world. This is a privilege whose origins are to be found with the architects of the Pharaohs. But progressive isolation, together with the strengthening of the architect's and the designer's faculties in the industrial era, has enormously increased the responsibilities. It is not by chance that the architects (the oldest skilled "modern" designers of history) bore the brunt of the industrial revolution. They answered the call a century ago and sustain the weight of it still, as is shown by the recent history of design, and particularly the important Italian chapter. If this has helped to mask or subdue the ideological failure of the modern avant garde, whose generous illusions have faded in little more than two generations, it is not an excuse to neglect or underrate the importance of unresolved questions and lingering open wounds.

The critical debate and the challenge posed to architecture, design and perhaps to art more generally, reside in the gap between contemporaneity and modernity, a gap which, though in some cases still marginal, may in others appear almost unbridgeable. The term "contemporary", without necessarily implying value judgements, refers to the purely chronological congruence of an event or work with its time, and hence to an intrinsically transitory condition, subject to continual change. On the other hand, "modern", or rather the idea of modern, while at times mistaken for contemporary, bears an indelible historical imprint and an ideological force than can be traced to that imprint. It is a concept which can be evaluated according to a given frame of reference, but which is also dynamic and susceptible to reincarnations in the present time.

Now that historical modern has ceased to be a contemporary phenomenon, it is evident that the sole fact of being contemporary, without any artistic or design objective and unsupported by any parallel ideological or moral tension, is insufficient to guarantee works which, besides belonging to their period, must also have significance and be able to represent it. And if our times can still be defined as modern, our works must also, in a sense, be modern works.

Some architects and designers continue uncritically and scrupulously reproducing "modern architecture and design" in order to feel contemporary. For the same reason others have felt the need to oppose it, taking refuge in creating alternative languages and theories. Still others question themselves, even through their work, on how to be and remain modern and not just contemporary. It is impossible to continue innocently in the historical modern experience, which is irremediably dated, though surely not yet exhausted.

So, one will have to keep using the modern when grappling with contemporary challenges, even in its new form as a dialectical balance between the need for, and the denial of, its roots and a plausible ideological tension. It is a modern now far removed from its ingenuous avant-garde beginnings. Nevertheless, it has become an inevitable and irreversible dimension, indispensable to understanding and designing in these unruly and uncertain times.

ABBREVIATIONS
Apart from H (height),
L (length), W (width),
D (depth) and
Di (diameter), the
following abbreviations
are used in the book:
ABS acrylo-butyl styrene
LCD liquid crystal display
MDF medium-density
fibreboard

MARIO BELLINI
Forum table for Vitra,
1986

1 · FURNITURE

Machine-age mass production this century has brought anonymity, but in these uncertain times that is no blueprint for living. Mario Bellini believes that mere style becomes a melancholy reduction of the true meaning of design within its natural context, that of production, manufacture and use. When a chair can be anything from a giant cube by Oswald Mathias Ungers to paper roses floating in Perspex by Shiro Kuramata it is clear we are at the point where art meets furniture, and furniture is art.

Where does that place industry? As Europe gets ready for the open market of 1992 and Japan sets up licensed production agencies in the world's major cities, a new industrial age is dawning. Regionalism is over, as design crosses every cultural border. With this new situation comes the new consumer. Environmentally conscious, office-orientated and interested in art, buyers of the Nineties want small runs of diverse pieces, often signed and numbered. Big manufacturers such as Alias, Zanotta and Vitra have been quick to respond, producing limited editions of artists' furniture alongside contract collections.

Design colleges today teach students to do everything. At the Royal College of Art Roger Bateman learned to carve, sculpt, forge, cast in bronze and panel beat. At the world's first-ever chair museum, the Vitra Museum which opened in 1989 near Basel, this evolution from craft to industry and back again is traced by exhibits which begin with the 1850 Thonet bentwood chair, to symbolize the end of the artisan era, and end with Kuramata's *Miss Blanche*, graphically underscoring the end of populism and machine-age mass production.

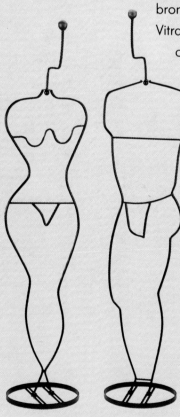

"Every chair, and especially every beautiful chair, is expected to be comfortable," says Bellini. He applies old-fashioned words such as comfort, durability, lightness, character, appropriateness and representativeness to make his selection shown here. Character, in particular, yields an appreciation of the human body and its sensuousness and also wit, as shown in Johanssen's clothes hangers for !kea.

Fashion fads do not really affect furniture buyers, since the industry cannot change tooling to produce temporary frivolities. Looks have to last.

1

NANNA DITZEL
Bench for Two
MAPLE FRAME, MAPLE-
VENEERED PLYWOOD SEAT
AND BACK
The plywood is silk-screen
printed while still flat
Limited batch production
H 97 cm (38¼ in) W 145 cm (57 in)
D 65 cm (25½ in)
Manufacturer: Gorm Lindum,
Denmark

3

FUMIO ENOMOTO
Stacking chair, *Bello*
STEEL, PLYWOOD
Prototype
H 73 cm (28¾ in) W 58 cm (22⅞ in)
D 49 cm (19¼ in)
Manufacturer: Ishimaru, Japan

2

MAURO CANFORI
Folding chair, *Matta*
COMPRESSED BEECH
LAMINATE
H 82 cm (32 in) W 60 cm (23½ in)
D 39 cm (15¼ in)
Manufacturer: Cidue, Italy

TOSHIYUKI KITA
Sofa, *Hop*
ALUMINIUM FRAME, FABRIC
OR LEATHER UPHOLSTERY
H 83 cm (32½ in) W 148 cm (57¾ in)
D 76 cm (30 in)
Manufacturer: Franz Wittmann,
Austria

Ackowledging the influence of the old masters Otto Wagner, Josef Hoffmann and, above all, Le Corbusier, Toshiyuki Kita believes that the relationship between creativity, innovation, man and nature was resolved in their work. "Design should not just be beautiful, it should be functional, too," he declares. Comfort is important in this little stacking chair for Casas. "It was my aim to find harmony between comfort and shape, and to create a piece of furniture that invites communication." Like Bořek Šípek, he believes that regionalism in design is an old-fashioned concept. "For me, design has no nationality, knows no borders. It has found a common language that transcends all borders."

TOSHIYUKI KITA
Chairs, *Mirai Yume*
CAST ALUMINIUM,
POLYURETHANE
H 81 cm (31¾ in) W 56 cm (22 in)
D 48 cm (18⅞ in)
Manufacturer: Casas, Spain

6
GUEN BERTHEAU-SUZUKI
Stacking chair, *Chiyono-fuji*
STEEL
Also available with a leather
seat
H 69 cm (27 in) W 54 cm (21 in)
D 45 cm (17½ in)
Manufacturer: Spend Co., Japan

7
MICHAEL GRAVES
Chairs, *Finestra* and *Oculus*
BEECH FRAME, FABRIC OR
LEATHER UPHOLSTERY
H 87 cm (34⅓ in) W 59 cm (23¼ in)
D 56 cm (22 in)
*Manufacturer: Atelier International,
USA*

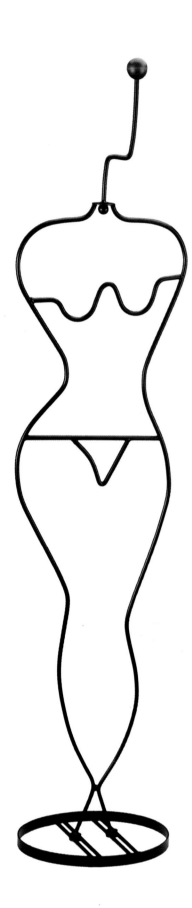

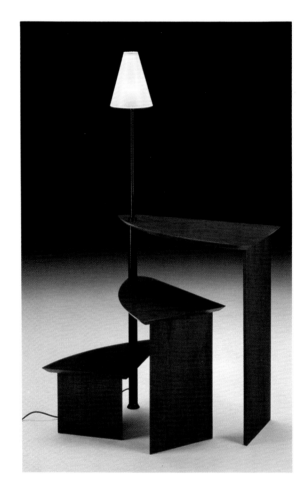

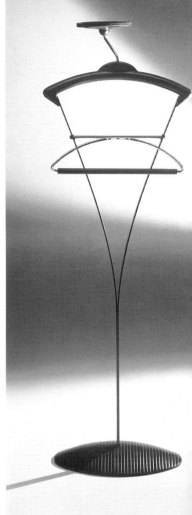

9

**ADRIANO BALDANZI
AND ALESSANDRO
NOVELLI**
Room valet, *Nottambulo*
STEEL, POLYURETHANE, CAST
IRON BASE
H 128 cm (50 in) W 46 cm (18 in)
D 23 cm (9 in)
*Manufacturer: Casamania by Frezza,
Italy*

8

**GIOVANNI
COLANTONIO, STEFANO
CONTINI AND
GIANCARLO STELLA**
Nest of tables, *Trio*
BEECH, STEEL
The three tables revolve
around the steel column,
surmounted by a lamp
H of lamp 130 cm (50¾ in) of tables
70 cm (27⅓ in) W 35 cm (13½ in)
L 65 cm (25¼ in)
Manufacturer: Disform, Spain

RAMON ARBOS

Lectern, *Tótems*

IRON, COPPER FITTINGS

H overall 110 cm (43¼ in) W of
lectern 22.5 cm (8⁴/₅)
L of lectern 31 cm (12¼ in) Di of base
30 cm (11⅞ in)

Manufacturer: Intent, Spain

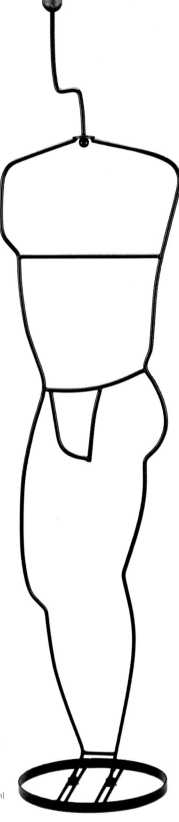

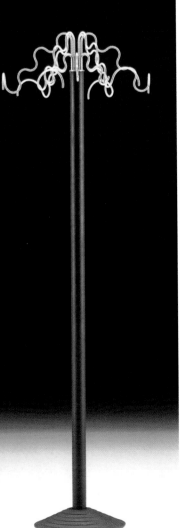

**JONATHAN DE PAS,
DONATO D'URBINO AND
PAOLO LOMAZZI**

Revolving coat stand,
Parruca

IRON, STAINLESS STEEL

H 180 cm (70⅝ in) Di 50 cm (19⅝ in)

Manufacturer: Disform, Spain

EHLEN JOHANSSEN

Valet stands, *Häpen F* and
Häpen M

METAL WIRE

H 185 cm (72⅞ in) W 45 cm (17¾ in)

Manufacturer: Ikea, Sweden

15

ALBERTO MEDA
Table, *Xlight*
ALUMINIUM FRAME, GLASS
AND CARBON FIBRE TOP
H 71 cm (28 in) W 88 cm (34⅝ in)
L 166 cm (65⅜ in)
Manufacturer: Alias, Italy

13

**BRUNO BORRIONE AND
BRUNO LEFEBVRE**
Table, *Monforte*
TUBULAR STEEL, FOLDED SHEET
METAL, GLASS
H 78.5 cm (30½ in) W 180 cm
(70¼ in) or 90 cm (35 in)
D 220 cm (85¾ in) or 90 cm (35 in)
Manufacturer: Elam, Italy

14

GEORG APPELTSHAUSER
Table, *1130*
STEEL, GLASS
The top swivels outwards to
form a double surface
H 71 cm (27½ in) W when open
140 cm (54½ in) Di 90 cm (35 in)
*Manufacturer: Draenert-Studio, West
Germany*

 16

**WOLFGANG
LAUBERSHEIMER**
Chair, *Kangaroo*
STEEL FRAME, ALUMINIUM
SEAT AND BACK
Prototype
H 67 cm (26⅜ in) W 48 cm (18⅞ in)
D 44 cm (17¼ in)
*Manufacturer: Wolfgang
Laubersheimer, West Germany*

 17

**JESSE MARSH FOR
FAUCIGLIETTI
ENGINEERING**
System, *Washington*
CHERRY WOOD, GLASS
Left to right:
Cabinet H 102 cm (40⅜ in) W 80 cm
(31½ in) D 40 cm (15¾ in)
Desk H 74 cm (29 in) W 70 cm
(27½ in) L 252 cm (99 in)
Glass top desk H 74 cm (29 in)
W 162.5 cm (63¾ in)
L 217 cm (84¾ in)
Bookcase H 173 cm (68 in)
W 76 cm (69 in) D 30 cm (11⅞ in)
Manufacturer: Arflex, Italy

**LOLA CASTELLÓ
COLOMER**

Armchair, *Ritmo*

RATTAN

H 85 cm (33 in) W 63 cm (24½ in)

D 58 cm (22½ in)

Manufacturer: En Canya, Spain

19

**LOLA CASTELLÓ
COLOMER**

Table, *Vira*

ASH, MDF, MOVEABLE GLASS

TOP

H 56 cm (21¾ in) Di 50 cm (19½ in)

Manufacturer: Punt Mobles, Spain

22

ALBERTO LIÉVORE

Chair, *Rothko*

BEECH PLYWOOD

H 74 cm (29 in) W 50 cm (19⅝ in)

D 55 cm (21½ in)

Manufacturer: Indartu, Spain

20

**ALBERTO LIÉVORE AND
JORGE PENSI**

Sofa bed, *Helsinoor*

STEEL FRAME, FABRIC
UPHOLSTERY

H 82 cm (32¼ in) W 228 cm (89 in)

D 93 cm (36½ in)

Manufacturer: Perobell, Spain

21

ALBERTO LIÉVORE

Table, *Manthis*

STAINLESS STEEL

H 69 cm (27⅛ in) Di 46 cm (18 in)

Manufacturer: Perobell, Spain

JOHN WERNER
Chair, *Popeye*
MDF, ALUMINIUM TUBE
Prototype
H 80 cm (31½ in) W 40 cm (15¾ in)
D 38 cm (15 in)
Manufacturer: John Werner, UK

DANILO SILVESTRIN
Chair, *2085*
BEECH, STEEL
H 89 cm (35 in) W 43 cm (16⅞ in)
D 53 cm (20⅞ in)
Manufacturer: Draenert, West
Germany

**BRUNO BORRIONE AND
BRUNO LEFEBVRE**
Chair, *Violetta*
VARNISHED TUBULAR STEEL,
VARNISHED PLYWOOD
H 75 cm (29¼ in) W 38 cm (14¾ in)
D 38 cm (14¾ in)
Manufacturer: Elam, Italy

 26

ENRICO BONA
Chair, *Enrica*
CHROME-PLATED TUBULAR
STEEL FRAME, LEATHER OR
FABRIC UPHOLSTERY
H 78 cm (30¾ in) W 48 cm (18⅞ in)
D 56 cm (22 in)
Manufacturer: Skipper, Italy

 27

TORD BJÖRKLUND
Table and chairs, *Anima*
SHEET METAL, MDF, LEATHER
UPHOLSTERY
Collapsible living-room
furniture
Chair H 92 cm (36 in) W 46 cm (18 in)
D 38 cm (15 in)
Table H 70.5 cm (27¾ in) W 80 cm
(31½ in) L 160 cm (63 in)
Manufacturer: Ikea, Sweden

 28

CARLO BARTOLI
Chair, *Nova*
WALNUT, LEATHER
UPHOLSTERY
H 83.5 cm (32½ in) W 44 cm (17 in)
D 51.5 cm (20 in)
Manufacturer: Novalia, Italy

30

**AFRA AND TOBIA
SCARPA**

Armchair, *Ronda 711*

STEEL FRAME, POLYURETHANE
AND DACRON UPHOLSTERY

H 82 cm (32¼ in) W 66 cm (26 in)
D 61 cm (24 in)

Manufacturer: Casas, Spain

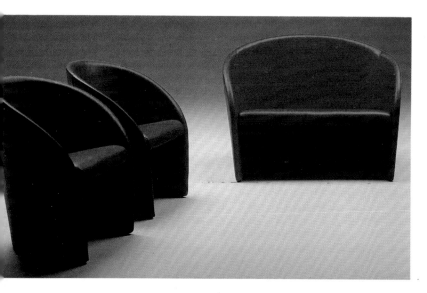

29

**LELLA AND MASSIMO
VIGNELLI**

Chair, *Intervista*

STEEL FRAME, LEATHER
UPHOLSTERY

Limited batch production

H 83 cm (32½ in) W 71 cm (28 in)
D 68 cm (26¾ in)

Manufacturer: Poltrona Frau, Italy

31

**LELLA AND MASSIMO
VIGNELLI**

Table, *Calice*

CAST IRON BASE, STEEL
COLUMN, SAND-BLASTED
GLASS TOP

H 60 cm (23½ in) or 72 cm (28½ in)
Di of top 70 cm (27½ in) or 120 cm
(47¼ in)

Manufacturer: Poltrona Frau, Italy

New Yorker Dakota Jackson revives a sense of workmanship and the adventurous use of fine materials for furniture with a future as brilliant as Art Deco's past. From unique commissions for collectors including Yoko Ono and Diane von Furstenberg, to limited production pieces and, this year, a newly accessible line of office and home furniture, Jackson's designs acknowledge the human shape. His heroes are Ruhlmann, Chareau and Le Corbusier: like Le Corbusier he believes that design *is* the decorative art.

 33

TOM DEACON
York Chair
EPOXY-PAINTED TUBULAR STEEL, PLYWOOD, POLYURETHANE AND DACRON UPHOLSTERY
H 74.5 cm (29 in) W 54 cm (21 in) D 56.5 cm (22 in)
Manufacturer: AREA Group, Canada

 32

DAKOTA JACKSON
PFM chairs from the *Ke-'Zu* collection
CHERRY WOOD, LEATHER UPHOLSTERY
Limited batch production
H 86.5 cm (34 in) W 55 cm (21½ in) with arms 62.5 cm (24½ in) D 64 cm (25 in)
Manufacturer: Dakota Jackson, USA

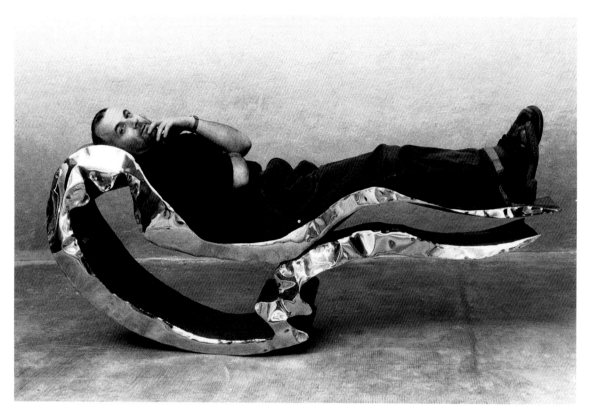

RON ARAD
Chaise longue, *Loop*
MILD STEEL, STAINLESS STEEL,
LEAD
The weight of the sitter
forces the chaise into a
horizontal position, while
lead cast into the head helps
create perfect balance
One-off
H 220 cm (85¾ in) W 50 cm (19½ in)
D 50 cm (19½ in)
Manufacturer: One Off, UK

RON ARAD
Table
STAINLESS STEEL, ACRYLIC
STRIPS
One-off
H 73 cm (28½ in) Di 280 cm (109¼ in)
Manufacturer: One Off, UK

 37

PHILIPPE STARCK
Table, *Miss Asahi*
Birch, Aluminium base,
MDF top
H 70 cm (27½ in) W 70 cm (27½ in)
D 70 cm (27½ in)
Manufacturer: Idée, Japan

 36

PHILIPPE STARCK
Table, *Miss Balù*
Composite thermoset,
polypropylene
H 72.5 cm (28½ in) W 60 cm (23½ in)
L 60 cm (23½ in)
Manufacturer: Kartell, Italy

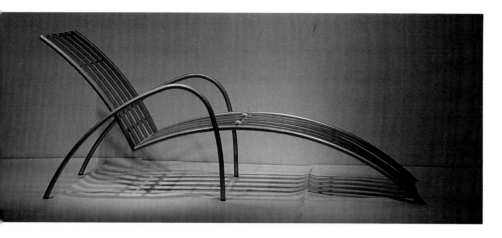

Stephan Lindfors was talent-spotted by Ingo Maurer at the Helsinki Fair with his *Scaragoo* insect light (see *The International Design Yearbook 1989/90*). His furniture is similarly zoomorphic. Jointed and vertebraed, it works in a natural way with a great deal of movement. It is never static, and has a certain sci-fi imagery. In his Foreword to the catalogue for an exhibition of his designs at the Galerie Binnen in the Netherlands he pointed out: "There are ten million insects on every habitable square kilometre of the surface of our planet."

Like a dragonfly, his *MVSEVM* table in either black-painted or chrome steel is teamed with a proboscis-shaped oval glass top. The legs, always a problem with extendable furniture, cluster like feelers to reinforce the imagery, while allowing the form to be segmented at will.

38

IDÉE ORIGINAL
Chair, *Neptune II*
ALUMINIUM FRAME,
WATERPROOF OAK SEAT
H 70 cm (27½ in) W 60 cm (23½ in)
L 150 cm (59 in)
Manufacturer: Idée, Japan

CHRISTIAN LEPRETTE

Table, *Bonaventura*

SHEET STEEL, GLASS

H 70 cm (27½ in) W 70 cm (27½ in)

L 190 cm (74⅞ in)

Manufacturer: Baleri, Italy

STEFAN LINDFORS

Tables, *MVSEVM*

STEEL, PVC SCREWS, WOOD

OR GLASS TOP

Oval H 72 cm (28½ in) W 72 cm

(28½ in) L 93 cm (36½ in)

Square H 72 cm (28½ in) W 72 cm

(28½ in) L 72 cm (28½ in)

Long H 72 cm (28½ in) W 72 cm

(28½ in) L 144 cm (56¼ in)

Manufacturer: Lilyriver,

Finland

POUL PETERSEN

Chaise longue, *Stepless*

STEEL FRAME, MAPLE VENEER

H 83 cm (32½ in) W 50 cm (19⅝ in)

L 200 cm (78¾ in)

Manufacturer: Poul Petersen,

Denmark

ALDO ROSSI

Desk, *Papiro*

LACQUERED WALNUT

H 115 cm (44⅞ in) W 144 cm (56⅛ in)

D 64 cm (25⅛ in)

Manufacturer: Molteni, Italy

"The foundation of an imaginative creation must be rigorous, indisputable and repetitive," Aldo Rossi reveals in his *Autobiografica Scientifica*. This pronouncement demonstrates the need for modern architecture to be based on a powerfully deliberate act of will, on a declaration of faith that shakes up the links between design and society. Rigorous is the word most often applied to his furniture designs which, like his buildings, are unembellished and at first glance deceptively simple. A strong, familiar image – the desk – is addressed with geometric simplification and articulated shapes that rely upon a rhythmic distribution of apertures, just like the façades of his buildings. Abstraction and reduction amount to the monumental.

ALDO ROSSI

Chair, *Parigi*

ALUMINIUM FRAME,
POLYURETHANE AND LEATHER
UPHOLSTERY

H 87 cm (34¼ in) W 76 cm (30 in)

D 98 cm (38½ in)

Manufacturer: Unifor, Italy

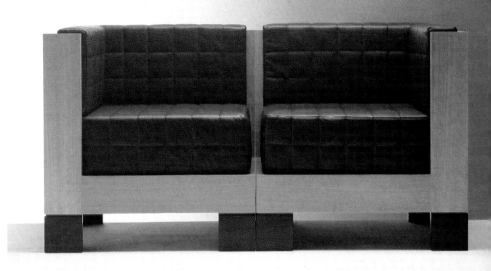

44

OSWALD MATHIAS UNGERS

Chair, *Sfera*

CHERRY WOOD, EBONIZED BASE AND INLAYS, LEATHER UPHOLSTERY OR FABRIC LOOSE COVERS

H 69 cm (27⅛ in) W 69 cm (27⅛ in) D 69 cm (27⅛ in)

Manufacturer: Sawaya & Moroni, Italy

45

OSWALD MATHIAS UNGERS

Sofa, *Cube*

CHERRY WOOD, EBONIZED BASE AND INLAYS, LEATHER UPHOLSTERY OR FABRIC LOOSE COVERS

H 69 cm (27⅛ in) W 138 cm (53⅞ in) D 69 cm (27⅛ in)

Manufacturer: Sawaya & Moroni, Italy

Rather than treat art as a decorative accessory to architecture, Site's work is a fusion of both disciplines. Their stated dislike of cityscapes punctuated by plaza sculptures and wall murals ("awkward intrusions rather than meaningful cultural resources") leads in to their furniture designs, which involve formalistic geometry upon artful bases.

46

SITE PROJECTS

Table, *Mountain Range*

MARBLE, GLASS

H 38 cm (15 in) W 76 cm (30 in) L 150 cm (59 in)

Manufacturer: Casigliani, Italy

ETTORE SOTTSASS
Chair, *Luxor*
PEAR WOOD, FABRIC
UPHOLSTERY
H 77 cm (30¼ in) W 40 cm (15¾ in)
D 50 cm (19⅝ in)
Manufacturer: Bros's, Italy

RICCARDO DALISI
Desk, *Idea*
ANODIZED ALUMINIUM,
GLAZED ALUMINIUM, BRASS
WHEEL COVERS, RUBBER
WHEELS
H 71 cm (27⅔ in) W 59 cm (23 in) or
104 cm (40½ in) L 245 cm (95½ in)
Manufacturer: Baleri Italia, Italy

**DANIEL WEIL AND
GERARD TAYLOR**
Games table, *Man-gioco*
OAK, STRING NETTING,
GREEN BAIZE, LINOLEUM
Limited batch production
H 73 cm (28¾ in) W 90 cm (35½ in)
L 160 cm (63 in) extended 200 cm
(78¾ in)
*Manufacturer: Anthologie Quartett,
West Germany*

Oxidization is the vital process that transform all materials, so the founders of Oxido chose the name to describe their alchemy. Architect Gianni Veneziano is more interested in art, while Prospero Rasulo is the designer. "Living with art on the domestic front has imposed a style in the last decade which has influenced architecture as well as design," says Rasulo. Small-scale production allows what they call "poetic design", full of expressiveness. This collection of lacquered pieces mimics classics from Art Nouveau, Art Deco and the Fifties.

According to Veneziano, "stylistic versatility is fashionable, but our creations spring from the theories of the Seventies, inspired by radical architecture and the theory of banal design. Breaks with tradition pave the way towards a sensual, metaphysical manner of understanding and creating objects." Even before the Seventies people like Sottsass moved in that direction, an artist who has been able to maintain his art through working with industries like Swatch and Alessi. In Milan these two are known as the "grandchildren" of Memphis. Veneziano says: "In the Nineties, I hope that tendencies developed during the Eighties stimulate industry towards more artistic products, closer to the times in which we live."

50

IGNAZIO GARDELLA, LUCA MEDA AND ALDO ROSSI

Chair, *Carlo Felice*

STEEL FRAME, WOOD ARMS AND BACK, FABRIC UPHOLSTERY

H 90 cm (35½ in) W 55 cm (21½ in)
D 68 cm (26¾ in)

Manufacturer: Unifor, Italy

51

PROSPERO RASULO AND GIANNI VENEZIANO

Chair, from the *Oxido Zoo* collection

BEECH

H 70 cm (27½ in) W 50 cm (19⅝ in)
D 40 cm (15¾ in)

Manufacturer: Masterly, Italy

53

SHIRO KURAMATA
Chair, *Miss Blanche*
ALUMINIUM PIPE, PAPER
FLOWERS CAST IN ACRYLIC
RESIN
Limited batch production
H 90 cm (35½ in) W 55 cm (21½ in)
D 60 cm (23½ in)
Manufacturer: Kokuyo Co., Japan

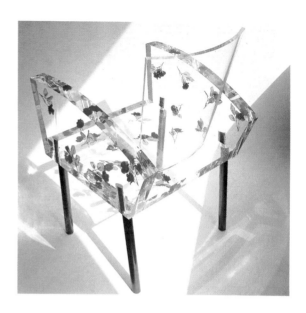

52

SHIRO KURAMATA
Stool, *Indian Rhapsody*
TUBULAR STEEL FRAME,
PLASTIC SEAT, ACRYLIC SHEET
BACK
H 116 cm (45¼ in) W 36 cm (14⅛ in)
D 36 cm (14⅛ in)
Manufacturer: Toyo Sash Co., Japan

54

DENIS SANTACHIARA
Chair bed, *Trans*
STEEL FRAME, BEECH
SUPPORTS, POLYURETHANE
UPHOLSTERY
Closed H 180 cm (70⅝ in) W 100 cm
(39 in) L 100 cm (39 in)
Open H 140 cm (55⅛ in) W 100 cm
(39 in) L 190 cm (74⅞ in)
Manufacturer: Campeggi, Italy

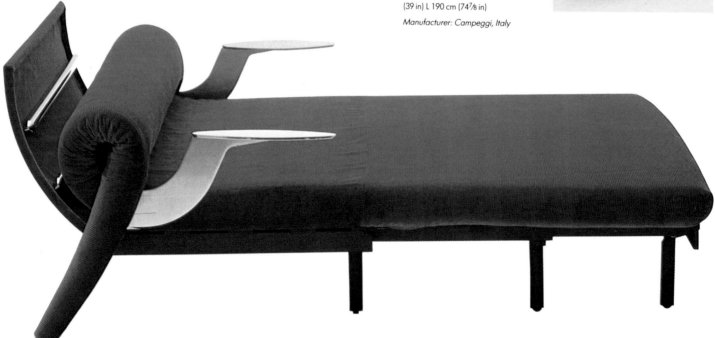

56

KAZUO KAWASAKI
Folding wheelchair, *Carna*
TUBULAR TITANIUM
Lightweight, 20 kg
Prototype
H 60.5 cm (23⅞ in) W 58 cm (22⅞ in)
D 83 cm (32½ in)
Manufacturer: Sig Workshop, Japan

55

134
Bench, *Airport*
STAINLESS STEEL, WOOD,
PLASTIC LAMINATE,
ALUMINIUM OR LEATHER
The backrests are
attachable in different
combinations of materials
H 43 cm (16⅞ in) W 140 cm (55⅛ in)
or 205 cm (80 in) D 58 cm (22⅞ in)
Manufacturer: Ibra, Denmark

 57

ROBIN DAY
Stacking chair, *Multo*
OVAL-SECTION TUBULAR
STEEL, PLYWOOD
H 84.5 cm (33 in) W 56.5 cm (22 in)
D 51 cm (20 in)
*Manufacturer: Mines & West Group,
UK*

59

RODNEY KINSMAN
Bench, *Trax*
ALUMINIUM, STEEL
H 76.5 cm (30⅛ in) W 240 cm
(94½ in) D 70 cm (27½ in)
Manufacturer: OMK Design, UK

 58

RONALD CARTER
Bench
STEEL FRAME, AFRICAN
MAHOGANY SEAT AND BACK,
POLYURETHANE FINISH
Made initially for use in the
Victoria and Albert Museum,
London
Limited batch production
H 67 cm (26 in) L 150 cm (58½ in)
W 62 cm (24 in)
Manufacturer: Miles Carter, UK

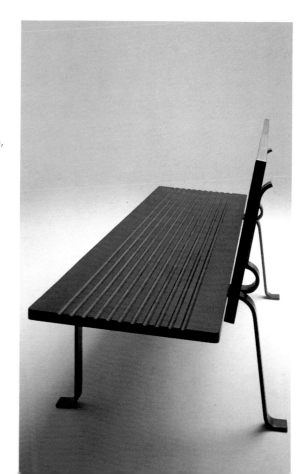

60

**MINALE, TATTERSFIELD
AND PARTNERS**

Bench

CONCRETE, GRANITE,
PERFORATED STAINLESS STEEL

Prototype

H 42.5 cm (16¾ in) W 150 cm (59 in)

D 52 cm (20½ in)

Manufacturer: Alan Zoeftig & Co., UK

61

**JOSEP MASSANA AND
JOSEP TREMOLEDA**

Bench, *Havana*

METAL, PLYWOOD

H 86 cm (33⅞ in) W 275 cm (107¼ in)

D 76 cm (30 in)

Manufacturer: Mobles 114, Spain

62

JOSEP LLUSCÁ

Hall furniture, *Indoor*

STEEL, GLASS, WOOD

Wall unit (left) H 190 cm (74⁷⁄₈ in)

W 45 cm (17³⁄₄ in) D 20 cm (8 in)

Console (right) H 190 cm (74⁷⁄₈ in)

W 106 cm (41³⁄₄ in) D 32 cm (12¹⁄₂ in)

Pegs D 8 cm (3¹⁄₈ in)

Manufacturer: Sellex, Spain

63

JOSEP LLUSCÁ

Bench, *BNC*

CHROME-PLATED TUBULAR

STEEL, POLYESTER AND

LEATHER OR FABRIC

UPHOLSTERY

H 78.5 cm (30⁷⁄₈ in) W total 267 cm

(104¹⁄₈ in) W of single seat 48 cm

(18⁷⁄₈ in) D 55 cm (21¹⁄₂ in)

Manufacturer: Enea, Spain

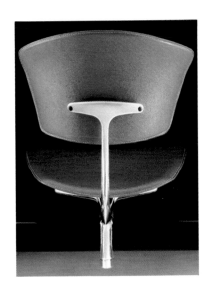

64

JOSEP LLUSCÁ
Table, *Nudo*
BEECH
H 90 cm (35½ in) W 130 cm (51 in)
L 130 cm (51 in)
Manufacturer: Muebles Dul, Spain

RICARDO BOFILL

Chairs and table, Swift II

BEECH, NICKEL-PLATED

BRASS, LEATHER UPHOLSTERY

Limited batch production

Table H 72 cm (28½ in)

W 90 cm (35 in) L 90 cm (35 in) or

Di 130 cm (51⅛ in)

Chair H 97 cm (38 in) W 39 cm

(15⅜ in) D 38 cm (15 in)

Manufacturer: Taller de Arquitectura,

France

66

CARLO FORCOLINI

Chair and stools, *Miro*

EPOXY-PAINTED STEEL,
RUBBER

Top to bottom:

H 91 cm (35½ in) W 40 cm (14¾ in)

D 54 cm (21¼ in)

H 47 cm (18½ in) W 40 cm (14¾ in)

D 42 cm (16½ in)

H 64 cm (25⅛ in) W 40 cm (14¾ in)

D 44 cm (17¼ in)

Manufacturer: Alias, Italy

67

TOSHIMITSU SASAKI

Chair, *Origin*

TUBULAR STEEL, BAMBOO

Prototype

H 80 cm (31½ in) W 42 cm (16½ in)

D 48 cm (18⅞ in)

Manufacturer: Minerva Co., Japan

68

**JORDI MIRALBELL AND
MARIONA RAVENTÓS**

Stools, *Nif Naf Nuf*

STAINED BEECH

Nif *(right)* H 28 cm (11 in) W 25.5 cm
(10 in) L 28 cm (11 in)

Naf *(left)* H 22 cm (8²/3 in) W 20 cm
(7⁷/8 in) L 37 cm (14¹/2 in)

Nuf *(centre)* H 25 cm (9⁷/8 in) Di 25 cm
(9⁷/8 in)

Manufacturer: Santa & Cole, Spain

69

SANTA & COLE DESIGN TEAM
Stacking chair, *Traviesa*
ANODIZED ALUMINIUM TUBE, POLYURETHANE-COATED BEECH
H 75 cm (29½ in) W 51 cm (20 in) D 61 cm) (24 in)
Manufacturer: Santa & Cole, Spain

70

BAÑO AND ASSOCIATES
Folding chair, *Sister Moon*
LAMINATED OR VENEERED ASH
H 81 cm (31½ in) W 56 cm (21¾ in) D 56 cm (21¾ in)
Manufacturer: Punt Mobles, Spain

71

ENNIO AROSIO AND SILVANO MARIANI
Chair, *Carlotta*
BEECH OR WALNUT, LEATHER SEAT
H 110 cm (43 in) W 50 cm (19½ in) D 45 cm (17½ in)
Manufacturer: Misura Emme, Italy

72

LLUIS PAU, JOSEP MARTORELL, ORIOL BOHIGAS AND DAVID MACKAY

Cabinet, *Serie Componibile ABAC (B)*

LACQUERED MDF, ASH

H 117 cm (45⅔ in) W 101 cm (39⅓ in)
D 50 cm (19⅝ in)

Manufacturer: Colur, Spain

73

ENRICO BALERI

Drinks cabinet, *Miss Maggie Bar*

SHEET AND TUBULAR EPOXY-PAINTED STEEL FRAME, GLASS DOOR AND TOP

The shelves are illuminated by two dichroic 50W bulbs activated when the door is opened

H 160 cm (62½ in) W 48 cm (18¾ in)
D 42 cm (16⅓ in)

Manufacturer: Baleri Italia, Italy

74
FLORIN BAERISWYL AND CHRISTOF WÜTHRICH
Storage unit, *Modus*
PLYWOOD, ALUMINIUM, FABRIC
The unit can be dismantled and reassembled for easy storage
Prototype
H 180 cm (70¼ in) W 90 cm (35 in)
D 45 cm (17½ in)
Manufacturer: Dai-Design, Switzerland

76
PIETRO AROSIO
Chair, *Fuseaux*
STEEL, LEATHER SEAT, CHROME FINISH
H 80 cm (31¼ in) D 50 cm (19½ in)
Manufacturer: Airon, Italy

75
PIETRO AROSIO
Storage system, *Push*
PEAR WOOD, ALUMINIUM
The drawers are opened by a catch in the central button
Left: H 72 cm (28 in) W 120 cm (46¾ in) D 54 cm (21 in)
Right: H 45 cm (17½ in) W 40 cm (15½ in) D 54 cm (21 in)
Manufacturer: Emmebi, Italy

77

RICHARD SAPPER
Computer workstation,
Secretaire
ALUMINIUM
H 145 cm (57 in) W 90 cm (35½ in)
D 56 cm (22 in)
Manufacturer: Unifor, Italy

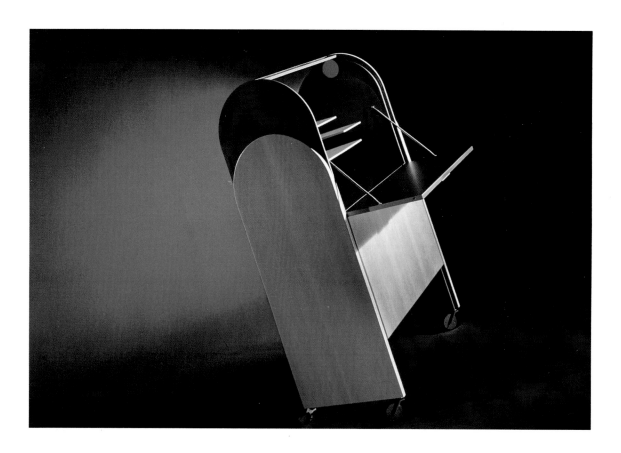

78

ALDO BARTOLOMEO
Secretaire, *Accademia*
WALNUT, BLACK SATIN
LINING
H 135 cm (52½ in) W 55 cm (21½ in)
D 45 cm (17½ in)
Manufacturer: Stildomus, Italy

79

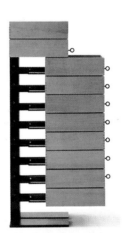

MARIO BOTTA

Chest, *Robot*

Epoxy-painted steel frame,
pear wood

Also available in black
lacquered MDF

H 121 cm (47¼ in) W 35 cm (13½ in)
D 35 cm (13½ in)

Manufacturer: Alias, Italy

The greatest exposure Jaime Tresserra Clapés has received for his beautiful but exclusively expensive furniture was in the film *Batman*. With high standards of craftsmanship, and only 25 pieces made of each design, his small collection is highly prized for its combination of ancient cabinet-making skills and an organic fluidity of form. His designs usually take one or two weeks to execute, but are two months in production. *Samuro* stands like the warrior of feudal Japan, the guardian of family possessions. Though touch-sensitive handles spring open at fingertip pressure, Tresserra Clapés believes that how one feels about furniture is more important than how well it works. The makers of this piece also make the traditional Spanish furniture seen on sets for television soap operas such as *Dallas* and *Dynasty*: "the hands are the same, but the mind is different."

All his pieces are handmade, which gives each piece a sinuous flow. Nothing is worked upon the set square. Inspired by Art Deco, he likes to think of his furniture as the evolution of Ruhlmann. Surprisingly, the architect he most admires is Norman Foster, whom he describes as organic like Gaudí, simply working in steel and glass rather than clay and tiles.

80

JAIME TRESSERRA CLAPÉS
Chest, *Samuro*
WALNUT, BRASS FITTINGS
Limited batch production
H 178 cm (69½ in) W 42 cm (16½ in)
L 116 cm (45¼ in)
Manufacturer: J. Tresserra Design, Spain

81

JAIME TRESSERRA CLAPÉS
Filing cabinet, *Buck Paralelas*
WALNUT, CHROME FITTINGS
Limited batch production
H 55 cm (21½ in) W 50 cm (19⅝ in)
L 45 cm (17¾ in)
Manufacturer: J. Tresserra Design, Spain

JOHN COLEMAN

Cabinet, *Javit*

MAHOGANY, BRASS

One-off

H 145 cm (56½ in) W 45 cm (17½ in)

D 33 cm (12¾ in)

Manufacturer: John Coleman

Furniture, UK

83

ANTONIO CITTERIO
Sofa and chairs, Baisity
POLYURETHANE-COATED
STEEL FRAME, LEATHER OR
FABRIC UPHOLSTERY

Two-seater H 85 cm (33½ in)

L 152 cm (59¾ in) D 104 cm (40½ in)

Three-seater H 85 cm (33½ in)

L 218 cm (85 in) D 104 cm (40½ in)

Chair H 85 cm (33½ in) W 81 cm

(31⅞ in) D 100 cm (39⅜ in)

Manufacturer: B & B Italia, Italy

84

ROBERTO LAZZERONI
Sideboard, *Tadao,* from the
Dedos Tenidos collection
Cherry wood or walnut,
maple or padouk
H 89 cm (35 in) W 175 cm (68⅞ in)
D 51 cm (20 in)
Manufacturer: Ceccotti, Italy

ROBERTO LAZZERONI
Settee, *Mosquito,* from the
Dedos Tenidos collection
CHERRY WOOD, ACRYLIC
FINISH
H 80 cm (31¹⁄₂ in) W 123 cm (48¹⁄₂ in)
D 50 cm (19⁵⁄₈ in)
Manufacturer: Ceccotti, Italy

JEANNOT CERRUTI
Chairs and table, *Damas,*
from the *Dedos Tenidos*
collection
PADOUK, INLAID
CHERRY WOOD DRAUGHT
BOARD, PAINTED MAPLE
TABLE BASE
Limited batch production
Chair H 79 cm (30³⁄₄ in) W 63 cm
(24¹⁄₂ in) D 53 cm (20¹⁄₂ in)
Table H 69 cm (27 in) W 55 cm
(21¹⁄₂ in) L 90 cm (35 in)
Manufacturer: Ceccotti, Italy

87

ATELIER ALCHIMIA
Ollo collection
Left to right, below:
Cabinet, *Colonna*
LACQUERED WOOD, GLASS
SHELVES
H 210 cm (82 cm) W 45 cm (17½ in)
Di at top and base 51 cm (20 in)
Wall hanging
PRINTED COTTON
H 196 cm (76½ in) W 166 cm (64¾ in)
Table
LAMINATED WOOD,
ALUMINIUM LEGS
The top opens to provide
storage
H 32 cm (12½ in) W 48 cm (18¾ in)
L 147 cm (57⅓ in)
Rug
WOOL
W 134 cm (52¼ in) L 198 cm (77¼ in)
Screen, *Stanza*
LAMINATED WOOD
Limited batch production
H 196 cm (76½ in) L 282 cm (110 in)
W 20 cm (7¾ in)
Bookcase, *Angoliera*
LAMINATED WOOD
H 217 cm (84½ in) W 24 cm (9⅓ in)
D 43 cm (16¾ in)
Manufacturer: Alchimia Trade, Italy

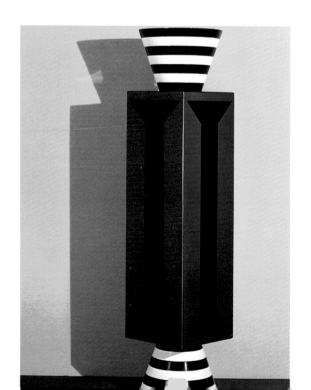

ATELIER ALCHIMIA
Soli collection
LACQUERED WOOD, GLASS
Limited batch production
Left to right:

Wardrobe Di 110 cm (43¼ in)

Dining table H 70 cm (27½ in)

Di of top 180 cm (70⅝ in)

Coffee table H 40 cm (15¾ in)

Di of top 110 cm (43¼ in)

Five-shelf unit Di 80 cm (31½ in)

Manufacturer: Alchimia Trade, Italy

Fashionable changes of style seldom affect the furniture industry. Mercurially for designers, Alchimia offers a completely different look each year. For 1990/91 it is a galaxy of spheres in a space-age set. Nose-cones upended on a black-and-white floor provide the setting for the launch of lacquered furniture like space capsules. The sphere they chose for the collection in their Milan showrooms expresses "centrality, calm, distance, concentration and dilation". It is the sphere of the sun, symbol of the universe. Alchimia revives craft skills such as marquetry, hand-painting and carving, and combines them with innovative technology. A new lacquer, for example, water-based and ecologically sound, is applied to wood, glass and metal.

The primary function of this collection is aesthetic; functionality comes second. Says Bruno Gregori of the Alchimia team: "We think of a house like the cosmos, the universe of life. The sphere is as ancient as its primordial past. We pay attention to the ecological condition of our life in the house, and refer to the arts as a corrective, surface or colour."

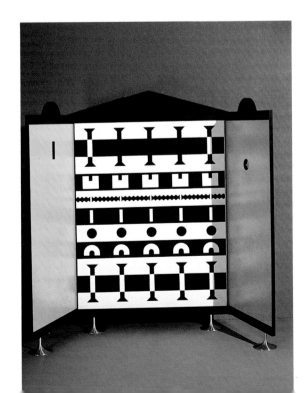

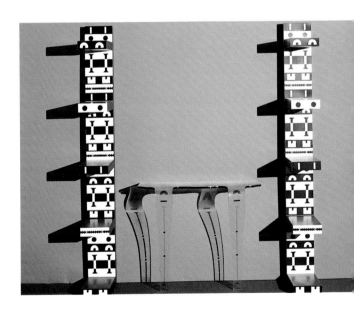

89

ERWIN EBENBERGER

Bed, *Liege*

LAMINATED LARCH PLYWOOD

Limited batch production

H 82.5 cm (33½ in) W 240 cm

(94½ in) L 264 cm (103 in)

Manufacturer: Ebenberger, Austria

90

ENZO MARI

Beds, *Tappeto Volante*

ALUMINIUM FRAME,

COMPRESSED ALUMINIUM

STRUTS, WOOD OR METAL

HEADBOARDS, LEATHER OR

FABRIC COVERING

Single H 32 cm (12½ in) W 86 cm

(33⅞ in) L 201 cm (78⅓ in)

Double H 32 cm (12½ in) W 141 cm

(55½ in) L 201 cm (78⅓ in)

Manufacturer: Interflex, Italy

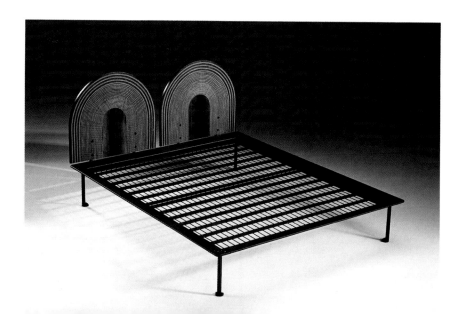

 91

GASPARE CAIROLI

Bed, *Conforete*

STEEL, POLYURETHANE-
COATED WOODEN SLATS

H 30 cm (11¾ in) W 180 cm (70¼ in)

L 200 cm (78 in)

Manufacturer: Refim, Italy

GAETANO PESCE
Bed, *New York*
ANODIZED ALUMINIUM
TUBES, RUBBER, FOAM RUBBER
HEADBOARD
Prototype
H 97 cm (38 in) W 213 cm (83 in)
256.5 cm (100 in)
Manufacturer: Galleria Fulvio Ferrari,
Italy

93

MONDO DESIGN TEAM
Bed, *Baldacchino*
Iron frame, fabric
H 210 cm (81⅝ in) W 182 cm (71 in)
L 202 cm (79 in)
Manufacturer: Mondo, Italy

94

MONDO DESIGN TEAM
Bed, *Wicker*
Iron frame, rattan
H 103 cm (40½ in) W 190 cm (74⅞ in)
L 220 cm (86⅝ in)
Manufacturer: Mondo, Italy

95

MONDO DESIGN TEAM
Bed, *Latta*
Iron frame with tinned
finish, wood
H 105 cm (41 in) W 89 cm (35 in)
L 202 cm (79 in)
Manufacturer: Mondo, Italy

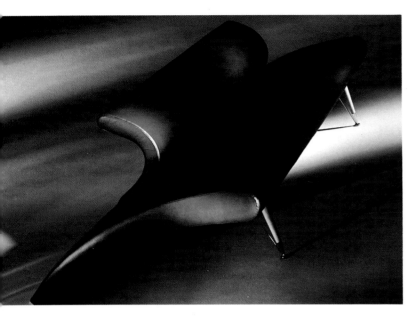

 96

MASSIMO IOSA GHINI

Settee, *Vertigine*

WOOD AND STEEL FRAME,
LEATHER UPHOLSTERY

H 65 cm (25½ in) W 224 cm (87⅓ in)

D 110 cm (43¼ in)

Manufacturer: Design Gallery

Milano, Italy

 97

MASSIMO IOSA GHINI

Shelving system, *Volgente*

GLASS

H 202 cm (78¾ in) W 55 cm (21½ in)

D 64 cm (25⅛ in)

Manufacturer: Fiam, Italy

Rising young furniture designer Massimo Iosa Ghini is the
leader of a group of architects, artists and designers who call
themselves Bolidiste, an allusion to speeding objects and
dynamic form. Ettore Sottsass first asked Iosa Ghini to design
an armchair for Memphis in 1985, and a year later he joined
the team. Today the Bolidiste want to be more accessible
than Memphis was, and design to affordable prices, so Iosa
Ghini works with leading manufacturers. His ambitious glass
shelving system, *Volgente*, brings dynamism to an essentially
stationary structure. Its wrap-around geometry appears to
shave off at one side, permitting the other to swoop forward
protectively.

Fiam's enthusiastic experiment with techniques and
equipment for glass cutting has pioneered a new precision
cutting system, the Paser, for thick float crystal. Now sheets
of any thickness can be cut to any shape, freeing the
designer from the old constraints of diamond-cutting, which
restricted curves.

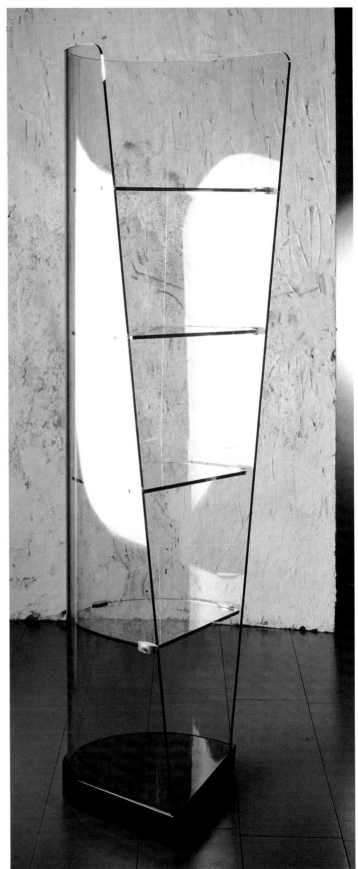

 98

MICHELE DE LUCCHI

Bookcase, *Platone*

OAK, GLASS, PLATE GLASS

H 142 cm (56 in) W 88 cm (34⅝ in) or

118 cm (46 in) D 50 cm (19⅝ in)

Manufacturer: Glass Design, Italy

 100

ISAO HOSOE

Rotating bookshelf, *Cactus*

CRYSTAL GLASS, STEEL BALL

BEARINGS

H 171 cm (66¾ in) W 50 cm (19⅝ in)

D 50 cm (19⅝ in)

Manufacturer: Tonelli, Italy

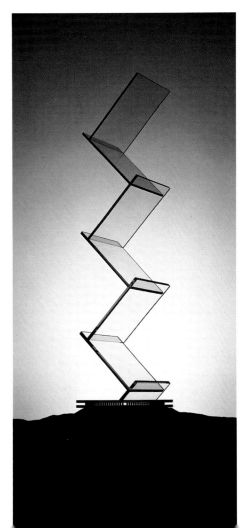

 99

ISAO HOSOE

Rotating bookshelf, *Albero*

CRYSTAL GLASS, STEEL BALL

BEARINGS

H 162 cm (63¾ in) W 50 cm (19⅝ in)

D 50 cm (19⅝ in)

Manufacturer: Tonelli, Italy

102

JORGE PENSI
Chair, *Orfilia*
ALUMINIUM FRAME,
PLYWOOD SEAT AND BACK
H 82 cm (32¼ in) W 55 cm (21½ in)
D 60 cm (23½ in)
Manufacturer: Thonet, West Germany

101

**JANE DILLON, PETER
WHEELER AND FLORIS
VAN DEN BROECKE**
Rocking chair, *Camber*
CHERRY WOOD FRAME,
NYLON BACK, LAMINATED
PLYWOOD BASE, WOOL
UPHOLSTERY
Limited batch production
H 72 cm (28 in) W 86 cm (33½ in)
D 120 cm (46¾ in)
Manufacturer: Thonet, West Germany

At the Vitra Design Museum at Weil am Rhein near Basel, the chair collection begins with the Thonet bentwood chair of 1850. The curator Alexander von Vegesack chose it to illustrate the beginning of industrial furniture and the end of artisan furniture, "that decisive moment when the great artisans died."

To mark the final decade of this century, Thonet invited nine European designers and architects to join the first European Design Forum. Their brief was to design "visions" for chairs with a characteristic expression of their countries. Of all the designs, Mario Bellini chose only two. Dillon, Wheeler and van den Broecke's *Camber* chair is named both after its curve and also to suggest the word *camera* or room. The design plays with the idea of the territory around a sitter, with relaxation and meditation encouraged by the chair's rocking motion.

Jorge Pensi says of his *Orfilia* chair: "Thonet is undoubtedly part of the historical evolution of the chair, so designing a contemporary chair capable of meeting the standards of such a historical landmark is a great challenge. *Orfilia* is a stackable chair which carries the features of all my designs – a totally identifiable object, independent of time. Its shape, symbolical values and technology link it to Thonet. It was conceived as a light structure in cast aluminium, with plywood seat, back and arms. The combination of different textures for the structure, and different varnishes for the plywood, results in wide variations."

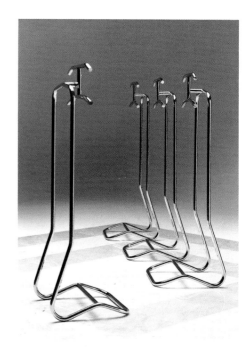

103

ECKART MUTHESIUS
Valet, *Mandu*
CHROMED TUBULAR STEEL
Re-edition from 1932
H 109 cm (42½ in) W 39 cm (15⅜ in)
L 38 cm (15 in)
*Manufacturer: Vereinigte
Werkstätten, West Germany*

104

CARLO SCARPA
Chair and table, *Series 1934*
Re-edition from 1976
Chair
WALNUT OR BEECH, WOOL
UPHOLSTERY
H 77 cm (30¼ in) W 67 cm (26⅜ in)
D 66 cm (26 in)
Table
WALNUT, FELT UPHOLSTERY
H 72 cm (28½ in) W 94 cm (37 in)
L 220 cm (86⅝ in)
Manufacturer: Bernini, Italy

The death in 1989 in Berlin of Eckart Muthesius at the age of 85 ended a highly productive life devoted to architecture and design. He designed not only buildings but game parks and even houseboats, as well as furniture, fittings and tableware. Muthesius is best known for Manik Bagh Palace, built and fitted for the Maharajah of Indore in the early 1930s. It proved to be an astonishing example of Art Deco design, with almost all the furniture made in Berlin under Muthesius's strict supervision. Special glues and veneers were used that would withstand the Indian climate. The sale of the furnishings by auction in 1980 (the palace now houses the Ministry of Finance) revived interest in Muthesius's work, and led to plans to put into production some of his furniture by the Vereinigte Werkstätten. The valet stand from the Maharajah's dressing room is one example.

The Italian company Bernini has remained faithful to its traditional craft heritage for two generations. Giancarlo Bernini met Carlo Scarpa in Tokyo in 1969, and they worked together until Scarpa's death a decade later. Their first project, which went into production in 1974 after five years' research, was a bookcase named *Zibaldone*. Scarpa also designed two tables, two chairs, four sideboard units and two bookcases. Two of his projects, for a chair and a small armchair dating back to 1934, were launched at the Milan Furniture Fair in 1989. Mario Bellini, despite an aversion to re-editions, approves of this collection, which was only ever made before in prototype for Scarpa's own home.

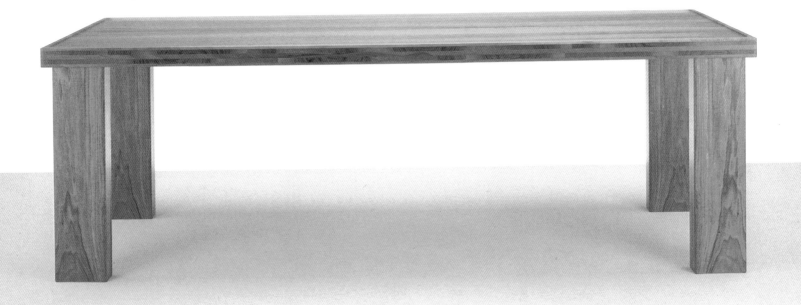

 107

ACHILLE CASTIGLIONI
Table, *T 89*
WOOD, CAST IRON
H 73 cm (28½ in) W 90 cm (35 in)
L 220 cm (85¾ in)
Manufacturer: Bernini, Italy

 105

ACHILLE CASTIGLIONI
Cabinet, *Camino*
MARBLE
Limited batch production
H 86 cm (33⅞ in) W 162 cm (63¾ in)
D 52 cm (20½ in)
Manufacturer: Up & Up, Italy

During his long career (he is now 73), Achille Castiglioni has never ceased to quest for new forms, techniques and materials capable of being mass produced. "Ultimately," he says, "design simply means designing. What counts is not so much the person designing the object as the practical use which can be made of it. The main thing is that it should become an object of common use, accessible to everybody. I always start from a function, the idea, then I gradually modify it and perfect it as I make it. There is a lot of modelling involved in my job. Also, I am the son of a sculptor and I always saw my father work with his hands to mould the material gradually into the desired shape." The character of his cabinet, given its shape and size, is its freestanding ability to double as a desk and a table within the room.

 106

VICENT MARTINEZ-SANCHO
Table, *Anaconda*
ASH
H 72 cm (28½ in) W 90 cm (35½ in)
L 150 cm (59 in)
Manufacturer: Punt Mobles, Spain

110

LODOVICO ACERBIS
Table, *Marco and Henry*
LACQUERED BEECH, WITH
WHEELS OR SOLID
ATTACHMENTS FOR LEGS
H 72 cm (28¼ in) W 80 cm (31¼ in)
L 150 cm (58½ in)
Manufacturer: Morphos, Italy

108

UMBERTO RIVA
Table, *UR 303*
ALUMINIUM IRON SUPPORTS,
PLYWOOD
H 86 cm (33⅞ in) W 90 cm (35½ in)
L 220 cm (86⅝ in)
Manufacturer: IB Office, Italy

109

**GIANFRANCO
GASPARINI**
Table
STEEL FRAME, PLYWOOD TOP
WITH EBONIZED WALNUT
VENEER
H 72 cm (28½ in) W 86 cm (33⅞ in)
L 280 cm (109¼ in)
Manufacturer: Poggi, Italy

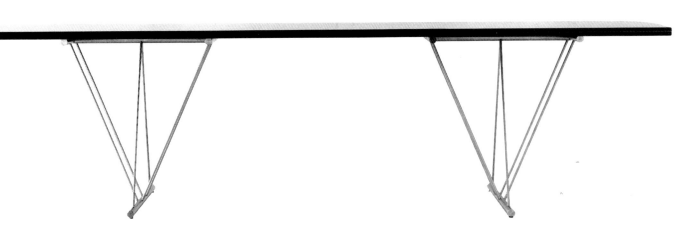

 111

CINI BOERI

Sofa, *Amado*

CHROMED TUBULAR STEEL
FRAME, WOOD,
POLYURETHANE FOAM AND
LEATHER OR FABRIC
UPHOLSTERY
H 70 cm (27$\frac{1}{3}$ in) W 90 cm (35 in)
L 180 cm (70$\frac{1}{4}$ in)
Manufacturer: Arflex, Italy

 112

JEAN NOUVEL

Sofa bed, *Profils*

ALUMINIUM FRAME, COLD-
CURED FOAM AND
POLYURETHANE COVERING
H 74 cm (29 in) W 200 cm (78$\frac{3}{4}$ in)
D 90 cm (35$\frac{1}{2}$ in)
Manufacturer: Ligne Roset, France

113

MICHELA BALDESSARI
Armchair and sofa from the
Palinsesto collection
ASH, METAL JOINTS,
POLYURETHANE AND LEATHER
OR FABRIC UPHOLSTERY
Limited batch production
Chair H 77 cm (30 in) W 79 cm
(30¾ in) D 63 cm (24½ in)
Sofa H 77 cm (30 in) W 143 cm
(55¾ in) D 72 cm (28 in)
Manufacturer: ICF, Italy

115

**LUIGI MASSONI AND
GIORGIO CAZZANIGA**
Settee, *Naga 213*
WOOD, POLYURETHANE
FOAM AND CALF LEATHER
UPHOLSTERY
H 83 cm (32½ in) W 160 cm (63 in)
D 97 cm (38¼ in)
Manufacturer: Matteo Grassi, Italy

114

GABRIEL TEIXIDO
Armchair, *Blues*
WOOD FRAME, LEATHER
UPHOLSTERY
H 80 cm (31½ in) W 114 cm (44½ in)
D 90 cm (35½ in)
Manufacturer: Tagono, Spain

116

ACHILLE CASTIGLIONI
Garden table, *Ovale del Giardiniere*
MARBLE
Limited batch production
H 73 cm (28 1/2 in) W 130 cm (50 3/4 in)
L 230 cm (89 3/4 in)
Manufacturer: Up & Up, Italy

 118

OSCAR TUSQUETS BLANCA

Fireplace surround, *Frontal Chimenea*

MARBLE

H min. 91 cm (35½ in) max. 119 cm (46⅜ in)

W min. 126 cm (49 in) max. 156 cm (60⅞ in)

Manufacturer: Bigelli Marmi, Italy

 119

UMBERTO RIVA

Table, *Marmo*

MARBLE, ALUMINIUM BASE

H 73 cm (28¾ in) W 90 cm (35½ in)

L 130 cm (51⅛ in)

Manufacturer: Bigelli Marmi, Italy

 117

FRANCESCO VENEZIA

Shelf, *Glifo*

TRAVERTINE MARBLE

H 252 cm (99 in) W 43 cm (16⅞ in)

D 21 cm (8¼ in)

Manufacturer: Bigelli Marmi, Italy

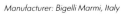

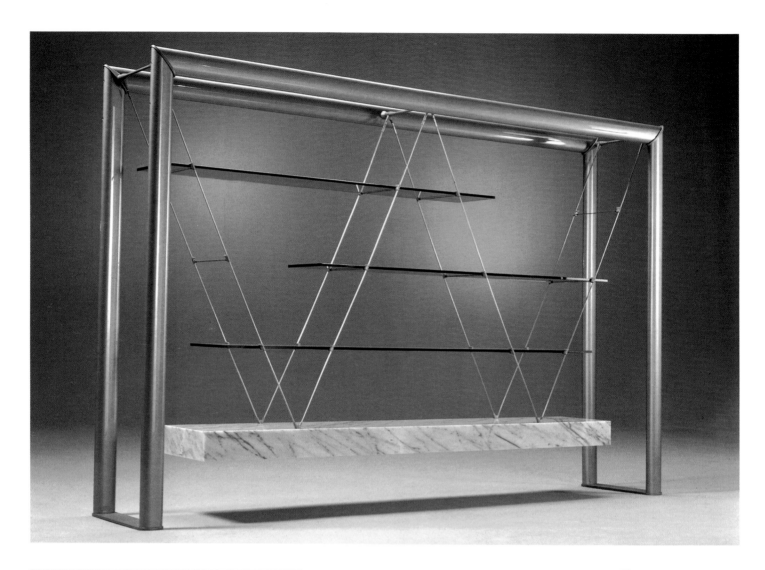

Andrea Branzi's bookcase is like a suspension bridge, stabilized through the weight of the suspended block of marble. Yet the crystal shelves among the pulleys create an architecture that is at the same time ordered and variable, and offer a light and stable frame based upon strong interior tension. His new collection of furniture for Cassina is intended to introduce the concept of a *genius loci* within a domestic environment. "Archetypal objects that are almost mythical, elaborations of primary structures, such as a bridge, an arch, the sea, a temple," is Branzi's description. Most Western design, he believes, is rebuilding domestic identity through industrial products that enhance and develop traditional domestic values. "A century of rapid and accelerated modernity has in fact erased the notion that man's abode is only a functional place, and not a place to be lived in. Man lives in places that he can love, in which he puts objects in a relationship that is not only functional but also symbolic, mysterious and cultural."

120

ANDREA BRANZI
Shelving system, *Berione*
STEEL, CRYSTAL, MARBLE
COUNTER-WEIGHT
H 190 cm (74 in) W 52 cm (20¼ in)
L 300 cm (117 in)
Manufacturer: Cassina, Italy

 121

**THOMAS EXNER AND
CHRISTIAN STEINER**
Bookshelf
BEECH PLYWOOD
H 187 cm (73 in) W 188 cm (73⅓ in)
D 37 cm (14½ in)
Manufacturer: Ebenberger, Austria

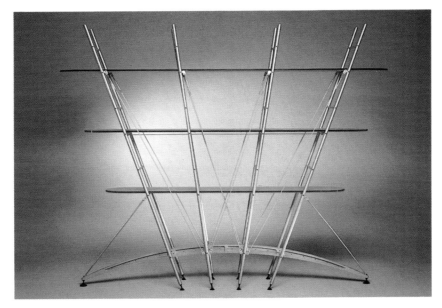

 122

ERIC RAFFY
Shelving system, *Triplan*
ALUMINIUM, GLASS
Limited batch production
H 205 cm (80 in) W 270 cm (105⅓ in)
D 40 cm (15¾ in)
Manufacturer: Farjon, France

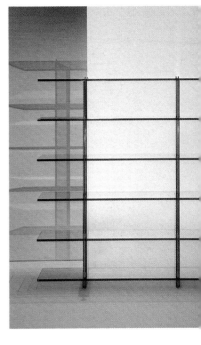

 123

RENZO PIANO
Bookshelf, *A Libreria Teso*
CRYSTAL GLASS, STEEL TIE-
RODS
H 200 cm (78¾ in) W 240 cm (94½ in)
D 35 cm (13¾ in)
Manufacturer: Fontana Arte, Italy

124

JONAS BOHLIN
Magazine rack, *Magasin*
PAINTED BIRCH
H 140 cm (54½ in) D 12 cm (4½ in)
Manufacturer: Källemo, Sweden

125

**MARILENA BOCCATO,
GIAN NICOLA GIGANTE
AND ANTONIO ZAMBUSI**
Shelving system, *Statica*
ALUMINIUM FRAME, TEMPERED
GLASS DOORS
H 203 cm (79 in) W 80 cm (31¼ in)
D 35 cm (13½ in)
Manufacturer: Industrie Secco, Italy

 126

GIANDOMENICO BELOTTI

Shelving system, *JA*

STEEL, CRYSTAL

H 180 cm (70¼ in) W 90 cm (35 in)
D 35 cm (13½ in)

Manufacturer: Alias, Italy

 127

MASAYUKI KUROKAWA

Bookcase, *Tana System Libro*

ALUMINIUM, RUBBER, ZINC DIECASTING

H max 300 cm (117 in) W of module 60 cm (23½ in) D 30 cm (11⅞ in)

Manufacturer: Toyo Sash Co., Japan

128

VICO MAGISTRETTI

Table, *Eleo*

LACQUERED WOOD,
LAMINATE, POLYESTER
DRAWER FRONT

H 36 cm (14⅛ in) W 80 cm (31½ in)

L 140 cm (55⅛ in)

Manufacturer: Morphos, Italy

129

VICO MAGISTRETTI

Sofa, *Portovenere*

STEEL FRAME, POLYURETHANE
FOAM AND LEATHER OR
FABRIC UPHOLSTERY

Two-seater H 88 cm (34⅝ in)

W 168 cm (65½ in) D 90 cm (35½ in)

Three-seater H 88 cm (34⅝ in)

W 234 cm (91¼ in) D 90 cm (35½ in)

Manufacturer: Cassina, Italy

130

VICO MAGISTRETTI

Coffee table, *Florian*

LACQUERED WOOD

Two-tiered H 100 cm (39½ in)

Di 40 cm (15¾ in)

Three-tiered H 108 cm (42⅛ in)

Di 40 cm (15¾ in)

Manufacturer: Morphos, Italy

131

VICO MAGISTRETTI
Chairs, *Silver I and II*
ALUMINIUM, POLYPROPYLENE
H 80 cm (31½ in) W 51.5 cm (20 in)
D 44 cm (17¼ in)
Manufacturer: Edizioni de Padova,
Italy

132

**UWE FISCHER AND
KLAUS-ACHIM HEINE
FOR GINBANDE**
Folding table, *Tabula Varia*
PLYWOOD, ALUMINIUM,
PLASTIC
H 80 cm (31½ in) W 80 cm (31½ in)
L 400 cm max (157½ in)
Manufacturer: Vitra, Switzerland

133

ANTONIO CITTERIO
Chair, *AC 1*
ALUMINIUM, POLYURETHANE
AND FABRIC UPHOLSTERY
H 102 cm (39¾ in) W 67 cm (26 in)
D 43 cm (16¾ in)
Manufacturer: Vitra, Switzerland

Charles Eames must be counted as one of the most significant proponents of contemporary design, who reinvented the chair with new technology, new materials, new forms. The chaise was originally designed, with his wife Ray, for a Museum of Modern Art competition in 1948. It is typical of Eames furniture: technically advanced, with an organic form that has emotional qualities. It was intended for use as a "one and a half" seater – for example, as a seat for a mother and child.

Jasper Morrison is the spokesman for minimal design. His collection entitled *Some new items for the house* is reduced and deliberately simple in line. Despite the careful arrangement of the pieces, he claims not to be an interior designer. "It interests me to make rooms with furniture and objects that you'd expect to see in a room, but to leave out the room itself. Interior design is essentially a one-off activity while design is about production. There is a danger in designing for production of ignoring the outcome, the final destination of the item. By making these imaginary rooms, it is possible to take into account the final destination and purpose of production design." His masking tape lines on the floor are used to describe the room without its actually being there.

The rarity value of a piece by Ron Arad is recognized in the saleroom prices his furniture is now attracting. No sooner had he conquered mild steel for his voluminous chairs balanced with lead (see *The International Design Yearbook 1989/90*) than he moved on to timber. This is a new material for him, but his chair shows a mastery of the material: the two pieces fit together as beautifully as dovetailed joints, yet can also be moved apart to form slender, single seats.

134

JASPER MORRISON

Some new items for the house

BIRCH PLYWOOD, ALUMINIUM, STEEL

Prototypes (the chair only is in production)

H 85 cm (33½ in) W 40 cm (15¾ in) D 40 cm (15¾ in)

Manufacturer: Vitra, Switzerland

136

RON ARAD

Chair, *Schizo*

LAMINATED WOOD, HIGH GRADE STEEL

The two parts of the chair slot together

Chair one H 89 cm (34¾ in) W 35 cm (13½ in) D 37 cm (14½ in)

Chair two H 86 cm (33½ in) W 35 cm (13½ in) D 35 cm (13½ in)

Manufacturer: Vitra, Switzerland

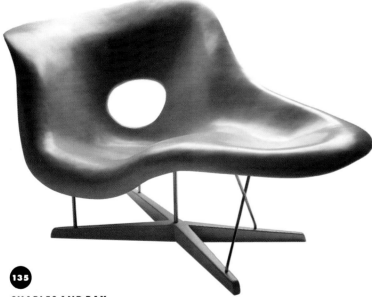

135

CHARLES AND RAY EAMES

Eames Chaise

FIBREGLASS SHELL, CHROMED TUBULAR STEEL STAND, OAK BASE

Re-edition from 1948

H 120 cm (47 in) W 180 cm (70⅝ in) D 80 cm (31½ in)

Manufacturer: Vitra, Switzerland

While art and craft companionably work together, design makes an uncomfortable ménage à trois. Designers need machine-age production for cost control, but in a way that does not inhibit craftsmanship or artistry. Oscar Tusquets Blanca's new collection for Aleph – easy chairs that are far from casual, capable of being produced in large runs – highlight what the manufacturers call "the spirit of joyful Renaissance characteristic of today's cultural front in the new Spain" alongside technical virtuosity. The supple shape of *Peineta* makes other slatted benches look wooden by comparison. The fact that individual flourishes are capable of being reproduced in many different materials (other pieces in the collection use metal and wire mesh) illustrates Tusquets Blanca's fiercely held principle: "One feature that distinguishes the art of design from other arts, such as sculpture, is that designs can be repeatedly reproduced by machines or by artisans other than the designer," he wrote in his Foreword to *The International Design Yearbook 1989/90*.

GORM HARKÆR

Folding garden furniture
BEECH, STAINLESS STEEL,
CONCRETE BASE, WOOL FELT
UPHOLSTERY
Chair H 70 cm (27½ in) W 48 cm
(18⅞ in) D 42 cm (16½ in)
Table H 70 cm (27½ in) W 84 cm
(33 in) L 84 cm (33 in)
*Manufacturer: Skovgaard &
Frydensberg, Denmark*

ANGELO MANGIAROTTI

Bench, *Clizia*
TRAVERTINE MARBLE
H 40 cm (15¾ in) W 50 cm (19⅝ in)
D 40 cm (15¾ in)
Manufacturer: Skipper, Italy

**OSCAR TUSQUETS
BLANCA**

Collapsible sofa, *Peineta*
TEAK, ALUMINIUM FITTINGS
H 90 cm (35½ in) W 114 cm (44½ in)
D 70 cm (27½ in)
Manufacturer: Aleph, Italy

 140

JOHN MAKEPEACE
Steamer Chairs
BEECH, COTTON UPHOLSTERY
Limited batch production
H 127 cm (50 in) W 60 cm (23½ in)
D 80/175 cm (31⅛/68⅞ in)
Manufacturer: John Makepeace, UK

Furniture by the British designer John Makepeace is in many private and public collections throughout the world. The finest furniture, he believes, has been the result of collaboration between designer and craftsman, a relationship he compares with that of a conductor working with virtuoso musicians to interpret a score. Most of his projects are privately commissioned. "There is little point in someone coming to me for a piece of furniture," he says, "unless it produces some fresh dimension which they could not have anticipated."

The *Steamer Chairs* are produced in limited edition. Evocative of another age in their craftsmanship, they have a certain practicality in their folding joints. They seem especially "English" in what Italians might call "Liberty Style". Makepeace comments: "Perhaps the style and feeling of the object is the result of my preoccupation with its function, as much as a part of my concern to develop ideas from a culture and history which is an intimate part of the designer."

 141

OSCAR TUSQUETS BLANCA
Bench, *Jofanco*
GRANITE
H 85 cm (33½ in) W 200 cm (78¾ in)
D 75 cm (29½ in)
Manufacturer: Escofet, Spain

Elaborate themes staged in the gloomy atmosphere of an abandoned abbatoir outside Milan make Pallucco and Rivier's unveiling of their furniture collection each year a crowd-pulling event. The pieces for 1990 cleverly market the concept of the end of a decade, with a symbolic bookcase, a *Necessary Angel* with arms outstretched ascending from a field of flowers, and the awakening of a new age with the finely engineered *Hero's Muscles* table and the armchair *Lilly of the Wind*. Buried beneath all the hype of the elaborate presentation is an interesting idea: communication with an audience.

Communication often seems more important that the objects themselves. "At one extreme it's an avant-garde attempt to talk about furniture," says Mario Bellini. "Their disconcerting geometry makes one insecure. It also challenges Cartesian principles." "*Hero's Muscles* is ruled by force," says Paolo Pallucco. "Its central handle supports four outstretched arms that hold all the power, upon which rests the thin top," a neat reversal of roles since most table tops are the weighty part. The surface is a clear, very thin glass pioneered by NASA for space-shuttle windows which allows stretch without fragmentation or buckling.

142

PAOLO PALLUCCO AND MIREILLE RIVIER
Shelving system, *Angelo Necessario*
Epoxy-painted steel frame, wood shelves
H 229 cm (89⅓ in) W 118.3 (46 in)
D 38.2/59.5 cm (15/23¼ in)
Manufacturer: Pallucco, Italy

143

**PAOLO PALLUCCO AND
MIREILLE RIVIER**

Table, *Hero's Muscles*

STEEL, GLASS

H 38.4 cm (15¼ in) W 114.6 cm

(44⅓ in) L 114.6 cm (44⅓ in)

Manufacturer: Pallucco, Italy

144

**PAOLO PALLUCCO AND
MIREILLE RIVIER**

Armchair, *Lilly of the Wind*

STEEL STRUCTURE,
POLYURETHANE AND LEATHER
UPHOLSTERY

H 86 cm (33⅞ in) W 81 cm (31¾ in)

D 71 cm (28 in)

Manufacturer: Pallucco, Italy

 145

**WOGG DESIGN AND
JOHANN MUNZ**
Wardrobe, *Wogg 4*
ALUMINIUM
The door folds around on
three sides of the structure
on ball-bearings and a steel
strap
H 205 cm (80 in) W 88.5 cm (34⅞ in)
or 126 cm (49 in) D 70 cm (27½ in)
Manufacturer: Wogg, Switzerland

 146

LUCA MEDA

Wardrobe, *7 Volte 7*

PAINTED WALNUT

H 242.5–297 cm (94½–115⅞ in)

W 45–120 cm (17¾–47¼ in) D 62 cm

(24⅜ in)

Manufacturer: Molteni, Italy

147

KAREN MÜCKEL

Living box, *Sparta-Sybaris*

BIRCH, ALUMINIUM

Prototype

Bookshelf H 90 cm (35½ in) W 150 cm
(59 in) D 45 cm (17¾ in)

Desk H 74.5 cm (29⅓ in) W 150 cm
(59 in) D 90 cm (35½ in)

Bed H 38 cm (15 in) W 96 cm (37¾ in)
L 200 cm (78¾ in)

Chair H 81 cm (31¾ in) W 45 cm
(17¾ in) D 50.5 cm (19⅞ in)

Wardrobe H 195 cm (76⅞ in)

W 98 cm (38½ in) D 75 cm (29½ in)

*Manufacturer: Berliner Zimmer, West
Germany*

"As with any new composition, I want to proclaim my variant of a well-known idea that furniture is a sculpture in space." Soviet graphic designer Mikhail Anikst (who planned *The International Design Yearbook 1988/89*) created these scale models for exhibition at the Museum für Angewandte Kunst in Cologne during the international furniture fair of 1990. Based on the Suprematist paintings of Malevich, they are a response to his transcendental abstraction, with primary colours a little dulled following the artist's own palette. Kazimir Malevich described the black square as "the window on the world", so Anikst has centred his collection on it. "Superimposing the red square or circle creates a new space. In the twentieth century the pattern created at the time of the Renaissance, in which everything from print to profiles was connected, composed and then framed, was broken. The use of the diagonal freed us expressively from that composition. I have played with simple forms to create more complicated abstractions. Comfort is not important to me."

148

MIKHAIL ANIKST
Chairs and table, *Homage to Russian Suprematism*
Plastic-coated cardboard
Prototypes
All dimensions are of scale models
Table H 3.5 cm (1⅗ in) W 12 cm
(4¾ in) L 12 cm (4¾ in)
Chair one H 10.5 cm (4⅛ in) W 11 cm
(4⅜ in) D 5 cm (2 in)
Chair two H 11.5 cm (4½ in)
W 4.5 cm (1¾ in) D 5 cm (2 in)
Chair three H 13.5 cm (5⅖ in) W 6 cm
(2⅜ in) D 5 cm (2 in)
Chair four H 14 cm (5½ in) W 7 cm
(2¾ in) D 4.5 cm (1¾ in)
Manufacturer: Mikhail Anikst, USSR

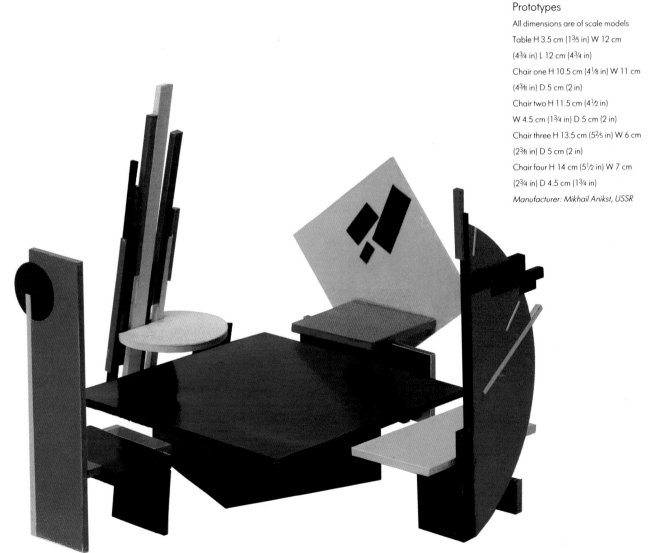

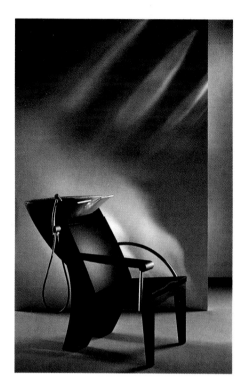  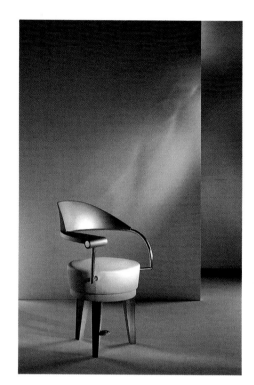

Furniture designed for the contract market, and a salon in particular, would not normally be represented in *The International Design Yearbook*, yet when Philippe Starck makes over a property commercial mass production of the more popular lines often follows. Designs for the Royalton Hotel in New York went into production soon after their launch in 1988: the horn-shaped lamp was made by Flos in Italy, and the fenders, firetongs, corkscrews and door handles were made by Starck's own small manufacturing company, Owo, in France.

Although hairdressing is essentially a fashion industry, salons are mostly fitted out in a clinical way: Starck believes that some of the necessary interaction between artist and client is lost as a result. He sought to make the salon both welcoming and more comfortable. "Beauty is a gift; receiving it should be a pleasure. Let us give the hairdressing salon its true meaning once again. Soulless equipment shall disappear, to be replaced with furniture which is elegant, discreet, well designed for the purpose and which, like the salon, will improve the wellbeing and comfort of the individual."

PHILIPPE STARCK
The *L'Oreal Coiffure* collection
Limited batch production
Above left:
Fauteuil de Lavage
POLYURETHANE AND STEEL STRUCTURE, FROSTED GLASS BASIN
H 95 cm (37½ in) W 53 cm (21 in) D 105 cm (41 in)
Above centre:
Fauteuil Techno
ALUMINIUM, MOULDED POLYURETHANE, HYDRAULIC BASE
H 95 cm (37½ in) W 53 cm (21 in) D 105 cm (41 in)
Above right:
Fauteuil Home
PEAR WOOD, POLYURETHANE, SKAI, SWIVEL SEAT OPERATED BY PEDAL
H 85 cm (33½ in) W 52 cm (20½ in) D 55 cm (21½ in)
Manufacturer: Présence Paris, France

150

PHILIPPE STARCK

Chair, *Tessa Nature*

BEECH, WOVEN PAPER OR

LEATHER SEAT

H 74 cm (29 in) W 48 cm (18⅞ in)

D 52.5 cm (20⅝ in)

Manufacturer: Driade, Italy

151

PHILIPPE STARCK

Chair, *Jane Paille*

BEECH, BEECH PLYWOOD,

WOVEN PAPER OR LEATHER

SEAT

H 89.5 cm (35 in) W 66 cm (26 in)

D 63 cm (24⅞ in)

Manufacturer: Driade, Italy

152

PHILIPPE STARCK

Chair, *Placide of Wood*

CHERRY, CHERRY PLYWOOD,

PEAR WOOD

H 91.5 cm (35¾ in) W 44 cm (17¼ in)

D 56.5 cm (22¼ in)

Manufacturer: Driade, Italy

"Designers should take the factory tool to make a better design for a better chair for everyone. That is really democratic design. One chair a minute. Astori of Aleph and Driade asked me to design a chair that could be prolifically produced. I sent in nine designs, and he made up nine prototypes, planning to put into production only one. But it was impossible to choose, so he produced seven. All have a different spirit – differences in colour, detail, different woods, from fruitwoods to hardwoods. Some are textural."

Starck's new collection for Driade is inspired by the technology of the conventional wooden chair. He explores familiar seats, with departures from the obvious. Legs are emphasized to become elements of sculptural relief in *Placide of Wood*, while the enfolding back support of *Jane Paille* transforms it into a protective club chair.

"My main ambition – no, production – this year has been to design with NO STYLE. For many years we all sought style. Now we need discretion, something invisible, something that provides a real service for people, a really generous idea, affordable, not too heavy for mobility. With a good product, there is no obligation to show its design." Starck believes that with so many projects in interior design today there is no more adventure to be had in it. So he has closed his own interior design projects; his final commission, for an interior in the Century Paramount Hotel, New York, opened in March 1990. Now he concentrates on architecture. "Perhaps in two years' time it will be right to stop designing furniture. Now, I think that in my production there are still some good pieces. You don't need to design more."

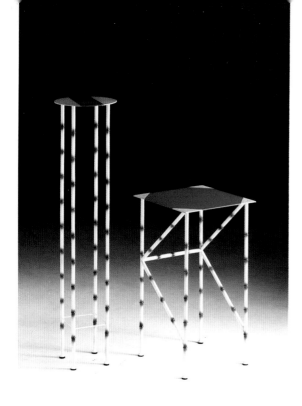

 153

ANDREA BRANZI
Vase holder, *Polinio*
STEEL FRAME, LACQUERED
WOOD TOP
One-off
H 130 cm (50²⁄₃ in) Di of top 32 cm
(12½ in)
Manufacturer: Zanotta, Italy

Stylish to the point of obsession, Milan guards its reputation as the design centre of the world. Cars, clothes, furnishing fabrics, furniture, office equipment – the shows to launch the new designs go on and on. Innovative manufacturing is the key. So at the thirtieth annual furniture fair it was interesting to observe that the leading manufacturers are shifting their position.

Zanotta, realizing that the future lies with avant-garde creativity as much as with modular seating systems for contract markets, produces élitist collections. Sometimes the editions are limited to one, numbered and signed by the artists or architects, all of whom also have design experience. This new collection recognizes new market trends: upmarket individuality runs alongside commercial lines for the mass market. Over forty limited-edition designs are intended to span the gap between furniture and art. The highly individual pieces are, claim Zanotta, "functional and poetic objects of interior design in which the poetic inspiration of the designers is freely expressed, without restraint." In aluminium and wood, with silk-screened fabrics and inlaid marquetry, each piece involves a degree of handwork not found in factory-assembled furniture. The work of the Neapolitan artist Riccardo Dalisi, for example, encapsulates the artistry and the craftsmanship involved. His *Mariposa* bench has an attenuated insect form, literally putting out feelers into a new market.

 155

ALESSANDRO MENDINI
Table, *Macaone*
LACQUERED WOOD
One-off
H 73 cm (28¾ in) W 140 cm (55⅛ in)
L 160 cm (63 in)
Manufacturer: Zanotta, Italy

 154

ANDREA BRANZI
Chair, *Cucus*
PLYWOOD, HAZELNUT
BRANCHES
Limited batch production
H 114 cm (44½ in) W 50 cm (19⅝ in)
D 57 cm (22⅜ in)
Manufacturer: Zanotta, Italy

ETTORE SOTTSASS
Desk, *Litta*
VENEERED COMPOUND
LAMINATE FRAME, LEATHER
INSERT, ASH DRAWERS, BRASS
HANDLES
One-off
H 76 cm (30 in) W 70 cm (27½ in)
L 130 cm (51⅛ in)
Manufacturer: Zanotta, Italy

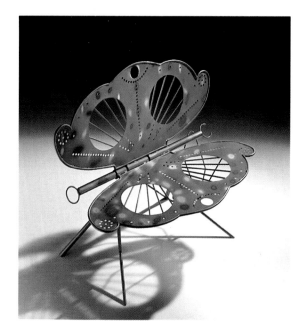

RICCARDO DALISI
Bench, *Mariposa*
STEEL
Limited batch production
H 88 cm (34⅝ in) W 102 cm (40⅜ in)
D 55 cm (21½ in)
Manufacturer: Zanotta, Italy

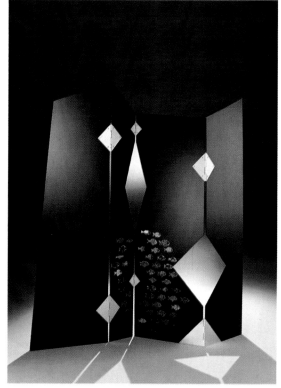

BRUNO MUNARI
Screen, *Spiffero*
ENAMELLED ALUMINIUM
PANELS, NICKEL-PLATED STEEL
HINGES, SILK-SCREENED
PRINTING
One-off
H 160 cm (63 in) W 161 cm (63⅓ in)
Manufacturer: Zanotta, Italy

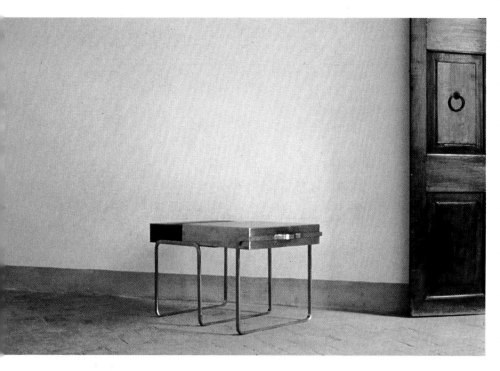

 160

SUSANA SOLANO
Table, *Valigia*
BURNISHED STEEL,
MAHOGANY
Limited batch production
H 58.5 cm (23 in) W 62 cm (24⅜ in)
L 95.5 cm (37½ in)
Manufacturer: Meta Memphis, Italy

 159

MIMMO PALADINO
Chest, *Ficcanaso*
MAPLE, PADOUK
Limited batch production
H 181 cm (71⅜ in) W 180 cm (70⅝ in)
D 45 cm (17¾ in)
Manufacturer: Meta Memphis, Italy

161

JOSEPH KOSUTH
Bed, *Modus Operandi*
WOOD FRAME, QUILTED
HEAD, JACQUARD BEDSPREAD
Limited batch production
H 75 cm (29½ in) W 85/170 cm
(33½/66⅓ in) L 210 cm (82⅝ in)
Manufacturer: Meta Memphis, Italy

162

FRANZ WEST
Chair
IRON
Limited batch production
H 85 cm (33½ in) W 72.5 cm (28⅔ in)
D 70 cm (27½ in)
Manufacturer: Meta Memphis, Italy

Dr Gregorini of Zanotta considered commissioning a small collection of signed and numbered pieces of furniture from artists, but replaced the idea with commissions to tried and tested designers because he felt it would be impossible to translate artists' drawings and sketches into three-dimensional form (see pages 90–91). Ernesto Gismondi of Artemide and Alias, however, was not deterred. For his Meta Memphis collection (on these and the following two pages), artists have taken on furniture design – tables, sofas, chairs, desks, lamps and clocks for the home. In the Foreword to the catalogue Marco De Michelis writes: "The whole history of contemporary design could be catalogued as the process of reciprocal investigations between the industrial world and the figurative arts. The former is still young and interested in giving the machine civilization a sense of heritage; the latter is willing to bring the themes of the aesthetic revolution into a new concept of daily life."

Ten artists were invited to participate. Pistoletto's iron structure, treated with lustreless paint, is reduced to an abstraction, finding new meaning in the crowded clutter of domestic objects as conceptual art. Paladino makes the chest a solitary hiding place, isolating and defining privacy and intimacy. Weiner, with a wastepaper basket of copper-plated brass and marble, builds a monument to waste, incapable of being emptied. He writes: "There are times when the only sense of accomplishment in a day is the amount of débris that accrues." Joseph Kosuth's allegorical bed is covered with a jacquard bedspread which reproduces the jacket of the first edition of Freud's *The Interpretation of Dreams*. Susana Solano's small table in welded steel is constructed to slide open effortlessly, reducing the stolid immobility of most tables and giving it a grace of movement. Franz West imbues a scrap-iron chain with the illusion of the Indian rope trick, holding aloft a bulb in a delicate sculpture.

 163

**MICHELANGELO
PISTOLETTO**
Mobile
MATT-PAINTED IRON
Limited batch production
H 220 cm (86⅝ in) W 100 cm (39½ in)
D 30 cm (11⅞ in)
Manufacturer: Meta Memphis, Italy

 164

LAWRENCE WEINER
Wastepaper basket
COPPER-PLATED BRASS,
MARBLE
Limited batch production
H 59 cm (23¼ in) W 32 cm (12½ in)
D 21 cm (8¼ in)
Manufacturer: Meta Memphis, Italy

 165

MIMMO PALADINO
Shelving system, *Solus*
BEECH, EBONY MIRROR-
FRAME, BRONZE COFFER
Limited batch production
H 175 cm (68⅞ in) W 165 cm (65 in)
D 50 cm (19⅝ in)
Manufacturer: Meta Memphis, Italy

 166

FRANZ WEST
Lamp
IRON, HALOGEN BULB
Limited batch production
H 170 cm (66⅓ in)
Manufacturer: Meta Memphis, Italy

A collection of Jasper Morrison's furniture – tables, a lounger and chairs, some of which were designed several years ago – was presented for the first time in 1989 as a popular line in mass production, all made by Cappellini International. This has similarities with the marketing of fashion, in which haute couture exclusivity makes it into ready-to-wear collections, and the point was emphasized by the furniture launch at the studio of fashion designer Romeo Gigli. It bears out Jasper Morrison's conviction that all furniture should be designed with mass production in mind. Though for years he relied on small-scale production within small workshops dotted around London, his designs have always avoided handwork. "The term designer-maker has been adopted in a half-hearted attempt to give the craftsperson a more modern profile," he says. "There is no room for craft in industry."

 169

JASPER MORRISON
Flower Pot Table
TERRACOTTA, GLASS,
CHROMED METAL PLATE
H 65 cm (25½ in) Di of top 40 cm
(15¾ in)
Manufacturer: Cappellini, Italy

168

JASPER MORRISON
Chair, *Three Chair*
ALUMINIUM, ASH PLYWOOD
H 72 cm (28½ in) W 78 cm (30¾ in)
D 50 cm (19⅝ in)
Manufacturer: Cappellini, Italy

 167

JASPER MORRISON
Day bed
WOOD, ALUMINIUM FEET,
POLYURETHANE FOAM
UPHOLSTERY
H 78 cm (30¾ in) W 71 cm (28 in)
L 216 cm (85 in)
Manufacturer: Cappellini, Italy

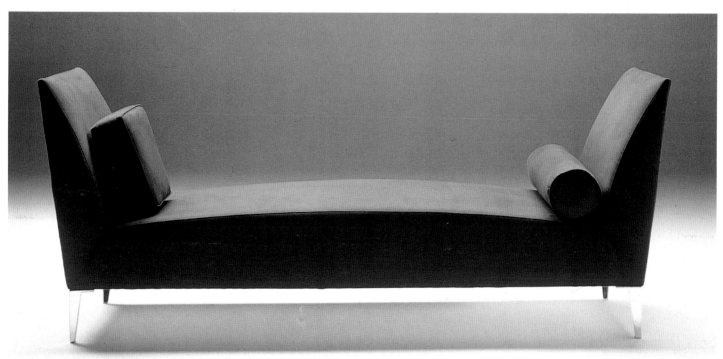

Danny Lane is a creative force whose furniture in glass has upended many of the concepts associated with the glass-topped table. His tables, chairs and towers are made through a controlled system of random breakage and fracture, and a technique for sandblasting clear float crystal. Expression comes before application. His strong ideological commitment to art and design comes from a feeling that exists independently of any design concept. He believes that one's personality manifests itself in one's field of endeavour, in "the way you solve problems, the way you apply yourself, be you an artist, designer or motor mechanic. The architecture of my pieces is constructed around a respect for materials, function and aesthetic performance. I have compressors, sandblasters, welders, grinders and large sheets of glass, but the most important instruments are myself and the team."

One of the symptoms of a halt in the mass production of modern furniture is that students of design are reviving age-old craft techniques alongside contemporary finishes such as panel-beating or airbrush painting. To make this ossuary (a reliquary for bones), postgraduate student at the Royal College of Art Roger Bateman hewed the column out of holly wood, set it in stone with a stonemason's skills, cast the helmet-like urn in bronze from a clay model, and panel-beat the doors from copper. The ossuary can be seen to symbolize the death of machine-age manufacturing.

2 · LIGHTING

Fittings are less important than the quality of light they shed, so the reflector, the baffle and the shield are now dominating lighting design. With the miniaturization of the source, there have been experiments with the housing, for example Meda and Rizzatto's *Titania*, in which the glare is shielded by colourful, interchangeable battens. The trend this year is to use metal halide discharge lamps, which give a light that is brighter yet at the same time cooler than the sparkle from dichroic low-voltage bulbs.

Bertheau-Suzuki makes his *Doping* lamp stalk on all fours, and De Pas, D'Urbino and Lomazzi adopt a playful approach with a ceiling lamp that undulates like the mythical Loch Ness monster. These are pure theatrics, designed to be eye-catching. Designs that move away from theatrical effects include Castiglioni's discreet *Parter*, with its glass diffuser sconce, designed to be unobtrusive when the lamp is switched off – the opposite of a decorative lamp. Jorge Pensi, whose streamlined *Olympia* put Spain in the running (see *The International Design Yearbook 1989/90*), has produced some additions to the series, as well as *Taps*, from which a simple stream of light is emitted.

Ingo Maurer also illustrates the wisdom of continuing with a good idea, extending the scope with his bird-like *Eclipselipse*, which hovers on the wall on touch-sensitive controls that eliminate all traditional wiring and switches. Red Square from New York employ an old trick for maximum illumination by putting rice paper shades on incandescent bulbs which are coated with heat-resistant paint to provide subtle colour. Jan Van Lierde from Belgium presents his innovative *Wind* lamps, which diffuse perfume in the heat; he is currently researching new developments in photosynthetic paper panels. Sant and Bigas explore the architectural qualities of light with an aluminium cornice that lights up where a lamp is clipped in; it can define stair treads or illuminate pictures.

Adjustment and angling are increasingly important, with telescopic lamps made of whiplash flexible carbon fibre, capable of extending like fishing rods. Tusquets Blanca's *Bib Luz* hanging lamp is extendable, Porsche's *Jazz* packs flat like a slim handset, while Stephan Copeland's *Tango* rotates on its jointed stem which is encased in a rubber concertina. Mario Bellini sought a good shape which provided a good direction and diffusion of light, and eliminated mechanical fussiness as well as lamps that were over-designed.

MARCO FERRERI
Table lamp, *Zan-Zo*
GLASS BASE, CHROMIUM-
PLATED BRASS CLOTH
DIFFUSER
Takes one 100W or 150W
incandescent or halogen
bulb
H 35 or 68 cm (13¾ or 26¾ in)
Di 22 or 30 cm (8⅔ or 11⅞ in)
Manufacturer: Fontana Arte, Italy

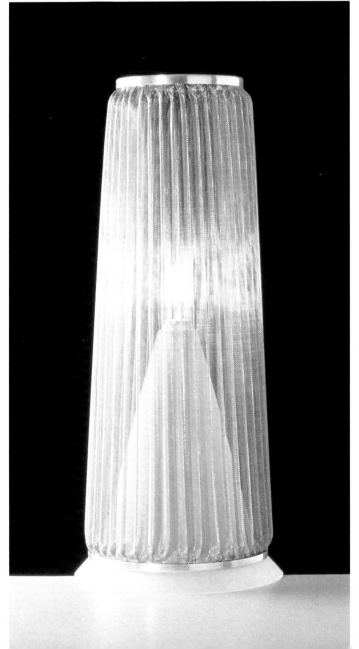

UMBERTO RIVA
Table lamp, *Franceschina*
ALUMINIUM, BRASS, GLASS
SHADE
Takes one 60W
incandescent bulb
H 35 cm (13¾ in) Di 17 cm (6⅝ in)
Manufacturer: Fontana Arte, Italy

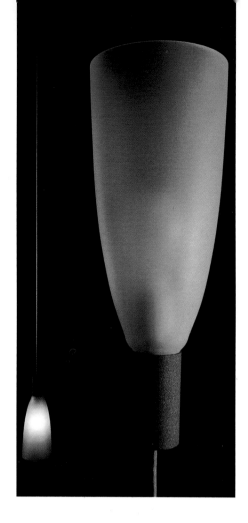

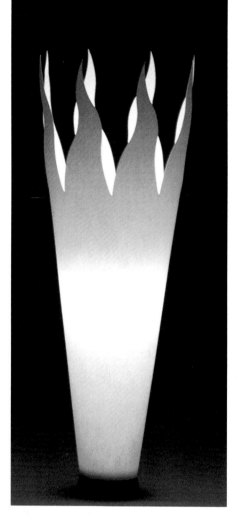

③

RED SQUARE DESIGN
Floor lamp, *Freddy*
Ceiling lamp, *Karl*
BASE METAL PLASMA-SPRAYED
WITH STAINLESS STEEL, SAND-
BLASTED GLASS SHADE
Each takes one 75W
incandescent bulb
H 180 cm (71 in) Di 25.5 cm (10 in)
Manufacturer: Red Square Design,
USA

④

RED SQUARE DESIGN
Table lamp, *Transforms*
METAL, RICE PAPER
Takes one 75W bulb, hand-
painted with heat-resistant
paint
H 61 cm (24 in) Di 30.5 cm (12 in)
Manufacturer: Red Square Design,
USA

⑤

RED SQUARE DESIGN
Table lamp, *LUZlamp*
CARBON STEEL, PARCHMENT
Takes one 75W
incandescent bulb
H 48.5 cm (19 in)
Di of shade 12.5 cm (5 in)
Manufacturer: Red Square Design,
USA

CHRISTIAN PLODERER
Oil lamp, *Feuerlichter*
Nickel-plated brass
Uses non-smelling
petroleum
H 15.5 cm (6⅛ in) Di 12 cm (4¾ in)
Manufacturer: Vest Leuchten, Austria

The aptly named *Doping Lamp* with its athletic steel carcass
(the matching chair is enclosed in wet-suit fabric) was
designed during the Olympic Games in Seoul when Ben
Johnson hit the headlines on drugs charges. "This lamp,
which seems to walk or break into a run, has in fact
swallowed too many medicines to run after fashionable
success," says Bertheau-Suzuki. "It refers to the
Deconstructivist movement in its asymmetry. I didn't want to
be just a 'fashionable' designer, but to parody this fashion."

**GUEN BERTHEAU-
SUZUKI**
Doping Lamp
Steel
Takes one 60W 210V
incandescent bulb
Prototype
H 45 cm (17¾ in) W 12 cm (4¾ in)
L 35 cm (13¾ in)
Manufacturer: Ishimaru, Japan

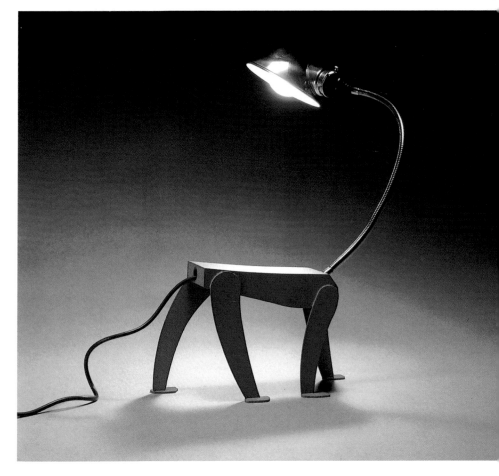

JOSÉ RIPOLL
Floor lamp, *Piscis*
POLYESTER AND FIBREGLASS
TUBE, STEEL BASE,
POLYCARBONATE FILM SHADE
Takes one 60 or 100W E27
incandescent bulb
H 186 cm (72½ in)
Manufacturer: Vapor, Spain

MAURIZIO PEREGALLI
Floor and table lamps,
Ventosa
EPOXY-PAINTED STEEL,
CERAMIC DIFFUSER
Floor lamp takes one 75W
halogen bulb
H 150 cm (59 in) Di of base 25 cm
(9⅞ in)
Table lamp takes one 50W
halogen bulb
H 60 cm (23½ in)
Di of base 15 cm (6 in)
Manufacturer: Noto, Italy

11

**DAVID FERRER AND
CARLES LA PUENTE**

Floor lamp, *Lámpara
Mitral*

CHROMED STEEL, FABRIC
SHADE, EBONY PULL SWITCH

Takes one 100W
incandescent bulb

H 92 cm (36 in) Di of shade: 55 cm
(21½ in)

*Manufacturer: Bd Ediciones de
diseño, Spain*

10

SERGE MEPPIEL

Wall lamp, *Hemera*

EPOXY-PAINTED SHEET STEEL,
GLASS DIFFUSERS

Takes one 300W halogen
bulb

W 50 cm (19⅝ in)

Manufacturer: Noto, Italy

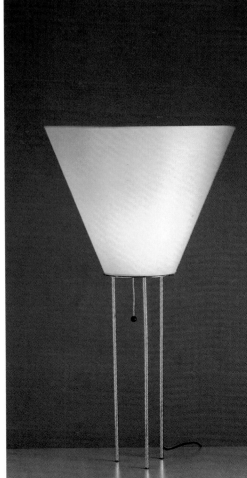

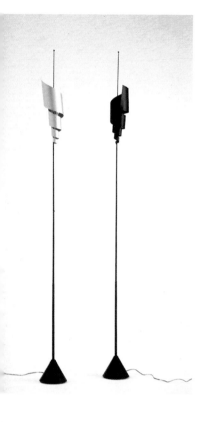

 CARLOS HAHN

Floor lamps, *Schleife, Baires*
CEMENT BASES, IRON PIPE,
FLEXIBLE BRONZE ARM
Each takes one 50W
halogen bulb
H 144–211 cm (56⅛–82⅜ in)
Manufacturer: Satō, West Germany

12 **PIERRE MAZAIRAC AND
KAREL BOONZAAIJER**
Floor lamp, *Lady Luck*
FIBREGLASS, ANODIZED
ALUMINIUM
Takes one 20W halogen
bulb
H 210 cm (81⅝ in)
Manufacturer: Scan Light,
Netherlands

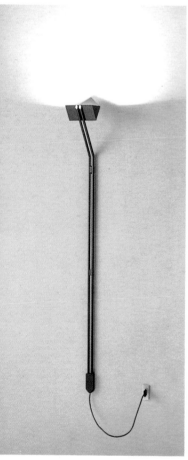

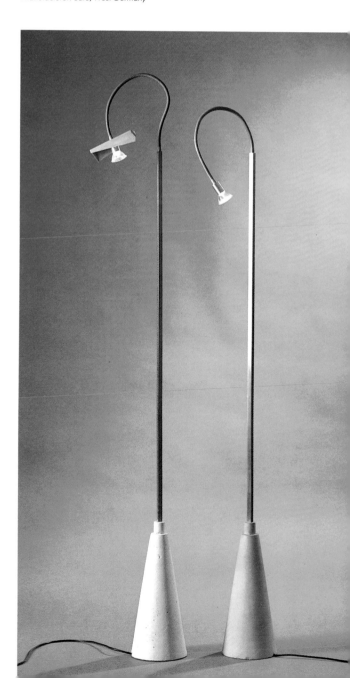

13 **MANLIO BRUSATIN**
Wall lamp, *Eidos P*
ANODIZED ALUMINIUM OR
18/8 STAINLESS STEEL
Takes one 300W tubular
halogen bulb
H 177 cm (69 in) W 18 cm (7 in)
L 20 cm (7⅞ in)
Manufacturer: Sirrah, Italy

This projectile shell, catapulted from a tiny red marble base, has a bowed tensile support. Like all Calatrava's work, it appears to defy gravity. In his sculpture, cubes of polished granite or marble held by frail pins and cables reflect his training as a bridge-builder and architect. He also designed the Zurich metro. Stress, tension, equilibrium and compression are his preoccupations, which he expressed in a thesis improbably entitled "The collapsibility of lattice-work structures". This slender lamp, with its unlikely diagonal support concealing the cord, has a grace that makes it a light sculpture as much as a fitting.

 15

CARLOS HAHN
Floor lamp, *Schwanschwan*
CEMENT BASE, FLEXIBLE
LACQUERED BRONZE ARM
Takes one 50W halogen
bulb
H 113-179 cm (44-69⅞ in)
Manufacturer: Satō, West Germany

 16

SANTIAGO CALATRAVA
Floor lamp, *Montjuic*
PAINTED SEMI-FOAMED FIBRE,
OPALINE METHACRYLATE
DIFFUSER
Takes one 500W tubular
halogen bulb
H 190 cm (74 in)
L of base 45 cm (17¾ in)
Manufacturer: Artemide, Italy

Behind every good patent, claims Achille Castiglioni, lies an unknown designer. His latest lamp adapts the simple idea of a sconce which projects from the wall. Connected to a power point near the floor, the name *Parter* suggests the Italian for both wall (*parete*) and floor (*terra*). "Normally, the sconce is seen as mostly decorative," says Castiglioni. "I don't think this is right. Why should it be a decorative item to light up a wall? So, starting from the idea of creating a lamp which would not be noticed too much when it was switched off, I used a glass diffuser which illuminates the wall. At the same time, it is hung so that no shadow falls on the wall. The distance of the reflector was then calculated to allow a halogen bulb to obtain the same effect. That's all."

MARCO ZANINI

Ceiling lamp, *Schiavone*

LACQUERED METAL, GLASS

Takes one 60W and ten tubular 25W incandescent bulbs

H 80 cm (31½ in)

Di max. 57 cm (22⅜ in)

Manufacturer: Venini, Italy

SERGIO MAZZA

Table lamp, *Rubin*

CHROME-PLATED BRASS, GLASS DIFFUSER

Takes one 20W 12V halogen bulb

H 22 cm (8⅔ in)

Di of shade 13.5 cm (5⅖ in)

Manufacturer: Quattrifolio, Italy

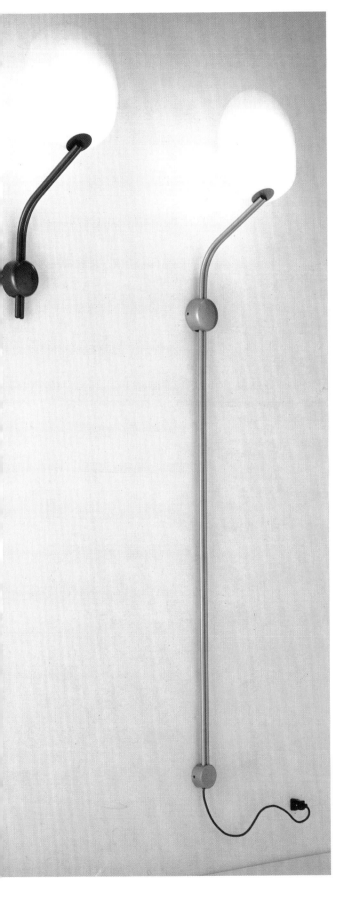

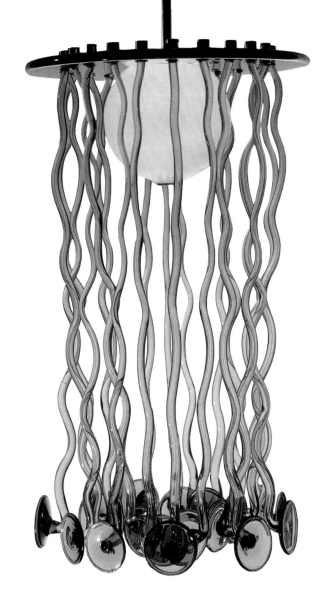

20

ETTORE SOTTSASS
Ceiling lamp, *Formosa*
GOLD-PLATED METAL, GLASS
Takes one 60W E14
incandescent bulb
H 70 cm (27½ in) Di 40 cm (15¾ in)

Manufacturer: Venini, Italy

19

ACHILLE CASTIGLIONI
Wall lamp, *Parter*
ENAMELLED METAL, PRESSED
GLASS DIFFUSER
Takes one 250W halogen
Halostar frosted bulb with
two shells or one 150W
incandescent bulb
Left: H 64.5 cm (25⅓ in)
W 29 cm (11⅜ in) D 33 cm (13 in)
Right: H 200 cm (78¾ in)
W 29 cm (11⅜ in) D 33 cm (13 in)

Manufacturer: Flos, Italy

 21

ROBERTO MARCATTI AND GIGI CONTI

Floor lamp, *Fantos*

STEEL, RUBBER, FIBREGLASS DIFFUSER

Takes one 150W halogen bulb

H 190 cm (74⅞ in)

Di of shade 30 cm (11⅞ in)

Manufacturer: Effetto Luce, Italy

 22

JACK WOOLLEY

Table lamp, *Cornet*

NYLON-COATED STEEL, TYVEK SHADE

Tyvek is a tear-resistant paper-like plastic made from high-density polyurethane fibres

Takes one 60W tungsten filament bulb

Limited batch production

H 70 cm (27½ in) Di 20 cm (7⅞ in)

Manufacturer: Toucan, UK

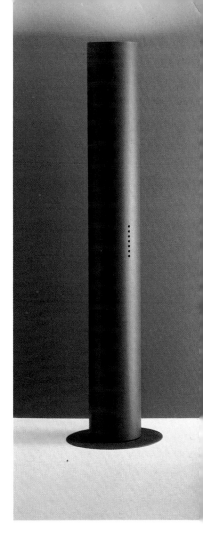

 23

JORGE GARCIA GARAY

Table and wall lamp, *Jet*

Chrome-plated steel rod

Takes one 60W E14 bulb.
The table lamp can also be
used as a wall lamp

Wall lamp (right) and table lamp

H 19 cm (7½ in) W 28 cm (11 in)

D 16 cm (6¼ in)

Small wall lamp (left) W 16 cm (6¼ in)

D 22 cm (8⅔ in)

Manufacturer: Garcia Garay, Spain

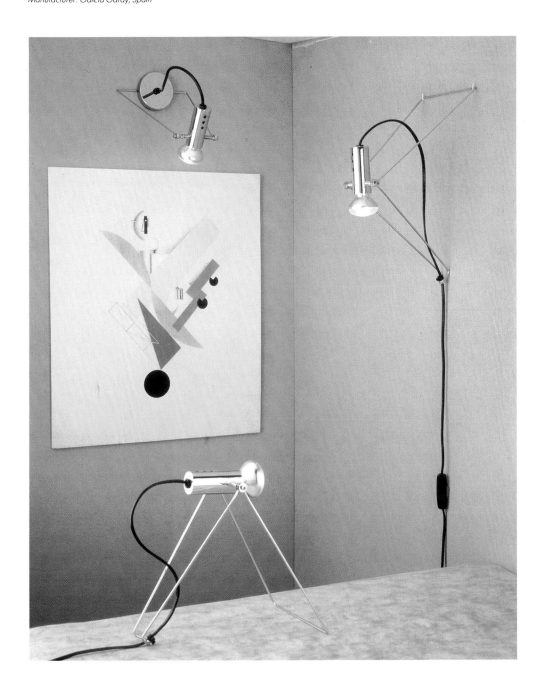

24

LELLA AND MASSIMO VIGNELLI

Floor lamp, *Sette Magie*

Metal

The copper reflector inside
the cylinder allows different
coloured light effects

Takes two tubular 330-
220W or 500-220W halogen
bulbs

H 200-240 cm (78-93½ in) Di 28 cm

(11 in) Di of base 51 cm (20 in)

Manufacturer: Morphos, Italy

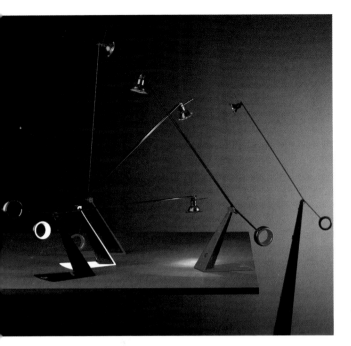

25

A & E DESIGN
Desk Lamp, *F1*
Floor Lamp, *F2*
ALUMINIUM, STEEL
COUNTERWEIGHT
Takes one 20W 12V
halogen bulb
H of base 25 cm (9⁷/₈ in)
W of base 14.5 cm (5³/₄ in)
L of arm 75 cm (29¹/₂ in)
Manufacturer: Belysia, Sweden

26

BENJAMIN THUT
Table Lamp, *Lifto*
STEEL SUPPORT WITH VARIOUS
FINISHES, GLASS DIFFUSER
Takes one 50W 12V
halogen bulb
L max. 130 cm (51¹/₈ in)
Manufacturer: Belux, Switzerland

27

SIGEAKI ASAHARA
Table lamp, *Z-618*
STEEL, PLASTIC
Takes one 70W halogen bulb
H 105 cm (41 in) W 25 cm (9⁷⁄₈ in)
Manufacturer: Yamada, Japan

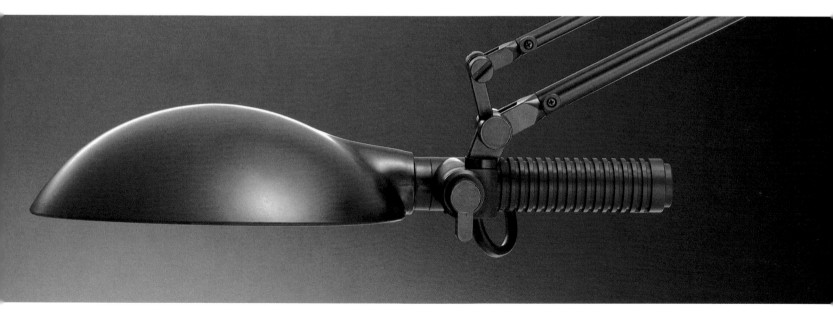

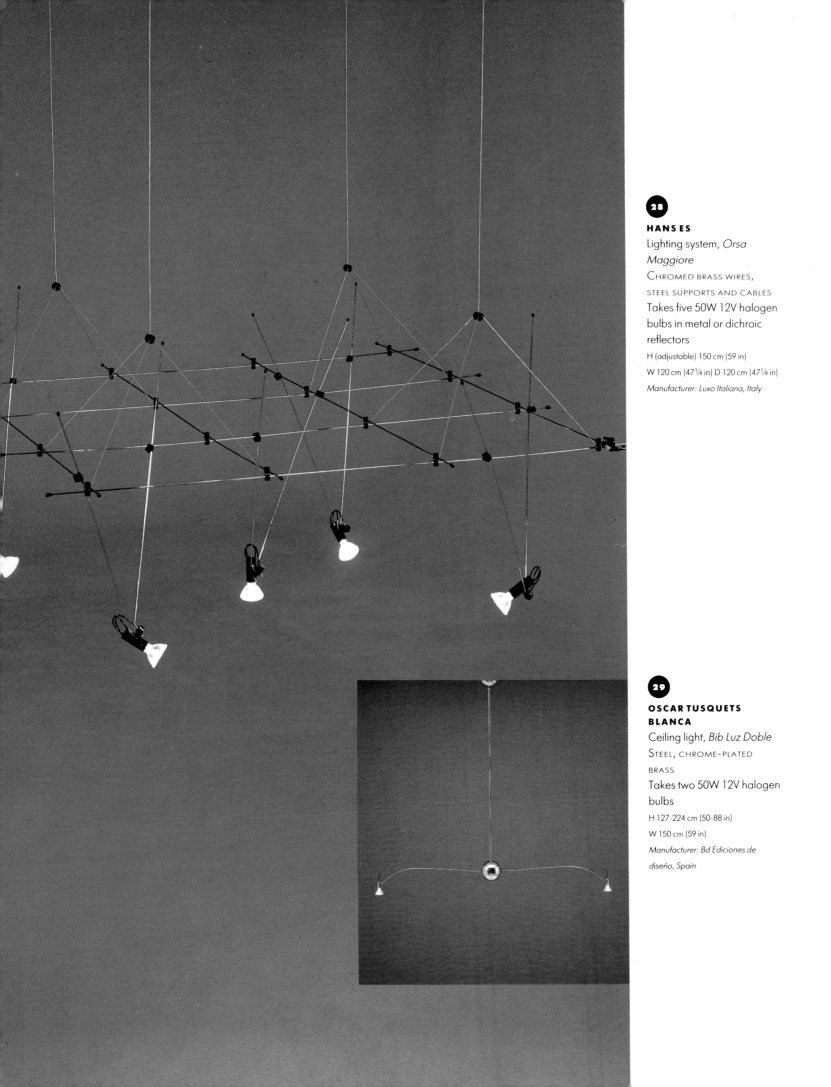

28

HANS ES
Lighting system, *Orsa Maggiore*
CHROMED BRASS WIRES, STEEL SUPPORTS AND CABLES
Takes five 50W 12V halogen bulbs in metal or dichroic reflectors
H (adjustable) 150 cm (59 in)
W 120 cm (47¼ in) D 120 cm (47¼ in)
Manufacturer: Luxo Italiana, Italy

29

OSCAR TUSQUETS BLANCA
Ceiling light, *Bib Luz Doble*
STEEL, CHROME-PLATED BRASS
Takes two 50W 12V halogen bulbs
H 127-224 cm (50-88 in)
W 150 cm (59 in)
Manufacturer: Bd Ediciones de diseño, Spain

31

JONATHAN DE PAS, DONATO D'URBINO AND PAOLO LOMAZZI

Ceiling lamp, *Nessie*
Lacquered or anodized metal
Takes five 20W or 50W 12V dichroic bulbs
L 100 cm (39 in)
Manufacturer: Stilnovo, Italy

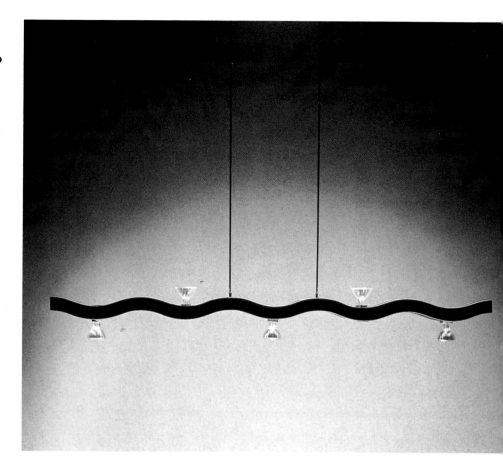

30

BORIS BROCHARD AND RUDOLF WEBER

Floor lamp, *Mobile*
Lacquered brass
Takes three 50W 12V halogen bulbs
H 240, 220 or 210 cm (93⅓, 86⅝ or 82 in) Di of base 30 cm (11⅞ in)
Manufacturer: Woka Lamps, Austria

Nessie is an interesting example of the playful form that lamps have taken since designers became more relaxed about the light source. As miniaturized bulbs provided longer light, designers could return to more amusing shapes, or harness the beam through reflectors and shields, as conscious of the shadow thrown as of the light itself. This Nineties version of an age-old myth, the Loch Ness monster, houses the dichroic bulb in an anodized, lacquered metal body to provide a suspension lamp with both direct and indirect lighting.

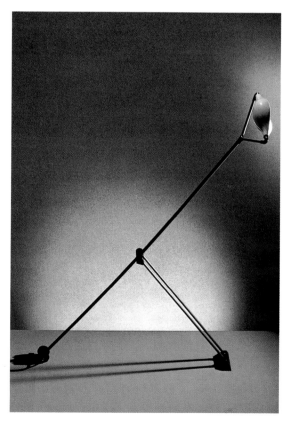

32

JONATHAN DE PAS, DONATO D'URBINO AND PAOLO LOMAZZI

Extendable floor or wall lamp, *Victory*
Lacquered metal, porcelain diffuser
Takes one 300W halogen bulb
H 210 cm (82½ in) W max. 180 cm (70½ in) L of diffuser 40 cm (15¾ in)
Manufacturer: Stilnovo, Italy

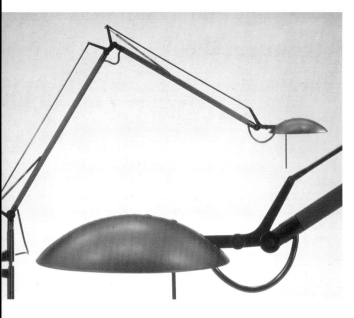

33

GABRIEL TEIXIDO
Table lamp, *Aladina*
ANODIZED ALUMINIUM
Takes one 50W 12V
halogen bulb
L 85 cm (33½ in)
Di of head 17 cm (6⅝ in)
Manufacturer: Carpyen, Spain

35

ALBERTO MEDA AND
PAOLO RIZZATTO
Ceiling lamp, *Titania*
ALUMINIUM STRUCTURE, STEEL
CABLES, SILK-SCREENED
POLYCARBONATE FILTERS
Takes one 150 or 250W E27
halogen bulb
H 8 cm (3⅛ in) W 27 cm (10½ in)
L 70 cm (27½ in)
Manufacturer: Luce-Plan, Italy

34

ALBERTO MEDA AND
PAOLO RIZZATTO
Wall lamp, *Screen*
ABS SUPPORT, TRANSPARENT
INJECTION-MOULDED
METHACRYLATE SCREEN
Takes one 150W E27
incandescent bulb
H 26 cm (10¼ in) L 36 cm (14⅛ in)
Manufacturer: Luce-Plan, Italy

Titania, Queen of the Fairies, adopts different raiments in
Meda and Rizzatto's halogen lamp. A magical
transformation of a grey or black aluminium ellipse occurs
when rib-like filters, which slot together on each side,
instantly change the colour of the reflection to green, blue,
yellow, red or mauve. Silk-screening of the polycarbonate
filters gives them a luminosity that no solid material could
achieve. The thin steel suspension cables, set independently
from the electrical point, make it possible to adjust the lamp
so that it is horizontal, almost vertical or set at the diagonal.

Alberto Meda and Paolo Rizzatto claim that most
suspension lamps do not have this flexibility of position or the
capability to be adapted to different interiors: most are
merely boring clones of each other. The simple function of
the *Titania*, its elliptical shape and aesthetic adaptability are
definite advances in design — and it is available to a wide
clientele through its moderate price.

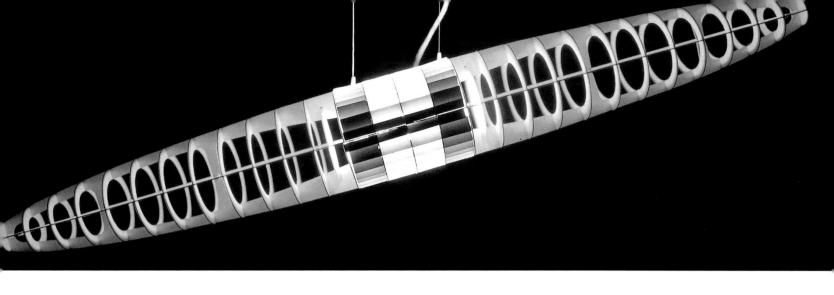

This thirty-year-old Canadian designer, living in Los Angeles, refers to the pivotal, enquiring cord of his *Tango* lamp as a gooseneck. The flamingo head of the lamp pivots while the reflector rotates in this most versatile of task lamps. The switch is located in the rubber boot at the head of the lamp. Copeland has always been fascinated by movement. While working as a merchant seaman he noticed that modern ships a thousand feet long could still safely flex with the waves: "It's amazing to see 50,000 tons of steel flowing like a piece of paper lying on top of the water. Similarly, it wasn't until we made office chairs that move with the human body that we began to understand sitting." Copeland has never followed any formal design training, yet this moving lamp undoubtedly has a disciplined fluidity.

His *China* task lamp is similarly dynamic in concept and simple in execution. The first lamp designed for Atelier International in the US outside their Italian collection, it provides direct dual-intensity light. Its reflector assembly rotates 270 degrees at the lamp head, while the stem assembly moves through 360 degrees at the base. The three-position switch is located on the reflector support. An in-line low-voltage transformer, built into the base, has a polarized detachable connection for use with workstation wireways.

36

STEPHAN COPELAND

Table lamp, *Tango*

ALUMINIUM, METAL SPRINGS, JOINTS COVERED IN POLYURETHANE, RUBBER AND ALUMINIUM HEAD

Takes one 50W 12V quartz halogen bulb

L 110 cm (43¼ in)

W of base 24 cm (9⅜ in)

Manufacturer: Arteluce Flos, Italy

37

STEPHAN COPELAND

Table lamp, *China*

BRUSHED STAINLESS STEEL STEM, ENAMELLED ALUMINIUM REFLECTOR, ENAMELLED CAST IRON BASE

Takes one 50W 12V quartz halogen bulb

H 36.8 cm (14½ in) L 77.4 cm (30½ in)

W of base 19.5 cm (7⅗ in)

Di of reflector 20.3 cm (8 in)

Manufacturer: Atelier International, USA

38

JAN VAN LIERDE
Table lamps, *Wind*
ALUMINIUM, GLASS
The heat from the lamp
diffuses the essence of
perfumed oils from a small
container
Each takes one 20W 12V
halogen bulb
Limited batch production
H 8 cm (3 in) W 8 cm (3 in)
L 8 cm (3 in)
Manufacturer: Kreon, Belgium

39

ARTURO SILVA

Ceiling or wall lamp, *Galileo*

DIE-CAST ALUMINIUM,
STAINLESS STEEL

An adjustable diaphragm
focuses the cone of light.
The basic lighting element is
available with a variety of
supports for wall or ceiling
attachment
Takes one 50W dichroic
bulb

H min. 27 cm (10½ in) max. 212 cm
(82⅝ in) L of lighting element 10 cm
(4 in)

Manufacturer: Antonangeli, Italy

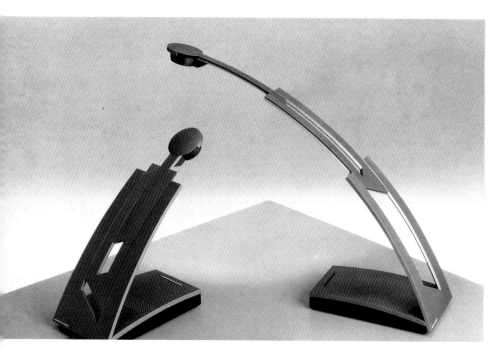

 40

**FERDINAND A. PORSCHE
AND CHRISTIAN
SCHWAMKRUG**
Table lamp, *Jazz*
PLASTIC
Compact reading lamp for
use when travelling:
the arm extends
telescopically with a sliding
electrical contact
Takes one 20W 12V
halogen bulb
H when closed 4 cm (1½ in)
W 13.5 cm (5²⁄₅ in)
L max. 63.5 cm (25 in)
Manufacturer: PAF, Italy

This small, flat, arc-shaped lamp, with a concealed cord, is
portable and packs flat: the brief was to design "an easily
transportable compact lighting element". The two-stage
telescopic arm allows a variety of positions and light
emphases. The idea was not to separate the three arm
elements (which would have destroyed the interrelationship
between them) but to create an overall graphic image that
would encourage variations. The *Jazz* also has an electronic
dimmer switch which ensures the same level of light intensity
each time the lamp is switched on. The luminous on/off
switch is easy to find in the dark.

 41

DANILO AROLDI
Wall lamp, *Soft*
CHROME-PLATED METAL,
OPAL GLASS DIFFUSER
Takes two 100W or 60W
halogen E14 bulbs
W 43 cm (16⅞ in) D 14 cm (5½ in)
Manufacturer: MA & MO, Italy

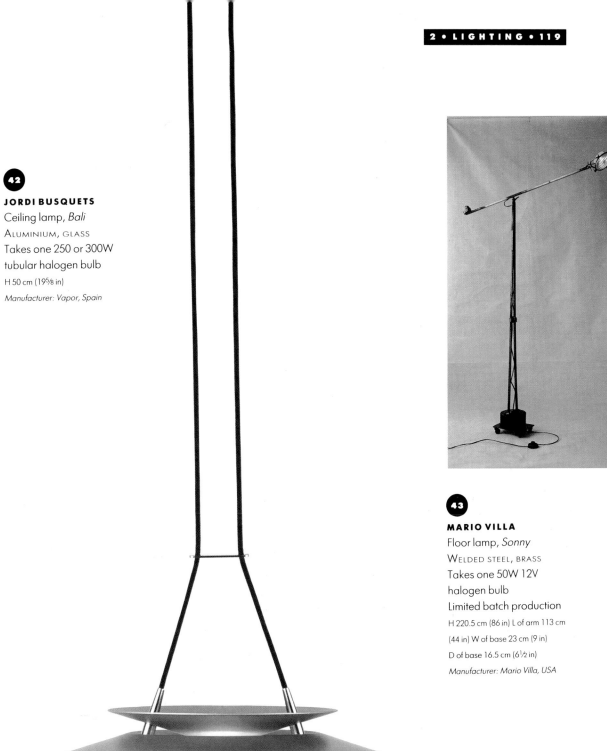

42

JORDI BUSQUETS
Ceiling lamp, *Bali*
ALUMINIUM, GLASS
Takes one 250 or 300W
tubular halogen bulb
H 50 cm (19⅝ in)
Manufacturer: Vapor, Spain

43

MARIO VILLA
Floor lamp, *Sonny*
WELDED STEEL, BRASS
Takes one 50W 12V
halogen bulb
Limited batch production
H 220.5 cm (86 in) L of arm 113 cm
(44 in) W of base 23 cm (9 in)
D of base 16.5 cm (6½ in)
Manufacturer: Mario Villa, USA

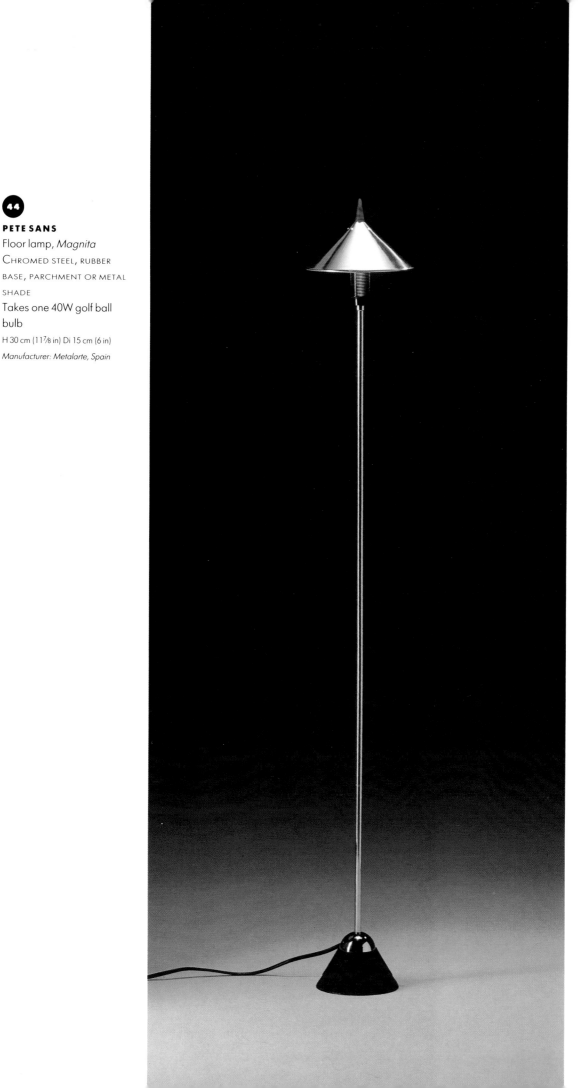

44

PETE SANS
Floor lamp, *Magnita*
CHROMED STEEL, RUBBER
BASE, PARCHMENT OR METAL
SHADE
Takes one 40W golf ball
bulb
H 30 cm (11⅞ in) Di 15 cm (6 in)
Manufacturer: Metalarte, Spain

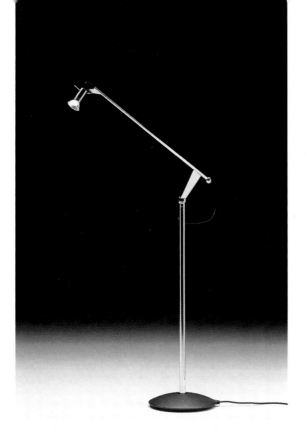

45

JOSEP LLUSCÁ
Reading lamp, *Saeta*
LACQUERED CAST IRON BASE,
CHROME-PLATED STEEL
Takes one 50W halogen
bulb
H 120 cm (47 in) W 48 cm (18⅞ in)
Manufacturer: Blauet, Spain

46

JOSEP LLUSCÁ
Table lamp, *Vaticana*
LACQUERED ALUMINIUM,
PERGACEL SHADE
Takes one 100W E27 bulb
H 70 cm (27½ in) W 28 cm (11 in)
Manufacturer: Metalarte, Spain

47

JOSEP LLUSCÁ AND
JOAQUÍN BERAO
Table lamp, *Ketupa*
CHROMED POLYCARBONATE
Takes one 50W 12V
halogen bulb
H 60 cm (23½ in) L 80 cm (31½ in)
Di of base 15 cm (6 in)
Manufacturer: Metalarte, Spain

**INGO MAURER AND
TEAM**

Table lamp, *Don Quixote*

STEEL, ALUMINIUM, RUBBER

Takes one 50W 12V
halogen bulb

H max. 45 cm (17¾ in)

W 27 cm (10½ in)

Manufacturer: Design M Ingo

Maurer, West Germany

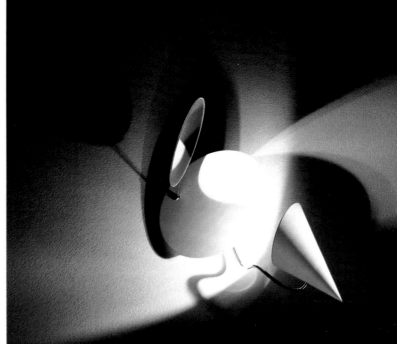

Eclipselipse combines and synthesizes form, function and
fantasy. "Never satisfied with function in its pure form, I
incorporate in all my designs a strong emotional
component," says Ingo Maurer. As a spotlight it is
augmented by the use of shadows and reflections, just as an
eclipse charts the interception of the light from a luminous
body. The light source is fixed while the mirror swivels: the
construction literally orbits around itself. "One's imagination
is thus an integral part of the design, as everchanging
pictures are created on the wall. I see it used both as a
picture/sculpture and as a bedside/table lamp."

**INGO MAURER AND
TEAM**

Spotlight, *Eclipselipse*

METAL, PLASTIC,
MIRRORGLASS

Takes one 50W halogen
bulb. The mirror reflects and
directs light from the spot,
rotating by 360 degrees

W 35 cm (13¾ in)

D of cone 15 cm (6 in)

Manufacturer: Design M Ingo

Maurer, West Germany

PEP SANT AND RAMON BIGAS

Wall lighting system,
Cornice

EXTRUDED ALUMINIUM,
METHACRYLATE

Takes 18 or 36W fluorescent
tubes or 300W halogen
bulbs

L 80-600 cm (31½-234 in)

W 8.5 cm (3⅜ in) D 11 cm (4⅜ in)

Manufacturer: Luxo Italiana, Italy

An architectural fitting like the old-fashioned dado rail but
made from an aluminium profile inspires the *Cornice* lighting
system, which can be a diffused uplighter or a more directed
downlighter, depending on the direction of the strip masking
the light source. It holds halogen bulbs, fluorescent compact
lamps or tubes with a concealed diffuser. Where there are
openings in a room, these modules can be coupled to reflect
the pattern on the other side. They are particularly useful in
halls or in stairways where they can act as handrails, with
light flooding below them on to the stair treads.

The system can become a two-dimensional column with
two profiles rising vertically, hiding two fluorescent tubes, or
a bathroom set framing four dichroic bulbs above the glass
and a crystal support shelf on the bottom to hold bottles. The
configurations of the system are vast, and the variety in the
type and direction of the light it can shed make it useful in
public places.

51

JORGE PENSI
Ceiling lamp, *Olympia*
POLISHED ALUMINIUM,
STAINLESS STEEL
Takes two 150W halogen
bulbs
H 90-170 cm (35-67 in)
W 80 cm (31 in)
Manufacturer: B-Lux, Spain

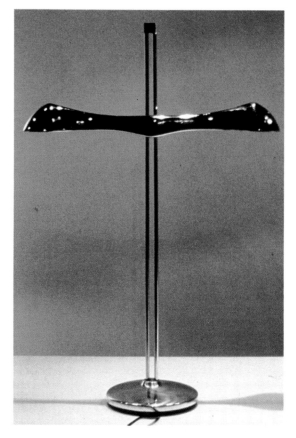

52

JORGE PENSI
Table lamp, *Marie*
POLISHED ALUMINIUM,
STAINLESS STEEL
Takes two 20W 12V halogen
bulbs
H 58 cm (22⅞ in) W 39 cm (15⅜ in)
Manufacturer: B-Lux, Spain

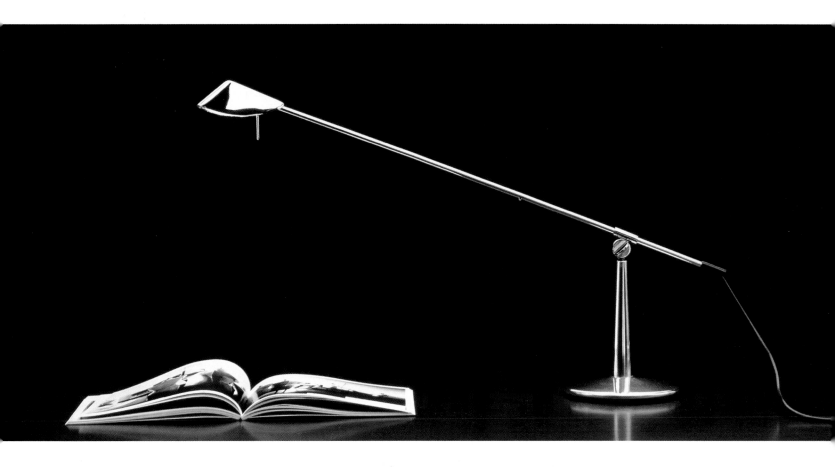

53

JORGE PENSI

Table lamp, *Taps*

CHROMED STEEL TUBING,
STAINLESS STEEL, CHROME OR
BLACK LACQUER FINISH

Takes one 50W 12V
halogen bulb

H 21 cm (8 in) L 75 cm (30 in)

Di of base 16 cm (6¼ in)

Manufacturer: B-Lux, Spain

3 · TABLEWARE

For the last decade tableware has been undervalued, while the packaging industry has expanded. Takeaway foods are presented with increasingly inventive wrapping, and changes in social customs have made it more acceptable to replace the milk jug with a carton and the plate with a polystyrene box. These fashions have made some items in the dinner service obsolete. As a consequence, Mario Bellini predicts that there will be an increasing demand for beautifully handwrought items to satisfy individualistic yearnings. Jennifer Lee's pots feature colour intrinsic to the handpinched clay, rather than as a later adornment, and Michael Rowe's conical vessels look like small volcanic eruptions.

Ironwork develops a few flourishes alongside its practical application. Mondo elevates it into wire frivolities, while Takenobu Igarashi's solid platters reveal a second layer beneath a rugged schism in the smooth contour. Enzo Mari's forged iron holders are, by contrast, a gentler image of natural growth, with sprouting buds and leaves. Matthew Hilton seeks zoomorphic forms in cast aluminium and Lino Sabattini turns to the galaxy for his *Cosmik* planets.

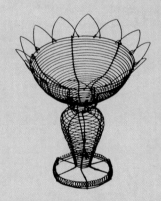

Knives, forks and spoons like music notes from Shozo Toyohisa address the crossover in cuisine between East and West, as do the ebony chopsticks finished with silver studs from British jeweller Marianne Forrest. Conscious of the need to protect tropical hardwoods, she recycles wood from broken guitar necks.

The Eighties was the decade that launched nouvelle cuisine, a phenomenon that led to some pretentious plates designed to frame highly styled food. Style came to triumph over substance. The only application of pattern upon plates this year are Awatsuji's black-and-white peonies, chrysanthemums, half-moons and leaf-tips, a graphic illustration of Japanese harmony in landscape in a two-dimensional medium.

Turning the tables on a moribund industry is the new collection by Bořek Šípek for Driade in Italy. Everything – from the glass candlesticks to Proustian table settings with blue-and-white fanned edges and ruffled bowls – recalls the elegance of a bygone era of banqueting. They look handcrafted but are in fact in mass production – a triumph of technology, since the forms defy conventional moulding, just as the results defy social typecasting around the table.

1

**BOREK SIPEK AND
DAVID PALTERER**

Champagne saucer

SILVER-PLATED BRONZE,
COBALT

Limited batch production

H 25 cm (9⅞ in) Di at rim 15 cm (6 in)

Manufacturer: Alterego, Netherlands

2

**BOŘEK ŠÍPEK AND
DAVID PALTERER**

Glass

BOHEMIAN CRYSTAL, BRONZE
BASE

H 14 cm (5½ in) Di at rim 7 cm (2¾ in)

Manufacturer: Alterego, Netherlands

BOŘEK ŠÍPEK

Vase

BOHEMIAN CRYSTAL

Limited batch production

H 47 cm (18¾ in)

Di at rim 16 cm (6½ in)

Manufacturer: Alterego, Netherlands

BOŘEK ŠÍPEK

Cutlery, *Alix*

SILVER-PLATED STEEL

Dinner fork L 24.7 cm (9½ in)

Fruit fork L 20 cm (7¾ in)

Tablespoon L 24.7 cm (9½ in)

Dessert spoon L 22.5 cm (8¾ in)

Coffee spoon L 14 cm (5½ in)

Dinner knife L 24.7 cm (9½ in)

Fruit knife L 18 cm (7 in)

Manufacturer: Driade, Italy

BOŘEK ŠÍPEK

Vase

BOHEMIAN CRYSTAL

Limited batch production

H 60 cm (24 in) Di at rim 21 cm (8½ in)

Manufacturer: Alterego, Netherlands

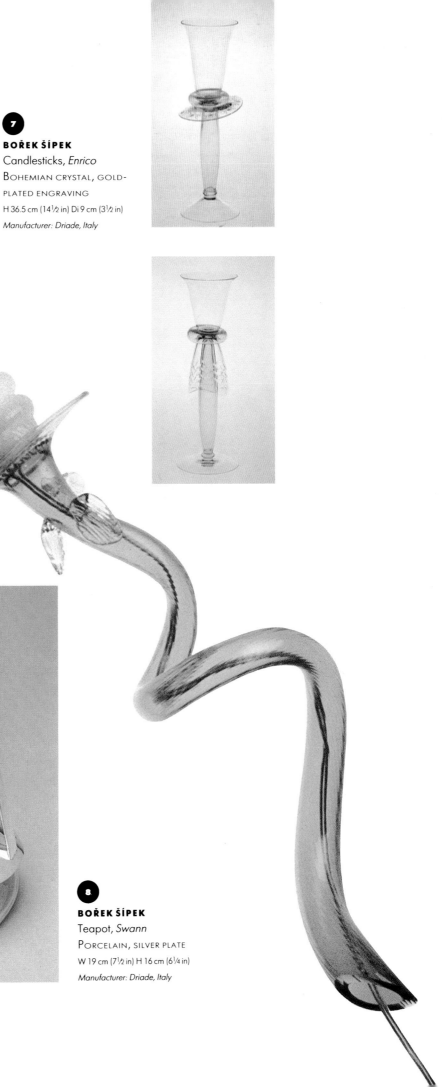

7

BOŘEK ŠÍPEK
Candlesticks, *Enrico*
BOHEMIAN CRYSTAL, GOLD-
PLATED ENGRAVING
H 36.5 cm (14½ in) Di 9 cm (3½ in)
Manufacturer: Driade, Italy

6

BOŘEK ŠÍPEK
Floor lamp, *Luigi III*
BOHEMIAN CRYSTAL
H 48 cm (18⅞ in) Di 15 cm (6⅛ in)
Manufacturer: Driade, Italy

8

BOŘEK ŠÍPEK
Teapot, *Swann*
PORCELAIN, SILVER PLATE
W 19 cm (7½ in) H 16 cm (6¼ in)
Manufacturer: Driade, Italy

9

BOŘEK ŠÍPEK

Dinner service, *Albertine*

PORCELAIN

Clockwise on these pages:

Dinner plate H 2.5 cm (1 in)

Di 28.5 cm (11 in)

Tea cup H 10 cm (4 in) W 15 cm (6 in)

Di at rim 10.5 cm (4⅛ in)

Egg-cup H 4.5 cm (1¾ in)

Di 11 cm (4⅓ in)

Soup plate H 8.5 cm (3⅓ in)

W 26 cm (10 in) D 24 cm (9⅓ in)

Side plate H 1.5 cm (½ in)

Di 21 cm (8¼ in)

Manufacturer: Driade, Italy

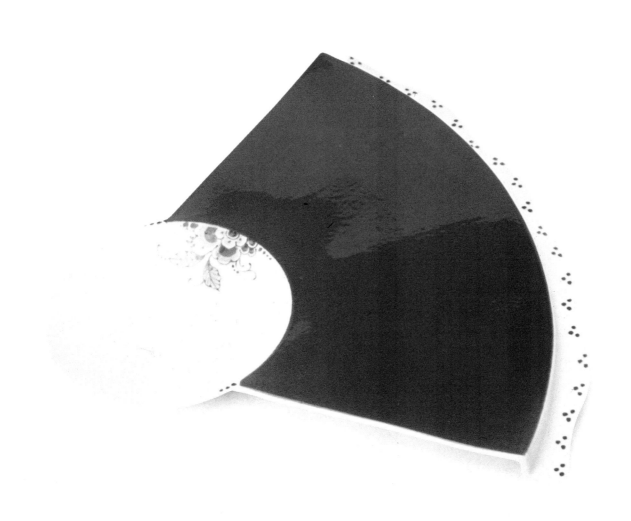

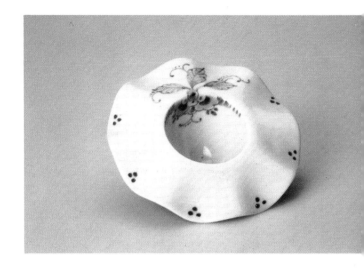

Bořek Šípek's designs for tableware have an emotional appeal. "Magical and mystical are exactly the titles I would most like to have applied to my work," he says. Born forty years ago in Prague, Šípek worked for many years in a small studio in Amsterdam and is now Professor at the Academy of Decorative Arts in Prague where he directs the faculty of art and design. He remains loyal to the few firms for whom he has always worked – Driade, Vitra, Leitner and Alterego – though he is now embarking on a new series for Daum. Driade, who market his furniture in leather and rattan, now concentrate on his glass and metalwork for tableware as well as porcelain named after characters in Proust.

"There is a lot of cruelty in my work. Cruelty is a phenomenon which has a constant fascination for me. When looked for it can be discovered in the glass designs, though in this medium it manifests itself more often in the expressive form of the piece rather than as a statement." Look at the champagne goblet crumpling under its own weight. Coloured droplets spill from the neck of one of his vases for Alterego, while on the other a delicate frill is laced around the neck, using a very old technique. "Very occasionally while working we attempt new forms and have to develop a technique on the spot to realize it, but in general the glass tradition is so very old that there's nothing new under the sun. Although in one piece several different techniques may have been applied, this is not meant to be described as a collage of styles. I hate collage."

10

SITE PROJECTS

Planter, *Liz*

GLASS, ALUMINIUM, SOIL

A terrarium wall layered with
soil surrounds the inner plant
pot

Di 15-50 cm (6-20 in)

Manufacturer: Baleri, Italy

11

ENZO MARI

Vase, *Sboccio*

FORGED IRON, CRYSTAL

Limited batch production

H 31 cm (12½ in) Di 16 cm (6¼ in)

Manufacturer: Bruno Danese, Italy

SYLVAIN DUBUISSON
Candlesticks, *73 Secondes*
SILVER OR TITANIUM
Limited batch production
H 20 cm (7⅞ in)
Manufacturer: Creative Agent, France

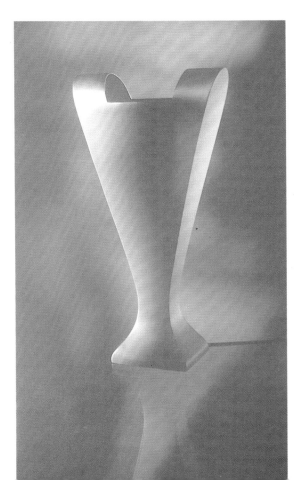

MASSIMO IOSA GHINI
Vase, *Ologramma*
SILVER-PLATED ALPACA
Limited batch production
H 31 cm (12 in) W 18 cm (7 in)
L 6.5 cm (2½ in)
Manufacturer: Design Gallery
Milano, Italy

ENZO MARI
Vase, *Viticcio*
FORGED IRON, CRYSTAL
Limited batch production
H 31 cm (12½ in) Di 16 cm (6¼ in)
Manufacturer: Bruno Danese, Italy

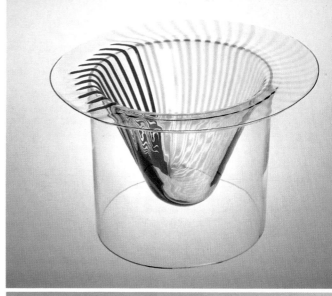

 16

TARU SYRJÄNEN
Centrepiece, *Summer,* from
the *Roundabout of Life*
collection
GLASS, COLOURED GLASS
STICKS
One-off
H 25.5 cm (10¼ in)
Di 40.5 cm (16¼ in)
Manufacturer: Iittala Glass, Finland

 15

ANNE NILSSON
Candlesticks, *Doremi*
GLASS, HAND-BLOWN AND
SHAPED
Top: H 16 cm (6¼ in) W 9.5 cm
(3¾ in)
Bottom: H 12.5 cm (5 in)
W at rim 9.5 cm (3¾ in)
*Manufacturer: Orrefors Glasbruk,
Sweden*

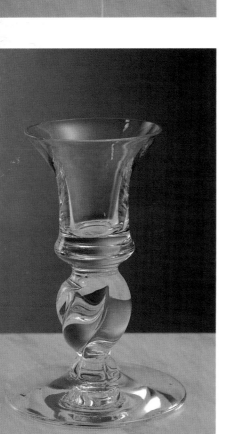

 17

MINAKO KUBOTA
Bowls, *Horizon* collection
25% HAND-BLOWN LEAD
CRYSTAL, COLOURED GLASS
ON RIM
Left: H 10 cm (4 in) Di 32 cm (12½ in)
Centre: H 15.5 cm (6 in)
Di 26 cm (10¼ in)
Right: H 13 cm (5 in) Di 21 cm (8¼ in)
*Manufacturer: Sasaki Glass Co.,
Japan*

JENNIFER LEE
Bowl
STONEWARE CLAY, OXIDES
One-off
H 12 cm (4¾ in) Di 21 cm (8¼ in)
Manufacturer: Jennifer Lee, UK

Craftsmanship always struggles to find a place in *The International Design Yearbook* since most selectors are concerned with the potential for mass production, or at least with machine-age prototyping. Jennifer Lee's handbuilt coloured stoneware has more to do with design than with decoration in its simplicity of form and its method of keeping colour intrinsic to the material. The clay is coloured with the knowledge of an alchemist and the persistence of an industrialist working with the vagaries of kiln-firing temperatures. Rather than applying glazes and slips, Lee adds oxides, stains and underglazes to the wet clay which give an even colour throughout the pot and a complete fusion of clay and stain. The colouring, which is coarsely ground with water then sieved before being added to the clay slip, gives an unusual speckled effect.

All the pots are handbuilt, the bases coiled, pinched or sometimes formed in pressed moulds. Flattened coils are added, the same width to avoid stress. Bands are smoothed upwards on the exterior and downwards on the interior, without smudging the colours. Lee believes that the placement of a coloured band can radically alter the balance of a pot. "My work changes slowly, but centres on the vessels seen on travels in the desert in Arizona, in Egypt and in Sinai. The early cultures have a cumulative influence rather than a direct one."

JENNIFER LEE
Asymmetric pot
STONEWARE CLAY, OXIDES
One-off
H 24 cm (9½ in) Di 12 cm (4¾ in)
Manufacturer: Jennifer Lee, UK

Mondo, better known for their furniture design (see page 61), are extending their production to include household objects. This new collection contains forty pieces, including fruit dishes, vases, chandeliers, trays and cake tins, in iron wire that is woven rather than welded, and treated to look aged. The idea is inherently the same as that for their furniture, says Rosa Maria Rinaldi: "Our goal is more ethnographic than designer-conscious." The irony is that these frivolities recall the pantry pieces of 17th-century France, and that they are made using old craft techniques, following research by Jean-Louis Ménard and Daniel Rozensztroch.

21

MONDO DESIGN TEAM
Filo di Ferro collection
COLOURED IRON WIRE
Candlestick H 14 cm (5½ in)
Di 18 cm (7 in)
Tall bowl H 36 cm (14½ in)
Di 30 cm (12 in)
Basket Di 32 cm (12¾ in)
Fruit basket Di 35 cm (14 in)
Glass-shaped candle holder
H 14 cm (5½ in) Di 8 cm (3 in)
Cake-dish Di 25 cm (10 in)
Oval tray L 32 cm (12¾ in)
Manufacturer: Mondo, Italy

20

VIC STANNARD
Vessel
PATINATED BRASS
One-off
H 25.5 cm (10 in) W 10 cm (4 in)
L 20.5 cm (8 in)
Manufacturer: Vic Stannard, UK

22

LINO SABATTINI
Centrepiece, *Giostra*
SILVER-PLATED BRASS ALLOY
The bowl and plate fit
together
H 12.5 cm (5 in) Di 38.5 cm (15½ in)
*Manufacturer: Sabattini Argenteria,
Italy*

23

LINO SABATTINI
Cup holder with lid and
cups, *Kyoto*
SILVER-PLATED BRASS ALLOY,
PORCELAIN
H 18.5 cm (7½ in) Di 10 cm (4 in)
*Manufacturer: Sabattini Argenteria,
Italy*

24

LINO SABATTINI
Serving piece, *Cosmik*
SILVER-PLATED BRASS ALLOY
W 22.5 cm (8¾ in) L 36 cm (14½ in)
*Manufacturer: Sabattini Argenteria,
Italy*

25

LINO SABATTINI
Series of bowls, *Sanae*
SILVER-PLATED BRASS ALLOY,
PORCELAIN

Left to right:
Soup bowl H 15 cm (6 in)
Di 18 cm (7 in)
Fruit salad cup H 9 cm (3½ in)
Di 10 cm (4 in)
Large soup bowl H 16.5 cm (6½ in)
Di 21 cm (8¼ in)
*Manufacturer: Sabattini Argenteria,
Italy*

From an industry moribund with Louis-the-something silver-plated lookalikes come some imaginative and stylish products from Algorithme to "enrich daily life". Their intention is to harness traditional silver techniques in new forms, inspired by the ideas of young designers such as the Argentinian Nestor Perkal.

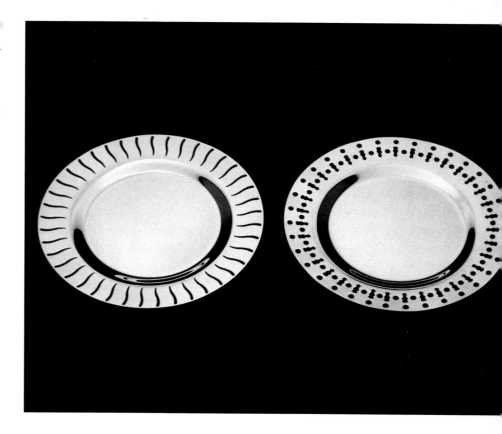

27

NESTOR PERKAL
Showing plates
SILVER-PLATED BRASS
Di 33 cm (13¼ in)
Manufacturer: Algorithme, France

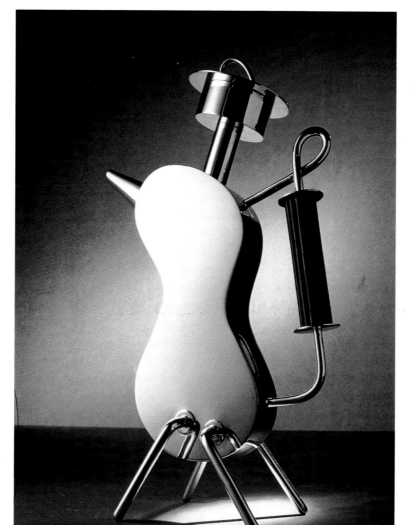

26

PETER SHIRE
Coffee pot, *Giotto*
SILVER-PLATED BRASS, EBONY
HANDLE
Limited batch production
H 40 cm (15¾ in) W 19 cm (7½ in)
Manufacturer: Design Gallery
Milano, Italy

MICHAEL ROWE
Conical vessel
BRASS, GOLD LEAF FINISH
One-off
H 26 cm (10½ in) W 34 cm (13½ in)
L 24 cm (9½ in)
Manufacturer: Michael Rowe, UK

MICHAEL ROWE
Conical vessel with corner-
relating base
BRASS AND COPPER, TINNED
FINISH
The piece is designed to be
seen across the corner of a
low wall
One-off
H 55 cm (22 in) W 44 cm (17½ in)
L 60 cm (24 in)
Manufacturer: Michael Rowe, UK

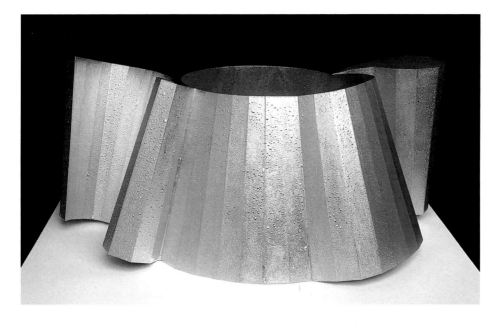

MICHAEL ROWE
Conical vessel
BRASS, TINNED FINISH
One-off
H 22 cm (8¾ in) W 28 cm (11¼ in)
L 52 cm (20¾ in)
Manufacturer: Michael Rowe, UK

CARSTEN JØRGENSEN
Cream jug
STAINLESS STEEL, BRASS
H 8.5 cm (3¼ in) Di 8.5 cm (3¼ in)
Manufacturer: Bodum, Switzerland

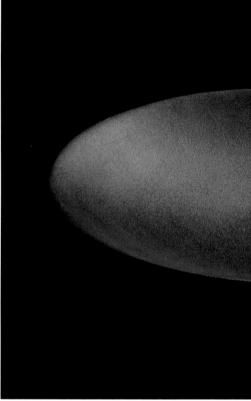

TAKENOBU IGARASHI
Platter, *Sukashi B Maru*
IRON
H 5.5 cm (2¼ in) Di 36.8 cm (14 in)
Manufacturer: Yamasho Casting Co.,
Japan

TAKENOBU IGARASHI
Platter, *Kariwari A Maru*
IRON
H 5.5 cm (2¼ in)
Di 36.8 cm (14 in)
Manufacturer: Yamasho Casting Co.,
Japan

34

TAKENOBU IGARASHI
Platter, *Arare Haru*
IRON
H 5.5 cm (2¼ in) Di 36.8 cm (14 in)
Manufacturer: Yamasho Casting Co.,
Japan

35

TAKENOBU IGARASHI
Platter, *Triangle Nami*
IRON
H 7.5 cm (3 in) W 38.5 cm (14¾ in)
L 45 cm (17½ in)
Manufacturer: Yamasho Casting Co.,
Japan

 36

MATTHEW HILTON
Bowl, *Di-ordna*
CAST ALUMINIUM
Limited batch production
H 11.5 cm (4½ in) W 26 cm (10¼ in)
L 43 cm (16¾ in)
Manufacturer: Matthew Hilton, UK

Like long-clawed lobsters, Matthew Hilton's bowls and candleholder are poised upon the table. But there is nothing explicit in his zoomorphic designs, rather a need to marshall volume and mass upon delicate supports so that they appear weightless, hovering above a tabletop. His cast aluminium tableware arose from a need to find the most commercial method of production since he wants to mass produce. "I began making tableware out of pottery, a huge oval dish, and then as I was trying to carve through a section the plaster fell apart. I took the piece to a caster and asked him to make it up in the cheapest material, which happened to be aluminium. When the pieces were joined I polished it to get rid of the joints. I liked the effect so much that I have used cast aluminium ever since. The alternative would be patinated bronze, but it would treble the costs and I don't want my work to be exclusive."

His preoccupation with flat dishes, scoops and vessels is to breathe life and movement into them. "For furniture, the poised leg on the antelope table is my best piece. Now I like to think these lobster bowls are, for aesthetic reasons, the most extravagant. They challenge the casters, too. Casters make moulds in sand, like sand-castle building in relief: the more curves and extrusions, the more opportunity for the sand edges to fall in." Matthew Hilton is currently designing furniture for two Spanish companies, Mobles 114 and Santa & Cole, and a rug for Nani Marquina.

 38

MATTHEW HILTON
Candle platform, *Arclumis*
CAST ALUMINIUM
Limited batch production
H 15.5 cm (6 in) W 17 cm (6¾ in)
L 43 cm (16¾ in)
Manufacturer: Matthew Hilton, UK

 37

ENZO MARI
Centrepiece, *Dronero*
FORGED IRON
Limited batch production
H 15.5 cm (6 in) W 13 cm (5 in)
L 65 cm (26 in)
Manufacturer: Bruno Danese, Italy

 39

MATTHEW HILTON
Bowl, *To-bor*
CAST ALUMINIUM
Limited batch production
H 10 cm (4 in) W 12 cm (4¾ in)
L 45 cm (17½ in)
Manufacturer: Matthew Hilton, UK

 40

ENZO MARI
Centrepiece, *Mazzucco*
FORGED IRON
Limited batch production
H 14.5 cm (5¾ in) Di 35.5 cm (14 in)
Manufacturer: Bruno Danese, Italy

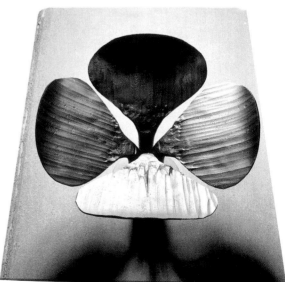

PHILIPS CORPORATE INDUSTRIAL DESIGN
Café Gourmet
CHROMIUM-PLATED STEEL, GLASS, PLASTIC
Employs a rapid heating and filtering process, a detachable cord-set and a hot plate that regulates the temperature of the coffee for up to twenty minutes
H 45 cm (17¾ in) W 19 cm (7½ in) D 19 cm (7½ in)
Manufacturer: Philips, Netherlands

The Café Gourmet coffee-maker heats the water drip by drip through a bulk heating element. A valve then opens so that the water flows rapidly on to the ground coffee and through the filter. This combination of a high temperature and a short contact time is designed to resemble as closely as possible the traditional way of brewing coffee in a jug. The Café Gourmet was awarded the top Innovation Award by the Netherlands Trade Market in 1989.

42

FERDINAND A. PORSCHE AND SIMON FRASER
Saucepans, *Luci e Ombre*
18/10 STAINLESS STEEL, ALUMAN, TITANIUM CERMET
The lids are corrugated to trap condensation and can also be used as heat-resistant stands
Front to back:
Low casserole Di 16 cm (6¼ in)
Boiling pot Di 12 cm (4¾ in)
Casserole Di 24 cm (9⅜ in)
Low casserole Di 20 cm (7⅞ in)
Stockpot Di 20 cm (7⅞ in)
Manufacturer: Barazzoni, Italy

(43)

ENZO MARI

Smith & Smith collection

SMALL STAINLESS STEEL

Saucepans H 7 cm (2¾ in)

Di 8 cm (3⅛ in), 10 cm (4 in) and

12 cm (4¾ in)

Cheese grater H 15.5 cm (6⅛ in)

D 9 cm (3½ in)

Funnel H 12 cm (4¾ in)

Di 9 cm (3½ in)

Manufacturer: Zani & Zani, Italy

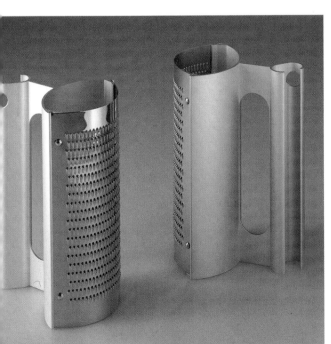

45

MARIANNE FORREST
Chopsticks
EBONY, SILVER
Limited batch production
L 23 cm (9 in)
Manufacturer: Marianne Forrest, UK

44

MIKE RYAN
Pepper mill
PEAR WOOD
H 11.5 cm (4½ in) Di 5.6 cm (2⅛ in)
Manufacturer: Alessi, Italy

46

MASSIMO IOSA GHINI
Cruet set, *Ogiva*
SILVER-PLATED ALPACA
Limited batch production
H 16 cm (6¼ in) W 9 cm (3½ in)
L 5 cm (2 in)
Manufacturer: Design Gallery
Milano, Italy

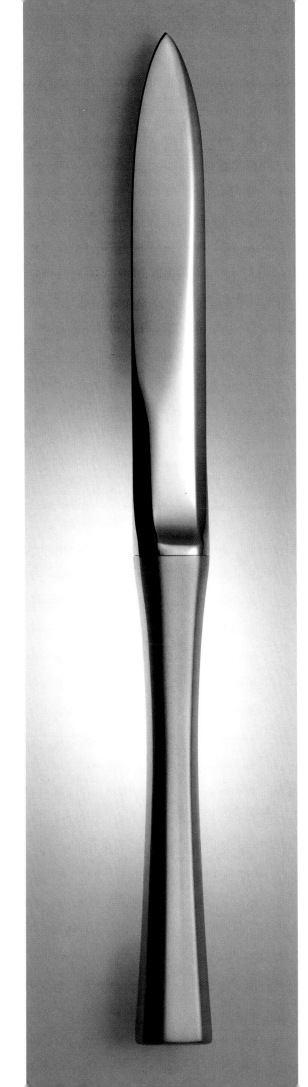

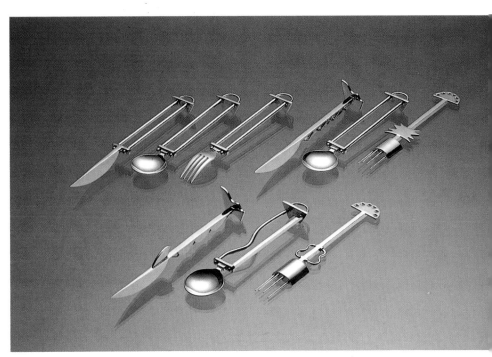

SHOZO TOYOHISA
Cutlery, *Nobile Produzione*
STAINLESS STEEL, SILVER- AND
GOLD-PLATED BRASS
Limited batch production
Knives L 20 cm (8 in) W 4 cm (1½ in)
Spoons L 20 cm (8 in)
W 4.5 cm (1¾ in)
Forks L 20 cm (8 in) W 3 cm (1¼ in)
Manufacturer: Koyo Sangyo Co.,
Japan

ALAIN CARRÉ
Dinner knife from the
Plein Jour collection
18/8 STAINLESS STEEL
L 23 cm (9 in)
Manufacturer: Sasaki Glass Co.,
Japan

SERGIO ASTI
Showing plate
PORCELAIN
Di 31 cm (12 in)
Manufacturer: Richard Ginori, Italy

MASANORI UMEDA
Startray
ALUMINIUM
Limited batch production
H 5.5 cm (2¼ in) Di 36 cm (14½ in)
Manufacturer: Nichinan, Japan

BARBARA SEIDENATH
Tea service
TOMBAC (COPPER AND ZINC
ALLOY), BRASS, SILVER-PLATED
INTERIOR
Prototype
Teapot H 22 cm (8½ in)
Di 18 cm (7 in)
Teapot warmer H 8 cm (3¼ in)
Di 8 cm (3¼ in)
Milk jug and sugar bowl
H 9 cm (3½ in) Di 11 cm (4¼ in)
Manufacturer: Barbara Seidenath,
West Germany

Seven Seas II is a plate like a flat fish suspended from a hook. Douglas Doolittle, a Canadian working for the Japanese firm Morimoto, designed it specially for the presentation of sushi in the Seven Seas Restaurant, but it has an application as a hanging, stackable plate in the home. A bar on the top separates the sauce from the fish slices, and the black bow helps to link the plates visually when they are arranged for buffets.

DOUGLAS DOOLITTLE
Sushi plate, *Seven Seas II*
LACQUERED ACRYLIC
Limited batch production
W 30 cm (11¾ in) L 30 cm (11¾ in)
D 3 cm (1¼ in)
Manufacturer: Morimoto, Japan

MICHAEL GRAVES
Coffee set
18/10 STAINLESS STEEL, HEAT-RESISTANT GLASS, POLYAMIDE HANDLES
Demitasse H 6 cm (2½ in) Di 5.8 cm (2¼ in)
Saucer Di 12 cm (4¾ in)
Mug H 10 cm (4 in) Di 7.5 cm (3 in)
Manufacturer: Alessi, Italy

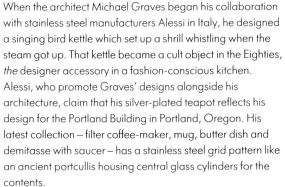

When the architect Michael Graves began his collaboration with stainless steel manufacturers Alessi in Italy, he designed a singing bird kettle which set up a shrill whistling when the steam got up. That kettle became a cult object in the Eighties, *the* designer accessory in a fashion-conscious kitchen. Alessi, who promote Graves' designs alongside his architecture, claim that his silver-plated teapot reflects his design for the Portland Building in Portland, Oregon. His latest collection – filter coffee-maker, mug, butter dish and demitasse with saucer – has a stainless steel grid pattern like an ancient portcullis housing central glass cylinders for the contents.

54

HIROSHI AWATSUJI
Dinner plate, *Kaze*
PORCELAIN
Limited batch production
Di 23 cm (9 in)
Manufacturer: Hiroshi Awatsuji,

Japan

55

HIROSHI AWATSUJI
Dinner plate, *Sono*
PORCELAIN
Limited batch production
Di 31 cm (12 in)
Manufacturer: Hiroshi Awatsuji,

Japan

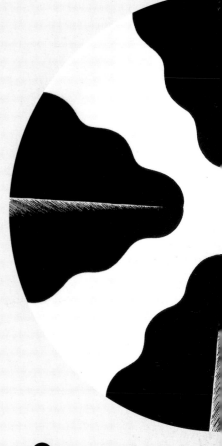

56

HIROSHI AWATSUJI
Dinner plate, *Umi*
PORCELAIN
Limited batch production
Di 31 cm (12 in)
Manufacturer: Hiroshi Awatsuji,
Japan

58

HIROSHI AWATSUJI
Dinner plate, *Kazari*
PORCELAIN
Limited batch production
Di 35 cm (13¾ in)
Manufacturer: Hiroshi Awatsuji,
Japan

57

HIROSHI AWATSUJI
Dinner plate, *Seki*
PORCELAIN
Limited batch production
Di 31 cm (12 in)
Manufacturer: Hiroshi Awatsuji,
Japan

4 · TEXTILES

The environment is the theme for textured fabrics this year, with strangely realistic images of nature which are the result of experimentation with printing on traditional warp and weft weaving. Ancient techniques are revived in Japan with interesting contemporary applications: Minagawa borrows the traditional Japanese technique of *fukuro ori* to weave

textiles in seamless tubes which are then cut in a spiral to create a flat-bias weave. Japanese designers continue to prove masters of the art of marshalling natural effects: Minagawa's criss-cross pattern recreates coconut tree trunks and silky willow bark, and Junichi Arai uses a jacquard technique on cotton, wool and polyurethane to create three-dimensional textured bark.

Vast repeat patterns are emerging for the first time. The group called Robert Le Héros have turned glazed printed linen into a wall-hanging, a giant allegorical canvas which is not an exclusive one-off but mass produced. "Tapestries of the new age", manufacturer Elio Palmisano calls the collages he commissions from designers. They involve cotton fabrics in different weaves laid on a canvas, then trimmed with embroidery stitches. The chromatic results are as dramatic as the geometric stylization of domestic landscapes. The dwellings in Sottsass's *Spring Day* and *Winter Day* are disquieting, with mysterious diagonals that deny the two-dimensional quality of the medium. Attempting to put borders on what constitutes art proves risky with Vorwerk's latest *Dialog* collections, designs by major artists and architects, marketed at a reasonable price.

Such artistry is always counterbalanced by the mainstays of architectural furnishing. Awatsuji's stripes are paced like ruler edgings, while Talli Nencioni's *Zanzibar* in cotton and linen recalls the interplay of light and shade in the souk. Gretchen Bellinger turns to a dressmaker's art for her cotton seersucker, in which the stripe is emphasized with small horizontal pleats right down the run of the cloth. Restrained designs in muted colours contain no surprises, but there are some good backgrounds, such as Anne Beetz's *Panier* in glazed linen upholstery basketweave, and *Arles* in cotton and natural silk upholstery. Andrée Putman gives *Longchamps* a metallic sheen with polypropylene threads in bronze, gold, pewter, topaz and turquoise.

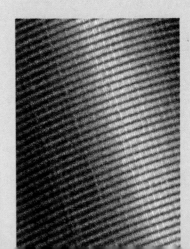

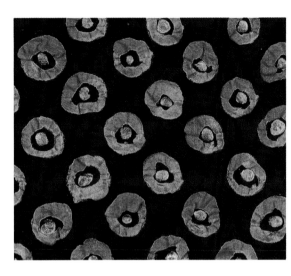

1

HELLE ABILD
Fabrics
COTTON CLOQUE,
HANDPAINTED WITH GOLD
AND COPPER PIGMENTS
One-offs
W 65 cm (24⅞ in) L 400 cm (156 in)
Manufacturer: Helle Abild, Denmark

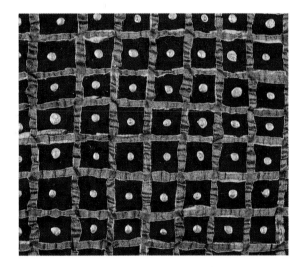

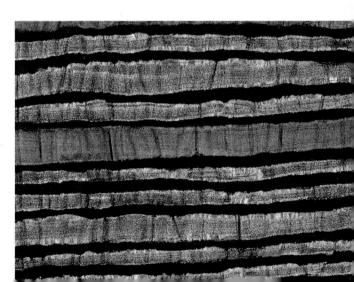

HIROSHI AWATSUJI
Fabric, *Radio*
COTTON, CHINTZ FINISH
W 137 cm (58¾ in)
Repeat 3 cm (1¼ in)
Manufacturer: Fujie Textile Co., Japan

MAKIKO MINAGAWA
Fabric, *Hikari*
COTTON CREPE WITH
RANDOM
IKAT DYE
Limited batch production
W 75 cm (29½ in)
Manufacturer: Miyatake, Japan

**MARIO TALLI
NENCIONI**
Fabrics
Left: *Zanzibar 5*
COTTON/LINEN
W 150 cm (60 in)
Repeat 41 cm (16⅛ in)
Right: *Senegal 2*
LINEN
W 150 cm (60 in)
Repeat 25 cm (9⅞ in)
Manufacturer: Telene, Italy

HIROSHI AWATSUJI
Fabric, *Shiki*
50% COTTON, 50%
POLYESTER
W 137 cm (58¾ in)
Manufacturer: Fujie Textile Co., Japan

MAKIKO MINAGAWA
Fabric, *Coco Sheath*
COTTON
Woven in a seamless tube
(*fukuro ori* or bag weaving),
the fabric is then cut in a
spiral to create a flat bias
weave
Limited batch production
W 150 cm (60 in)
Manufacturer: Miyashin, Japan

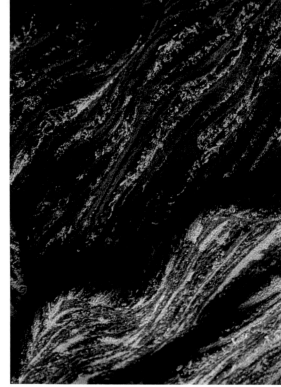

9

JUNICHI ARAI
Fabric, *Bark*
COTTON, WOOL AND
POLYURETHANE JACQUARD
A double-weave jacquard
fabric, with different textures
created by the polyurethane
yarn connecting both faces
W 85 cm (34 in)
Repeat 26 cm (10½ in)
Manufacturer: Nuno Corp., Japan

7

JUNICHI ARAI
Fabric, *Must*
RAYON AND NYLON
JACQUARD
A double-weave jacquard
in which the ground layer is
very dense but elastic,
creating puckers in the
second layer which is a
translucent film
W 71 cm (28½ in) Repeat 2.3 cm (1 in)
Manufacturer: Nuno Corp., Japan

8

JUNICHI ARAI
Fabric, *Blanket Cloth*
COTTON AND WOOL DOBBY
The fabric uses a dobby
technique whereby the
surfaces are created by the
sateen structure of the
bundle threads
W 90 cm (36 in) Repeat 2.2 cm (5½ in)
Manufacturer: Nuno Corp., Japan

10

JUNICHI ARAI
Fabric, *Tube Weave*
COTTON AND WOOL
JACQUARD
During the finishing process
the woollen threads of the
fabric float away from the
structure
W 55 cm (22 in) Repeat 3 cm (1¼ in)
Manufacturer: Nuno Corp., Japan

JUNICHI ARAI
Fabric, *Dots and Checks*
COTTON JACQUARD
W 30 cm (12 in) Repeat 11 cm (4¼ in)
Manufacturer: Nuno Corp., Japan

JUNICHI ARAI
Fabric, *Swollen Patterns*
COTTON AND WOOL
JACQUARD
W 125 cm (50 in)
Repeat 19 cm (7½ in)
Manufacturer: Nuno Corp., Japan

JUNICHI ARAI
Fabric, *Korean Carrot*
WOOL JACQUARD
The three-dimensional
textures are created by a
felted finishing process
W 140 cm (56 in)
Manufacturer: Nuno Corp., Japan

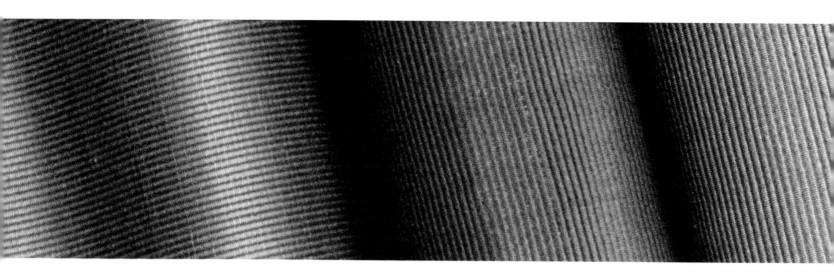

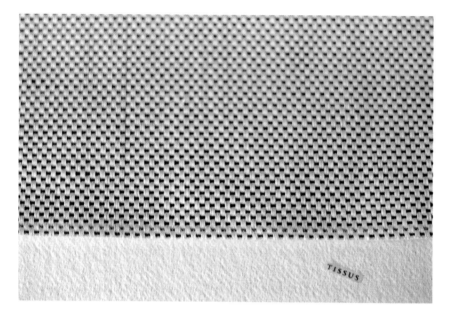

Andrée Putman's new collection in browns and what she calls "oysters" is inspired by the soft earth colours of the century-old kiln-fired bricks at the Hotel im Wasserturm in the Rhineland. "I had never seen brick coloured like that. So subtle, that interplay of natural earth colours, impossible to replicate today in the bricks we needed for the restoration of the hotel." So she picked up the palette and planned a collection of fabrics for Stendig in which the weave is as important as the colour range.

"I wanted to create a collection where colours could be combined in some unexpected way and where the patterns would create vibrations." In *Longchamps*, cotton with a polypropylene backing replicates the famous horsehair weave, as sophisticated as the most authentic version with the added advantage that it can be broad. *Varenne* is a rayon and polyester weave in nine colourways; the collection was assembled by Merle Lindby Varenne.

14

ANNE BEETZ
Upholstery fabric, *Panier*
GLAZED LINEN
W 120 cm (48 in)
Manufacturer: Knoll Textiles, USA

15

ANDREE PUTMAN
Fabric, *Longchamps*
50% COTTON, 50%
POLYPROPYLENE
W 135 cm (54 in)
*Manufacturer: Stendig International,
USA*

17

ANDRÉE PUTMAN
Fabric, *Varenne*
54% RAYON, 46% POLYESTER
W 135 cm (54 in)
Repeat 12 cm (4¾ in)
*Manufacturer: Stendig International,
USA*

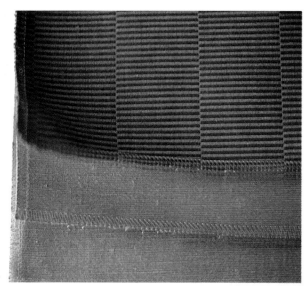

16

ANNE BEETZ
Upholstery fabric, *Arles*
73% COTTON, 27% SILK
W 130 cm (52 in)
Manufacturer: Knoll Textiles, USA

Emilio Ambasz, born in Argentina, lives in the USA but works everywhere: Europe, Asia and in the Americas. He is an architect and designer of unique relevance on the international scene. Alessandro Mendini, in his Foreword to *Emilio Ambasz, the Poetics of the Pragmatic*, points out that his work is not Post-Modern. "His vocabulary is not made up of references and ready-made sentences, thus it is free from the decay of fashions and styles." His glass house in San Antonio, Texas; the Frankfurt Zoo; the Houston Center Plaza in Houston, Texas; the Plaza Mayor in Salamanca, Spain, are just some of the world-famous schemes he has designed. In one of his major projects, the Nichii Department Store on Japan's second-largest island Hokkaido, he created a winter garden where people can gather beneath a skylight to look at plants, listen to water cascades and stroll in the courtyard. Ambasz has a lyrical love of nature, and a determination to celebrate it in architecture.

These printed cotton repeat patterns collage fragments from other cultures – from Gothic, Roman and Arabic numerals to the stylization of nature – without sentiment. Just as he uses paper cut and folded to make models of his buildings, he uses the two-dimensional quality of fabric as a shield to suggest what is behind it: literally, a curtain with strange symbols and portents to be read.

EMILIO AMBASZ
Fabrics
PRINTED COTTON
Fabrics for a range of home furnishing applications, including Japanese house slippers
Limited batch production
W 135 cm (54 in) Repeats 7.5-90 cm (3-36 in)
Manufacturer: Nichii Department Stores, Japan

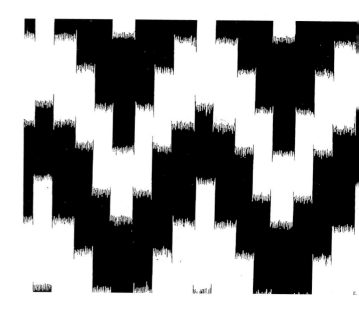

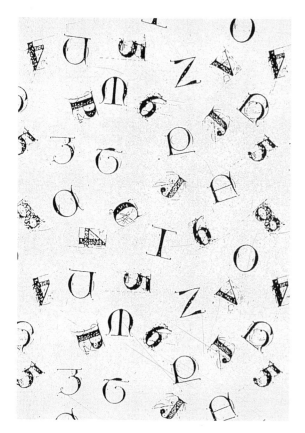

19

**OSCAR TUSQUETS
BLANCA**
Fabric, *Garofani*
COTTON
The fabric is hand-printed
by Ratti
W 140 cm (56 in)
Repeat 60 cm (23½ in)
Manufacturer: Driade, Italy

20

FINN SKÖDT
Upholstery fabric, *Lakota*
PRINTED COTTON
W 140 cm (56 in)
Repeat approx. 63 cm (25¼ in)
Manufacturer: Kvadrat, Denmark

21

FINN SKODT
Upholstery fabric, *Arapaho*
PRINTED COTTON
W 140 cm (56 in) Repeat approx.
63 cm (25¼ in)
Manufacturer: Kvadrat, Denmark

22

ANGEL JOVÉ
Fabric, *Fulles d'Aigua*
PRINTED COTTON
W 160 cm (64 in)
Repeat 84 cm (33½ in)
Manufacturer: Transtam, Spain

In Javier Mariscal's graphic poster entitled "Look of the Nineties", a pedestal typist's chair in a corporate office is more reminiscent of Dallas, Texas, than Valencia, but Spain is now moving into the wealthy stakes. Lurching, swaying, rioting, Mariscal's graphics tumble across the fabrics he designs for Marieta. Pop themes and his penchant for Fifties kitsch predominate in day-glo bright colours. In *Muchos Pesces* he uses the cross weave of the jacquard loom to control the weft threads which are lifted to illustrate thousands of fish in raised relief, elaborately figured and multi-coloured. He looks constantly for a balance between art and design: "Always I search for new frontiers between the kiosk or shop and the art gallery. I make things that are sold as art when they're actually commercial products, and which sell as commercial products when they're really art."

23

JAVIER MARISCAL
Upholstery fabric, *Muchos Pesces*
COTTON JACQUARD
TAPESTRY
W 160 cm (64 in) Repeat 90 cm (36 in)
Manufacturer: Marieta Textil, Spain

Four designers – Corinne Helein, Christelle Le Déan, Blandine Lelong and Isabelle Rodier – hide behind the name "Robert the Hero". All four graduated from the Ecole des Arts Décoratifs in 1985, worked for a while as stylists, then united in 1986 to design furnishing fabrics that evoke mythical figures and the classical past. Drawn freehand, the designs are printed on raw textures such as wild linen and pure cotton. They can be used for upholstery, but their painted texture and the absence of any repeat pattern lead the manufacturers Nobilis Fontan to recommend their use as wallhangings.

ROBERT LE HÉROS
Upholstery fabric or wall
hanging, *Le Pilleur d'Epave*
GLAZED, PRINTED LINEN
W 110 cm (44 in)
Repeat 94 cm (37½ in)
Manufacturer: Nobilis Fontan, France

« Nous allions aux pèlerinages comme on va à des fêtes. Nous prenions de
routes frémissantes de cantiques — routes de Rumengol (...), d'Auray. Nous cro
sions des élans, des villages, des troupes pleines d'un christianisme sauvage e
sonore. Les saints aimés, ils étaient les fils de nos terres. Les saintes avaient l
visage de nos femmes. C'était rugueux, plein de rire et de vent. Il y avait là quelqu
chose que Gauguin aurait aimé : une sorte de primitivisme et de pureté que ce
temps nouveaux, paraît-il intelligents, ont fait disparaître. (...) Oh ! ces mains ver
es fontaines, ce goût du miracle, cette candeur dans les gestes, cette enfanc
eau, le ciel, le bois, tout cela aussi en quelque sorte honoré, sanctifié par un pe
ple qui décidément avait écouté les secrets de la nature avant les exhortations de
docteurs. Entre les choses de la Terre et celles du Ciel, il y avait un accord profond

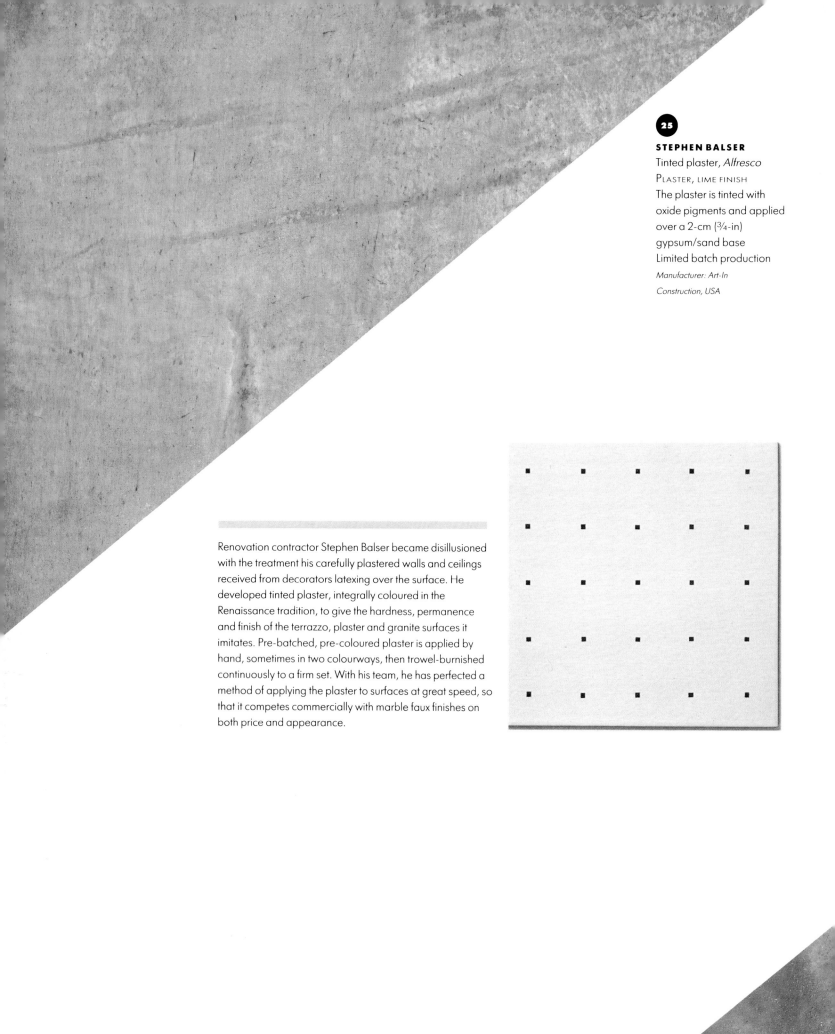

25

STEPHEN BALSER
Tinted plaster, *Alfresco*
PLASTER, LIME FINISH
The plaster is tinted with
oxide pigments and applied
over a 2-cm (¾-in)
gypsum/sand base
Limited batch production
Manufacturer: Art-In

Construction, USA

Renovation contractor Stephen Balser became disillusioned
with the treatment his carefully plastered walls and ceilings
received from decorators latexing over the surface. He
developed tinted plaster, integrally coloured in the
Renaissance tradition, to give the hardness, permanence
and finish of the terrazzo, plaster and granite surfaces it
imitates. Pre-batched, pre-coloured plaster is applied by
hand, sometimes in two colourways, then trowel-burnished
continuously to a firm set. With his team, he has perfected a
method of applying the plaster to surfaces at great speed, so
that it competes commercially with marble faux finishes on
both price and appearance.

26

DIETER SIEGER
Tiles, *Picto*
CERAMIC
W 30 cm (11⅞ in) L 30 cm (11⅞ in)
Manufacturer: AGROB Wessel
Servais, West Germany

The Adirondack Mountains, holiday homeland of rich New Yorkers, has a casual, earthy style that every designer including Ralph Lauren has used in fashion and furnishing. Tartan rugs, appliqué and quilting are stolid, homespun values. Gretchen Bellinger has added the *Boathouse* fabrics to her *Adirondack* collection, pure cotton woven in Belgium and true seersucker in the best Preppie style. "The collection reflects an understated, relaxed elegance, and the colours depict the weathered, bleached shades of the boathouse."

Bellinger's colour palette is derived from six neutrals of cotton bouclé. Multi-tonal combinations of beiges, taupes and greys are interwoven into a landscaped natural ground. The two-tone woven pattern of diminutive houndstooth is pleated, and highlighted with a contrasting second tone to produce the plain weave or "stripe" of the seersucker.

27

ETTORE SOTTSASS
Wall hangings, *Spring Day, Winter Day*
COTTON
Hand-woven with different weaves, plain and jacquard, the fabric is cut into various shapes and sewn on to canvas, then trimmed by cable stitches
Limited batch production
W 100 cm (40 in) L 125 cm (50 in)
Manufacturer: Elio Palmisano, Italy

28

GRETCHEN BELLINGER
Fabric, *Boathouse,* from the
Adirondack collection
Cotton seersucker
W 150 cm (59 in)
Repeat 3.8 cm (1½ in)
Manufacturer: Gretchen Bellinger,
USA

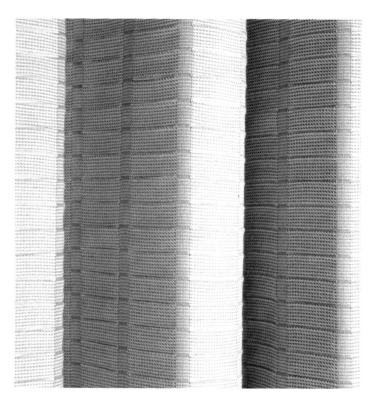

29

RUSHTON AUST
Wall hanging, *Plankton*
Cotton
A cotton calico, dyed and
overprinted using a paper
stencil and photo stencil
screen-print
One-off
W 125 cm (50 in)
L 250 cm (100 in)
Manufacturer: Rushton Aust,
UK

30

**JOSÉ LUIS RAMON-
SOLANS PRAT**

Rug

HAND-KNOTTED WOOL

W 360 cm (144 in) L 475 cm (190 in)

Manufacturer: Rica Basagoiti

Alfombras, Spain

 37

ANDRÉE PUTMAN
Rug, *Camille et Sophie*
MACHINE-WOVEN WOOL
W 180 cm (72 in) L 270 cm (108 in)
Manufacturer: Toulemonde Bochart,
France

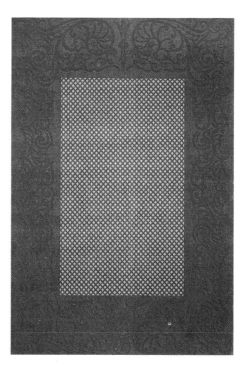

 38

ANDRÉE PUTMAN
Rug, *Paoli Paolo*
MACHINE-WOVEN WOOL
W 180 cm (72 in) L 270 cm (108 in)
Manufacturer: Toulemonde Bochart,
France

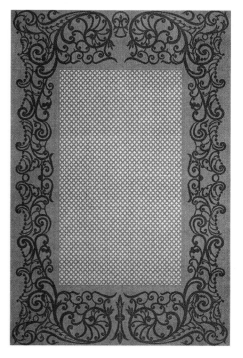

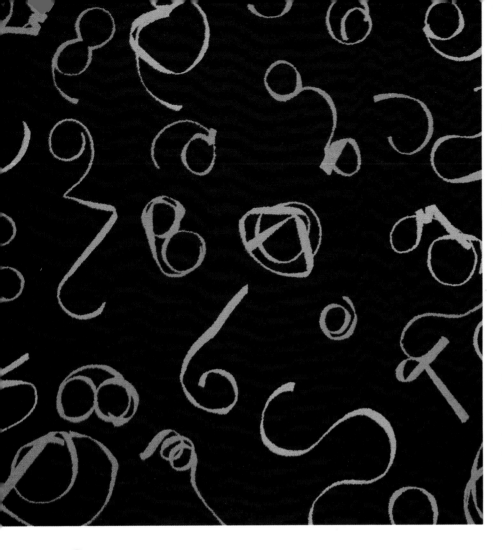

The West German carpet company Vorwerk attracted attention last year with *Dialog*, wall-to-wall artwork from internationally famous artists and architects at an affordable price. *Dialog 2* (on these and the following two pages) and *Dialog 3* (pages 180–1) are the result of new designs by the same people, and ideas by five new recruits: Milton Glaser, Zaha Hadid, Richard Meier, Jean Nouvel and Mimmo Paladino. Once again contributing designs are Sam Francis, David Hockney, Arata Isozaki, Sol Le Witt, Roy Lichtenstein, Oswald Mathias Ungers and Gerhard Richter.

   "The new trend in furnishing is transparent lines based on a minimum of furniture, bringing floor design to the forefront," claim Vorwerk. "*Dialog* is expressly not a signed artists' collection in limited edition, not an art substitute, but a consumer article." Emphasizing this crossover between art and consumerism, the carpets in the first collection have been exhibited at the German Museum of Architecture in Frankfurt, a building designed by Oswald Mathias Ungers. The Museum of Modern Art in New York offers the carpets for sale through its mail order catalogue.

39 MILTON GLASER

40 GERHARD RICHTER

41 SAM FRANCIS

43
MILTON GLASER

44
RICHARD MEIER

42
MIMMO PALADINO

Carpets from the
collection *Dialog 2*
POLYAMIDE
W 400 cm (157½ in)
Repeat 92.5 cm (36 in)
Manufacturer: Vorwerk, West
Germany

45

DAVID HOCKNEY

46

JEAN NOUVEL

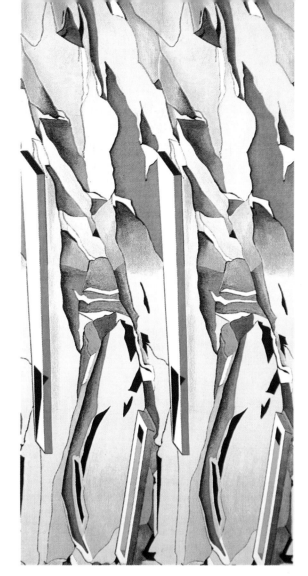

49
ZAHA HADID

48
ZAHA HADID

47
ZAHA HADID

50
MIMMO PALADINO

51
MIMMO PALADINO

52

ARATA ISOZAKI

Repeat 160 cm (62½ in)

53

ROY LICHTENSTEIN

Repeat 212 cm (82½ in)

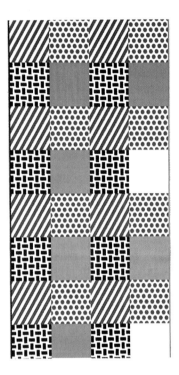

Carpets from the collection *Dialog 3*
POLYAMIDE
W 200 cm (78¾ in)
Manufacturer: Vorwerk, West Germany

54

OSWALD MATHIAS UNGERS

Repeat 110 cm (43 in)

55

OSWALD MATHIAS UNGERS

Repeat 55 cm (21½ in)

58

MILTON GLASER

Repeat 40 cm (15½ in)

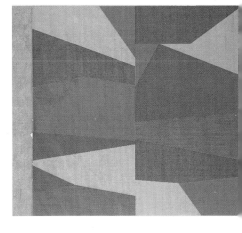

59

SOL LE WITT

Repeat 203 cm (79¼ in)

57

MILTON GLASER

Repeat 42 cm (16⅓ in)

56

DAVID HOCKNEY

Repeat 80 cm (31¼ in)

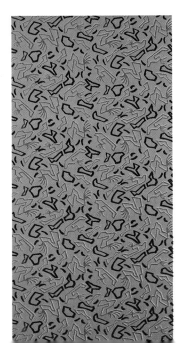

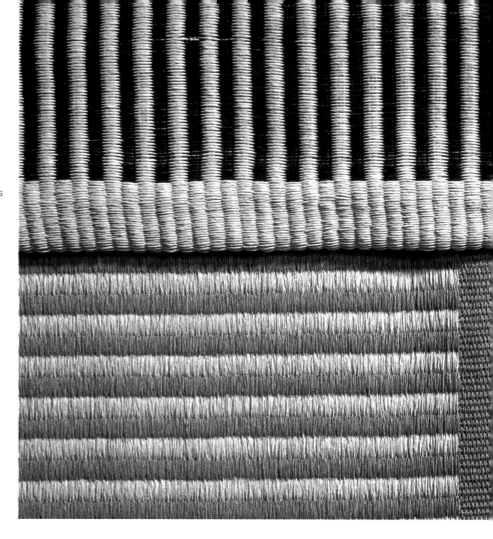

Ritva Puotila's first experiments with paper string woven with Japanese paper led her to make these weavings of wood fibre and strong cotton. The lightweight result is strong and easy to clean. The technique permits a subtle study of shades within a chromatic reduction of white, black and beige. The interplay of light and shade has a strong aesthetic effect, with carpets that look like ploughed fields, sand combed by wind or gravel stirred by water. Relationship with nature is celebrated in a ritualistic way by this Finnish designer, who acknowledges the physical properties of the materials with which she works, yet transcends both the limitations and the demands of the substance. The combination of textures, unequivocal colour and clarity of focus give these weaves a natural strength far from the mechanized world.

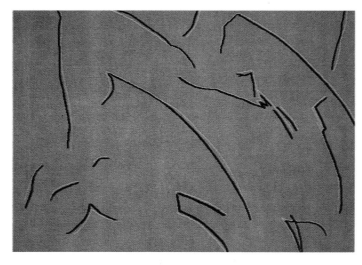

NANI MARQUINA
Rug, *Altamira*
WOOL
W 170 cm (68 in) L 240 cm (96 in)
Manufacturer: Nani Marquina, Spain

61

RITVA PUOTILA
Fabrics, *Papertex*
COTTON, PAPER STRING
W 90-200 cm (35½ in-79 in)
L 200-300 cm (79-117 in)
Manufacturer: Ritva Puotila, Finland

Jack Lenor Larsen's carpets graphically illustrate the symbiosis between a major designer and a manufacturer, who together constantly push forward the frontiers of technology for quality products. No other textile is as rigorously tested as flooring, and no other product in the home or public area takes so much rough handling. The cooperation between the American Larsen and the Swiss company Ruckstühl has created a product that meets both aesthetic and practical tests.

"The floor is the largest single furnished area in a room," says Larsen. "The larger the room, the more important the floor becomes." His exhibition at the Musée des Arts Décoratifs in the Louvre, Paris, testifies to his creativity. Next to lighting, he believes that floor covering is most essential to the successful manipulation of space.

 63

JACK LENOR LARSEN
Carpet, *Quadrangle*
WOOL
Repeat H 91 cm (36½ in)
W 68 cm (27¼ in)
Manufacturer: Ruckstühl, Switzerland

 62

HELEN YARDLEY
Rug
HAND-KNOTTED WOOL
W 213 cm (83¾ in)
L 304 cm (119½ in)
Manufacturer: A-Z Studios, UK

 64

**ELIZABETH BROWNING
JACKSON**
Rugs, *Winter, Spring,
Summer,* from the *Seasons*
collection
Hand-knotted wool
One-offs
W 210 cm (84 in) L 270 cm (108 in)
*Manufacturer: Elizabeth Browning
Jackson, USA*

PATI NÚÑEZ
Rug, *Polok i Ulises*
WOOL
W 200 cm (80 in) L 250 cm (100 in)
Manufacturer: Nani Marquina, Spain

CARLOS RIART
Rug, *Racan*
WOOL
W 170 cm (68 in) L 240 cm (96 in)
Manufacturer: Nani Marquina, Spain

**ELIZABETH BROWNING
JACKSON**
Rug, *Set*
HAND-KNOTTED WOOL
One-off
W 90 cm (36 in) L 210 cm (84 in)
*Manufacturer: Elizabeth Browning
Jackson, USA*

5 · PRODUCTS

Designs that tidy everything up lead to the ubiquitous black boxes which make hi-fi systems indistinguishable from microwave ovens. Household products that begin from a silicone chip or an electronic circuit highlight the big difference in silhouette between a power drill, a torch and a food mixer. Using overt metaphoric form tackles the demand for perceived value and individuality: now design is able to translate new technology into developed products. Designers break down faceless neutrality by using metaphors for an object's function, making the invisible become visible. This spirit of collaboration with engineering, of exploration and adventure, permeates the objects here. Under Bellini's rigorous eye, simulation and post-Memphis packaging are ruled out in favour of technology that delivers its message clearly and emphatically.

Thought-provoking and iconoclastic, the new designs are driven by function, not pretty packaging. Manufacturers who relied on in-house design departments for new ideas are now turning to smaller, less hidebound studios. Look at the loudspeakers shaped like musical instruments from Morten Warren, at Lonczak's *Bag Hog* bin, and at Moore's *Julie and Emily* keyboard and monitor set up like the familiar image of a notepad.

In Japan, "lifestyle" research is so important that of Sanyo's 400 designers 80 concentrate on lifestyle alone. Only with this research can a designer fully understand the implications of decisions that have far-reaching effects. Yet economists predict that in the Nineties Japan will become a net importer of products, a forecast that fits the notion of globalized manufacturing — a series of remote assembly operations, skilfully marketed according to prevailing trends. In the hugely successful *O-Product* for Olympus, Water Studio made a graphic package of Nineties technology contained in a Thirties-style aluminium camera body, numbered in a limited edition for exclusivity.

Obvious, well-designed accessories for contemporary life address the familiarity of everyday objects without drawing undue attention to their appearance, which tends to be rather streamlined and unobtrusive: bathroom ware from Porsche, personal organizers from De Lucchi and Waibl, a glass cleaner from Ziba. Product design can be a synthesis of research and technical innovation, but as a designer's contribution has to do with subjective values the most obvious criterion is appearance.

1

BRUNA RAPISARDA
Bathroom accessories,
Atlantide
SANDED GLASS
Toothbrush holder H 13 cm (5⅛ in)
Di at rim 10.5 cm (4⅛ in)
Toilet brush holder H 33.5 cm (13 in)
W 15 cm (6 in) D 12.5 cm (5 in)
Toilet roll holder H 7.5 cm (3 in)
Di 15 cm (6 in)
Manufacturer: Ceramica Mauri, Italy

2

**FERDINAND A. PORSCHE
AND SIEGFRIED EBNER**
Bathroom system,
Design Line
CERAMIC, WOOD
Basin H 21 cm (8¼ in)
W 69 cm (27⅛ in) D 60 cm (23½ in)
Wings H 75 cm (29½ in) W 40 cm
(15¾ in) D 38.5 cm (15¼ in)
Base H 55 cm (21½ in)
W 66 cm (26 in) D 38.5 cm (15¼ in)
Manufacturer: Öspag, Austria

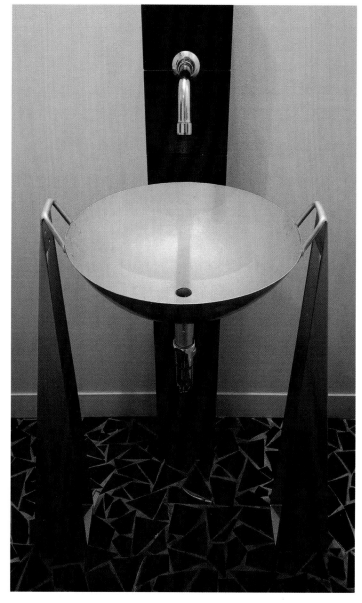

3

**GUEN BERTHEAU-
SUZUKI**
Sink unit, *China Town*
STEEL
The basin is a Chinese wok,
designed for the washroom
of a Tokyo bar
One-off
H 80 cm (31½ in) Di 65 cm (25½ in)
D 40 cm (15¾ in)
Manufacturer: Ishimaru, Japan

A surprising new patron of design emerged in the late Eighties – the hotel industry. Hotels launched their logos and new looks with total makeovers from penthouse suite to wine cellar by internationally acclaimed designers, such as Philippe Starck at the Royalton in New York, Aldo Rossi at Il Palazzo in Japan and Andrée Putman at the Hotel im Wasserturm in Cologne and Morgan's in New York. The custom-built furniture and fittings that result from this exclusivity are now in production in the Nineties for the home buyer. Souvenirs from celebrity hotels now include everything from Starck's corkscrew and door handles designed for the Royalton and made by Owo (see *The International Design Yearbook 1989/90*), to Andrée Putman's bath fittings designed for Morgan's and now in production by Sanistyl in France. Everything, from washbasins and taps to cabinets and mirrors, including the small accessories like soap dishes and towel rails, replicates the flattering bathrooms at Morgan's Hotel.

"The best bathrooms are always totally unpretentious, abstractly comfortable, always flattering," says Andrée Putman. "International hotels play an odd game trying to keep the rooms like being at home. I like the idea of the complete opposite. Nobody stays in a hotel room for long; the average stay in New York is one and a half days. I propose schemes which are creative, while never trying to copy the standard bathroom you have at home."

4

ANDRÉE PUTMAN
Bathroom accessories
NICKEL-PLATED BRASS
Top to bottom:
Shelf L 43 or 60 cm (17 or 23½ in)
D 9 cm (3½ in)
Toilet roll reserve H 12 cm (4¾ in)
W 15.5 cm (6⅛ in)
Robe hooks H 9.5 cm (3¾ in)
W 5 cm (2 in)
Ashtray or soap dish H 9 cm (3½ in)
W 11.5 cm (4½ in)
Towel rail H 11.5 cm (4½ in)
W 60 cm (23½ in)
Rack H 17.5 cm (6⅞ in)
W 60 cm (23½ in)

Mirror H 80 cm (31½ in)
W 35 cm (13¾ in)
Toilet roll holder W 9.75 cm (3⅞ in)
L 14 cm (5½ in)
Toilet brush holder H 36 cm (14⅛ in)
W 16.5 cm (6½ in)
Dustbin H 25.5 cm (10 in)
W 23 cm (9 in)
Mixer tap H 25 cm (9⅞ in)
W 23 cm (9 in)
Tap levers H 12 cm (4¾ in)
L 14 cm (5½ in)
Basin stand H 90 cm (35½ in)
W 40 cm (15¾ in)
Washbasin H 30 cm (11⅞ in)
W 40 cm (15¾ in)
Manufacturer: Sanistyl, France

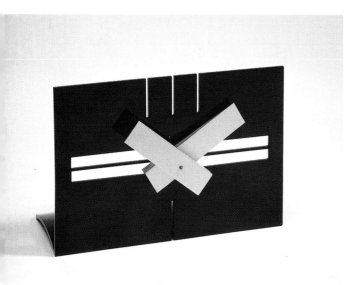

6

JOAQUÍN BERAO
Ainda
BRONZED BRASS, PVC
H 20.5 cm (8 in) W 30 cm (11⅞in)
D 16.5 cm (6½in)

7

CRISTIAN CIRICI
Equilibrio
STEEL, STAINLESS STEEL
Di 109 cm (42½ in) D 6 cm (2⅜ in)

5

**OSCAR TUSQUETS
BLANCA**
Ballesta
ALUMINIUM AND STEEL
FRAME,
CHROMED BRASS CHAIN,
CARBON FIBRE AND EPOXY
RESIN HANDS
H 172.5 cm (67¼ in) W 135 cm
(53¼ in) D 12.5 cm (5 in)

From the collection
Around the Clock
All prototypes
*Manufacturer: Bd Ediciones de
diseño, Spain*

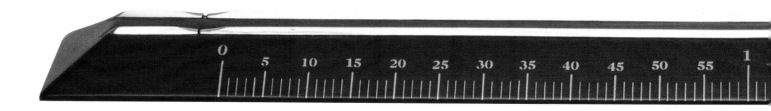

 9

PEP BONET

Horaria

STAINLESS STEEL, CHROMED
BRASS HANDS WITH GLASS
TIPS

H 166 cm (65⅜ in) W 50 cm (19⅝ in)

Di of base 23 cm (9 in)

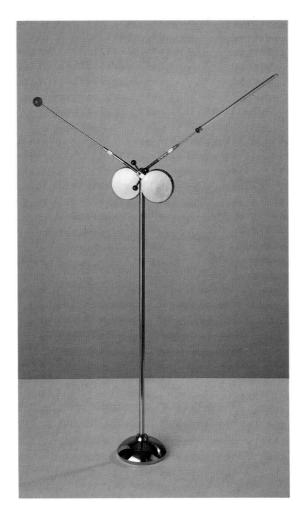

 8

PEDRO MIRALLES

Estación

STEEL, ANODIZED ALUMINIUM
HANDS

H 111 cm (43½ in) W 65 cm (25½ in)

D 25 cm (9⅞ in)

10

**SARA BOSSAERT AND
JOSEP FORT**

Regloj

ASH, BRASS, METHACRYLATE

H 8 cm (3⅛ in)

W 46 cm (18 in) D 6 cm (2⅜ in)

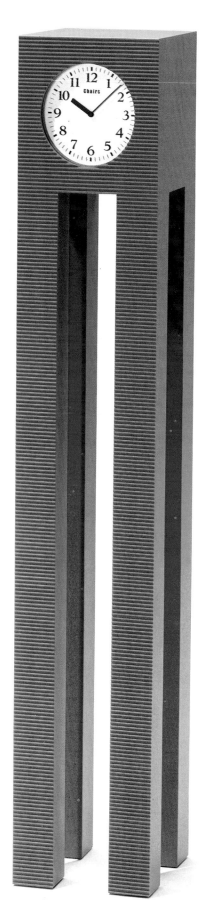

12

SHIGERU UCHIDA
Clock, *Dear Morris*
CORRUGATED BIRCH
PLYWOOD, BATTERY OPERATED
H 134.5 cm (53 in) W 24 cm (9⅜ in)
D 24 cm (9⅜ in)
Manufacturer: Chairs, Japan

13

**ACHILLE CASTIGLIONI
AND MAX HUBER**
Watch, *Record*
CHROMIUM-PLATED BRASS,
MINERAL CRYSTAL, NYLON
STRAP
Water resistant to 30 metres,
quartz mechanism
Di 3 cm (1⅓ in)
Manufacturer: Alessi, Italy

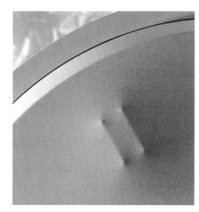

11

**MASAHIKO UCHIYAMA
FOR STEP DESIGN**
Relief Clock
POLYESTER, PVC
Prototype
D 5 cm (2 in) Di 30 cm (11⅞ in)
Manufacturer: Step Design, Japan

 14

MARIO BOTTA

Watch, *Eye*

STAINLESS STEEL, LEATHER STRAP, QUARTZ MECHANISM, SAPPHIRE GLASS

Pocket, table and wrist watch, water resistant to 30 metres

Di 3.5 cm (1⅗ in)

Manufacturer: Alessi, Italy

 15

CONSTANTIN BOYM

Clock, *Zvezdà*

BLACK DIE-CAST ALUMINIUM, CHROME-PLATED HOUR HAND, COPPER COLOURED MINUTE HAND, BATTERY OPERATED QUARTZ MECHANISM

Prototype

Di 45 cm (17¾ in)

Manufacturer: Morphos, Italy

**FERDINAND A. PORSCHE
AND SIMON FRASER**
Television, *M55-911*
Gʟᴀss, ABS
Flat screen, removable
stereo loudspeakers, built-in
remote control
H 55 cm (21½ in) W 58.5 cm (23 in)
D 39.5 cm (15⅝ in)
Manufacturer: Grundig, West

Germany

18

**FERDINAND A. PORSCHE
AND SIMON FRASER**
Car radio, *5500 RDS*
ABS
Remote control, with anti-
theft device
H 5 cm (2 in) W 18 cm (7 in)
D 16 cm (6¼ in)
Manufacturer: Grundig, West

Germany

17

**YAMAHA CORPORATION
DESIGN**
Electronic woodwind *EW 20*
PLASTIC
L 43 cm (16⅞ in) Di 3.8 cm (1½ in)
Manufacturer: Yamaha Corporation,

Japan

19

PRODUCT FIRST
3-band radio, *RR-4*
ABS
H 14 cm (5½ in) W 7 cm (2¾ in)
L 21 cm (8¼ in)
Manufacturer: Ross Consumer

Electronics, UK

 20

KOMPLOT DESIGN
Compact disc holder,
Disc-Desk
INJECTION-MOULDED
PLASTIC
Can be placed horizontally
or mounted vertically on a
wall
H 2.5 cm (1 in) W 17 cm (6⅝ in)
L 23 cm (9 in)
*Manufacturer: Hofstatter & Ebbesen,
Denmark*

Audio equipment gives the most extreme examples of styling, with exaggerated shapes that can be retrospective, organic, kinetic, aerodynamic. Pirate Design's amplifiers make a diagrammatical representation of their function: the relationship between the four elements of power in, audio signal in, waste heat out and power signal out.

In Morten Warren's loudspeakers, on the other hand, the shape – a trombone and tuba cross-breed – has an acoustic function. The taper allows lower frequencies to resonate, removing the need for a separate bass unit; the high-frequency tweeter is isolated and mounted on the side of the casing. B & W Loudspeakers plan to produce them at about £3,000 a pair.

According to Hideo Watanabe, Chairman of the Sony Corporation, "Design cannot only be concerned with colours, forms and balance of shape. Now designers should think of – and design – the corporate philosophy itself. I call this corporate dynamics." Created on a 3D Fresdam computer-aided design system, Sony's headphones combine high technology with timeless packaging. The diaphragm is in bio-cellulose, a natural fibre produced by the bacterium *acetobacter aceti*, developed jointly by Sony and the Ajinomoto Research Institute for Polymers and Textiles to offer a good level of amplification and acoustic spacing. The casing, of 200-year-old hardwood, gives concert-hall sound quality.

 21

MORTEN V. WARREN
Loudspeakers, *Emphasis*
FIBREGLASS, CAST IRON,
BRASS
A resonant pipe is built in to
the housing, with the
speaker system placed a
third of the way down to
increase base output
Limited batch production
H 140 cm (55⅛ in) W 45 cm (17¾ in)
D 45 cm (17¾ in)
*Manufacturer: B & W Loudspeakers,
UK*

23

**PIRATE DESIGN
ASSOCIATES**
Hi-fi mono power amplifiers
ALUMINIUM, COPPER
H 35 cm (13¾ in) Di 25 cm (9⅞ in)
*Manufacturer: B & W Loudspeakers,
UK*

22

SONY CORPORATION
Stereo headphones,
MDR R10
BIO-CELLULOSE DIAPHRAGM,
ZELKOVA WOOD HOUSING
Di 50 cm (19⅝ in)
Manufacturer: Sony, Japan

Mario Bellini's own keyboard designs for Olivetti made him a severe judge in this over-subscribed field. He liked the cultural and historical exchange in Loyd Moore's design. The paper, pencil and notebook contrast with a post-Gutenberg flat-screen LCD and mechanical keyboard. Images of earlier methods of collecting and conveying information are applied to electronic circuitry: an exploitation of the past and a celebration of the future.

24

LOYD MOORE
Monitor and keyboard,
Julie and *Emily*
ABS, ALUMINIUM
The flat screen LCD
resembles paper, pencil and
notebook
One-off
Julie H 30 cm (11⅞ in) W 38 cm (15 in)
D 16 cm (6¼ in)
Emily H max. 4.5 cm (1¾ in)
W 38 cm (15 in) D 30 cm (11⅞ in)
Manufacturer: Synapse/Technology
Design, USA

 25

**COLIN BURNS AND BILL
VERPLANK FOR ID TWO**

Interactive keyboard
ABS
Keyboard compatible with
personal computer for
bonds trading systems.
Long LCD provides soft
labels for personal
computer function keys;
square LCD is a 'scratch'
pad and calculator display
H 5 cm (2 in) W 48.5 cm (19 in)
D 25.5 cm (10 in)
Manufacturer: Micrognosis, USA

 26

ZIBA DESIGN

Personal computer,
Emerald LANstation
INJECTION-MOULDED ABS
Desktop IBM-compatible
PC with data and word-
processing capability. It can
also be used as a LAN (local
area network) workstation,
connecting with other
computers
H 23.5 cm (9½ in) W 36.5 cm (14¼ in)
D 13.5 cm (5¼ in)
*Manufacturer: Emerald Computers,
USA*

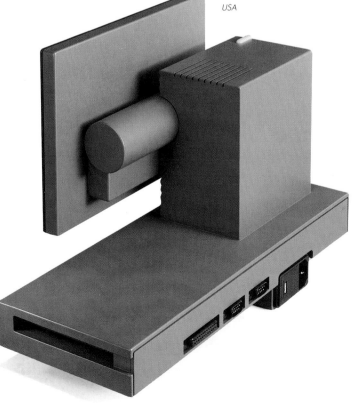

Elemental, bold and graphic, the *Kirk Plus* wall phone is a topic of conversation in itself. Simple lines slice across each other; the red triangle is the detail which ensures balance and harmony in the form. Marianne Stokholm and Gad Zorea maintain that Danish design is defined here, with the asymmetrical crossing of handset and wall bracket: it is practical and streamlined in its geometric simplicity. The keypad on the underside of the handset has rounded, quick-response keys which are comfortable to touch; pre-programmed facilities such as last-number redial and the privacy switch are easy to activate. Alcatel Kirk's patented transducers in receiver and transmitter provide perfect sound reproduction.

27

MARIANNE STOKHOLM AND GAD ZOREA
Telephone, *Kirk Plus*
ABS
Handset H 22 cm (8⅔ in)
W 7 cm (2¾ in)
Wall bracket L 23 cm (9 in)
Manufacturer: Alcatel Kirk, Denmark

28

GEOFF HOLLINGTON

Videophone

INJECTION-MOULDED ABS,
THERMOPLASTIC ELASTOMER

The still image is transmitted
while the user is speaking,
controls are in the handset,
unit is adjustable for angle
of tilt

Prototype

Videophone H 22 cm (8²/3 in)

W 27 cm (10¹/2 in) D 13.3 cm (5²/3 in)

Handset H 22 cm (8²/3 in)

W 4 cm (1¹/2 in) D 3 cm (1¹/3 in)

Manufacturer: Panasonic, Japan

KAZUO KAWASAKI
Weather gauge, *Frigg*
ABS
H 23.5 cm (9½ in) D 3 cm (1⅓ in)
Di 20 cm (7⅞ in)
Manufacturer: Takata, Japan

ZIBA DESIGN
Wall thermostat, *Encore*
INJECTION-MOULDED ABS
Senses and monitors
changes in temperature
H 11.5 cm (4½ in) W 6.5 cm (2½ in)
D 1.75 cm (¾ in)
Manufacturer: Cadet
Manufacturing, USA

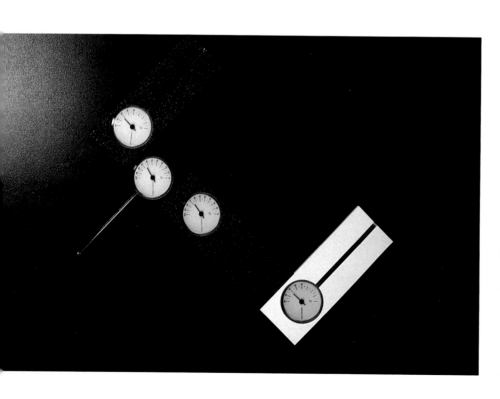

KAZUO KAWASAKI
Thermometer and
hydrometer, *Shu* and *Tefnut*
ABS
H 20 cm (7⅞ in) W 7 cm (2¾ in)
D 3 cm (1⅓ in)
Manufacturer: Takata, Japan

Pirate Design was set up in 1986 by graduates of the Royal College of Art, London. With simple, innovative ideas they have cut a swashbuckling path through mainstream product design. They regard themselves as "really unusual in the way we work, the way we make things and the way the product looks. We recognize that the working parts that drive a product can be used as an intrinsic part of the design. Design doesn't have to tidy up after the engineering. The outer shell should express what the inside is doing."

These electronic devices are voice-activated so they must be worn near the mouth and ear. The battery, contained in the ball which is also the head of the brooch pin, is activated when the pin is pushed into clothing. The idea is driven by changes in miniature electronics, such as whistling key rings. Says Mike Ganss of Pirate, "We took the idea and activated the pins to respond to a single command, 'Time', 'Weather' or 'Pass'. The task was to design a shape that would accurately express the function of the five pieces."

Each is based on components of steam machinery, the invention that marked the beginning of the industrial age. The security pass represents the valve gear controls that meter flow. The navigational aid is inspired by the mechanism that directs the movement of components. The timepiece uses the bearings that show the passage of motion, while the radiation detector is simply an abstract depiction of the firebox. The weather forecaster is a cross-section of the copper boiler: the wavy lines at the top symbolize boiling water, the springs indicate pressure, and the fuzzy stuff around the perimeter simulates lagging. They are all beautifully made, and recognition of the craft processes in the finished products adds to their symbolic value.

32

PIRATE DESIGN ASSOCIATES
Top: security pass
Above left: radiation detector
Above right: time piece
Far left: weather forecaster
Left: navigation aid
BRASS, STEEL, ALUMINIUM, POLYMERS
These personal electronic products are designed to be worn as brooches. They are voice-controlled with voice-synthesized information, and battery operated
Prototypes
W 4 cm (1½ in) L 12 cm (4¾ in)
Manufacturer: Pirate Design Associates, UK

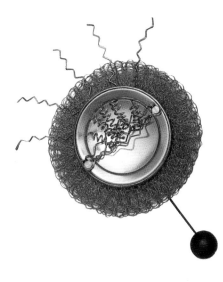

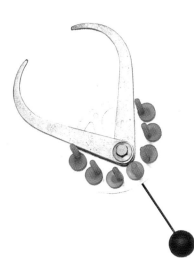

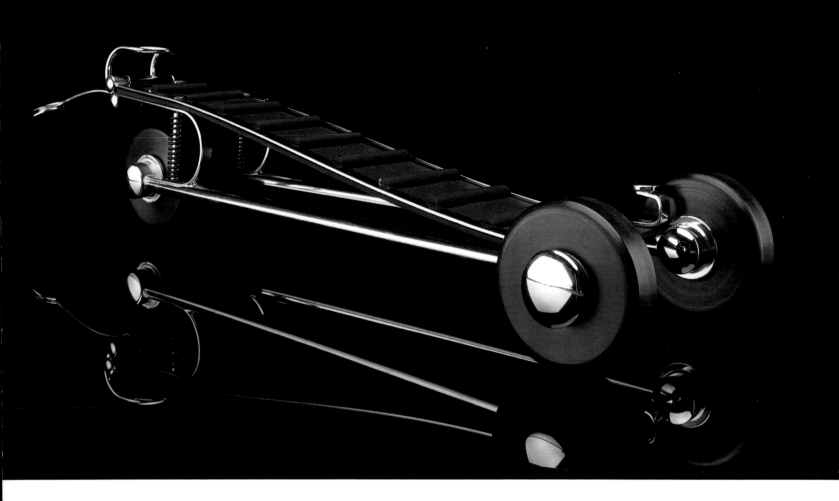

33

CORDULA NIES-FRIEDLÄNDER

City Skates

STEEL ROD, CHROMED OR GILT

Men's and women's roller-skates for urban travel. The women's are gilt and designed for wear with high heels

Prototype

H 8 cm (3¹⁄8 in) W 10 cm (4 in)

L 20 cm (7⁷⁄8 in)

Manufacturer: Cordula Nies-Friedländer, UK

34

TAKENAO SHISHIKURA

Binoculars, *8 × 42 DCF*

POLYCARBONATE, POLYURETHANE RUBBER COATING

Compact, water-resistant binoculars with large-aperture lenses

L 16.7 cm (6²⁄3 in) W 13 cm (5¹⁄8 in)

Manufacturer: Asahi Optical Company for Pentax, Japan

 35

KUNO PREY
Credit card holder,
Penny Pack
PLASTIC
W 6.4 cm (2½ in) L 10.5 cm (4⅛ in)
Manufacturer: Nava Milano, Italy

Paper cutting and folding acquires a new practicality with John Lonczak's *Bag Hog* rubbish bag holders. Shapes in polyethylene plastic, packaged flat, are assembled in seconds by rolling and latching together the patent system of hooking tabs. After use, the holders can be flattened immediately by hitting the right spot. *Manufold* is a scale model for modelmakers, originally made jointly by Lonczak and Turett Freyer as part of a model for a newstand for a New York competition. When Lonczak could not buy the correct scale model to show on a prototype chair, he made his own in paper glued with sticky tape. This version packs flat to sell in artists' suppliers and gift shops. More than a design tool, it drew a crowd when he demonstrated it outside his New York office. The *Manufold* dog which emerged to join it is purely for fun and, says Lonczak, awaits a kennel.

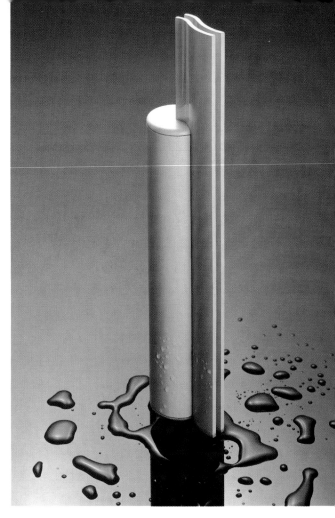

36

ZIBA DESIGN
Glass cleaner, *Cleret*
Extruded and injection-moulded ABS, santoprene
Two-sided cleaner for mirrors, tiles and windows
L 25.5 cm (10 in) Di 4.5 cm (1¾ in)
Manufacturer: Hanco, USA

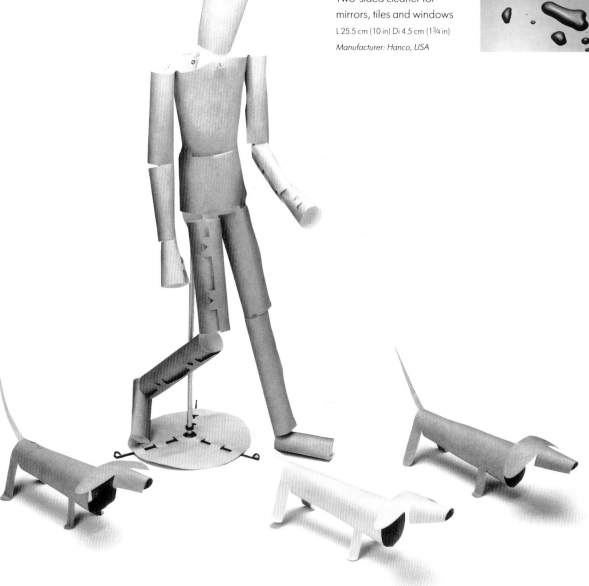

37

JOHN LONCZAK
Manufold
Tyvek
¼-scale mannequins for use as a children's toy or for anatomical study or design scale-modelling. Tyvek is a tear-resistant, paper-like plastic made from high-density polyurethane fibres
Man H 40.5 cm (16 in)
W 12.5 cm (5 in) D 2.5 cm (1 in)
Dog H 4.5 cm (1¾ in) W 7.5 cm (3 in)
L 23 cm (9 in)
Manufacturer: Form Farm, USA

JOHN LONCZAK
Bag Hog
POLYETHYLENE
Collapsible bin-bag holder
H 46 cm (18 in) or 61 cm (24 in)
Di 34.5 cm (13½ in)
L when flat 120 cm (47½ in)
Manufacturer: Form Farm, USA

MILES KELLER
Dustpan and brush
INJECTION-MOULDED
PLASTIC
Brush clips to pan for
storage
H 4 cm (1½ in) W 18 cm (7 in)
L 24 cm (9⅜ in)
Manufacturer: Umbra, Canada

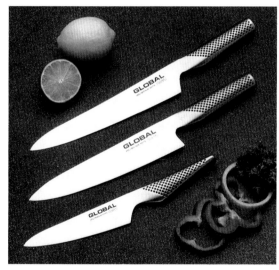

KOMIN YAMADA
Kitchen knives, *Global*
MOLYBDENUM/VANADIUM
HIGH-CARBON STAINLESS
STEEL
W 3-4 cm (1¼-1½ in) L 21.5-33 cm
(8½-13¼ in) D at handle 2 cm (¾ in)
Manufacturer: Yoshikin, Japan

FRANZ A. STUTZER
Lighter, *RO 455*
PLASTIC, COATED BRASS
Electronically controlled
quartz ignition
H 18.6 cm (7¼ in) Di 1.9 cm (¾ in)
*Manufacturer: Rowenta-Werke, West
Germany*

42

**JACOB BRAHE-
PEDERSEN**

Padlocks

HARDENED STEEL, SEMI-MATT
BLACK CHROME

The locks are colour-coded
for insurance purposes,
indicating the size and
extent of protection they
offer

Prototype

Blue: H 10 cm (4 in) W 6 cm (2⅜ in)
D 2.5 cm (1 in)

Red: H 10.5 cm (4⅛ in)
W 8 cm (3⅛ in) D 3.3 cm (1½ in)

Manufacturer: Ruko, Denmark

43

**PIRATE DESIGN
ASSOCIATES**

Camping stove

PHOSPHOR BRONZE,
STAINLESS STEEL, BRASS

Runs on petrol, with the
control handle operating
flame ignition, heat intensity
and an internal jet-clearing
device

H 150 cm (59 in) Di 130 cm (51⅛ in)

Manufacturer: A. B. Optimus, Sweden

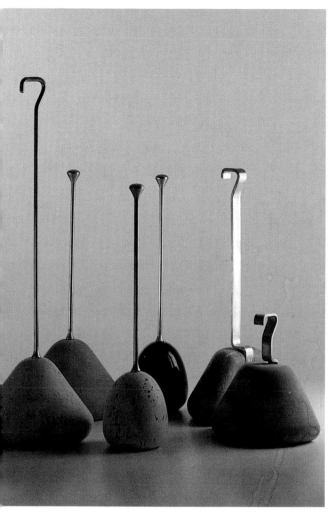

PEP BONET
Fire tongs, *Leina*
BURNISHED STEEL, BLACK
VARNISHED HOLDER
H 103 cm (40½ in)
Manufacturer: Alessi, Italy

**LUIGI CACCIA
DOMINIONI**
Doorstops, *Buffalmacco*
STONE OR MARBLE, BRASS
HANDLE
Left to right:
H 59 cm (23¼ in) W 20 cm (7⅞ in)
H 43 cm (16⅞ in) W 11 cm (4⅜ in)
H 57 cm (22⅜ in) W 12 cm (4¾ in)
H 33 cm (13 in) W 12 cm (4¾ in)
Manufacturer: Bigelli Marmi

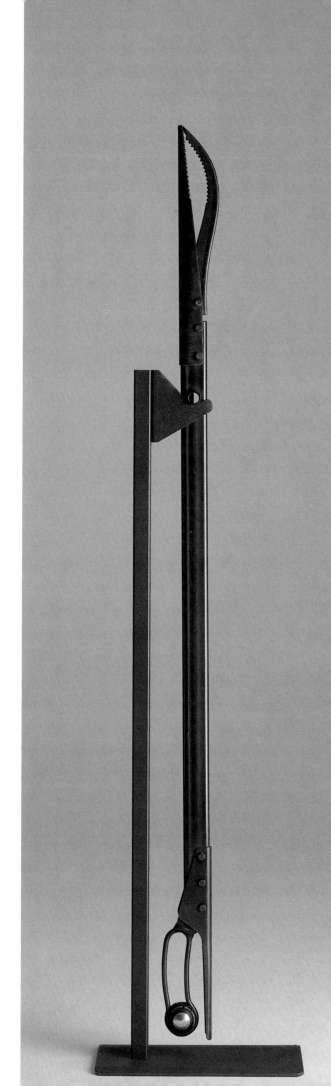

46

JOSEP LLUSCA

Door handles, *Arista*
BRASS WITH POLISHED
CHROMIUM OR BLACK
GRAPHITE FINISHES
Sliding-door handle L 15 cm (6 in)
Di 2 cm (¾ in)
Crank L 11.5 cm (4½ in)
Di 2 cm (¾ in)
Keyhole Di 5 cm (2 in)
Manufacturer: Sellex, Spain

49

TAKENOBU IGARASHI

Garden kit, *Hyvälysti*
ABS, ELASTOMER, POM
Compact garden kit
consisting of planter, fork,
trowel, secateurs, tool case
and belt which fit inside the
basic container, half of
which serves as a watering
can
H 24.5 cm (9⅔ in) W when closed
29 cm (11⅜ in) D 11 cm (4⅜ in)
Manufacturer: Kai Corporation,
Japan

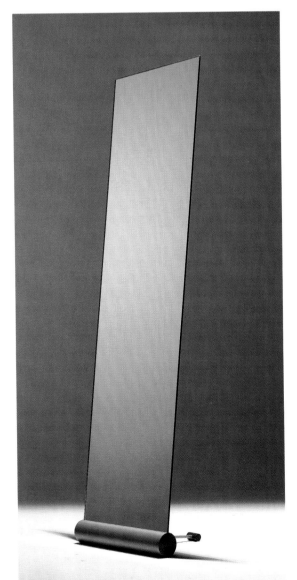

48

ISAO HOSOE

Mirror, *Soglia*
CRYSTAL GLASS, STEEL
Mounted on a mirrored
rotating base
H 180 cm (70⅝ in) W 35 cm (13¾ in)
Di of base 50 cm (19⅝ in)
Manufacturer: Tonelli, Italy

47

MAX LESER

Floor mirror
PVC, GLASS, STAINLESS STEEL
The mirror is supported by a
lateral arm projecting from
the roller
H 152 cm (59¾ in) W 46 cm (18 in)
Manufacturer: Becker Designed, USA

Mass production has reduced style and individuality in camera design. So while mass marketing cuts costs to increase the availability of high-performance cameras, there is a demand for individual packaging – particularly of a kind which makes products look like their antecedents. Recognizing the desire for exclusivity in the higher-income purchasing groups, Olympus restricted production of their *O-Product* to 20,000. Each burnished aluminium camera case is numbered, as well as the black cardboard packaging. Within two months of issue it is a collector's item. In an era when classic design can be neglected for the sake of pure functionalism, no black box with finger grips, however fluid in form, can rival its emotional appeal.

Combining early traditional box camera values with the latest floppy disc film, British designer Ross Lovegrove says of his prototype that he intends to "break down the barriers of conventional manufacture to elevate the product to a personal acquisition status". So he uses leather fascia panels and ABS plastic for the case, with a gold-plated lens bezel, shutter release and self-timer button. "As the leather ages and the gold tarnishes, the contrast between new and old, plastic and natural, becomes more apparent and potentially timeless."

This year witnessed the marketing of still video cameras, of professional quality but designed for use by amateurs. Conventional silver halide film for printing into snapshots has been replaced with a magnetic floppy disc. With Canon's *Ion*, single-frame images are recorded on to the disc for instant screening on a television or home computer screen. No processing is necessary. They can also be made into colour prints or transmitted via telecommunication lines. Pictures can then be erased and the disc re-used.

In the year of the tenth anniversary of the Sony Walkman, Sony launched the world's smallest and lightest camcorder, which fits in a briefcase, a backpack, or the palm of the hand. Equipment which once weighed in as heavy as a futon has shrunk to the size of a box of chocolates, without any loss in performance. It sold 50,000 in the first ten days after its launch in Japan. Sony forecast that by the end of the Nineties the screening of home movies will have replaced the photograph album.

CANON DESIGN TEAM
Still video camera,
Ion RC-251
ABS, Polycarbonate
For use with video floppy disks and a range of accessories for projection, reproduction and transmission of images
H 3.5 cm (1⅗ in) W 14 cm (5½ in)
D 10.5 cm (4⅛ in)
Manufacturer: Canon, Japan

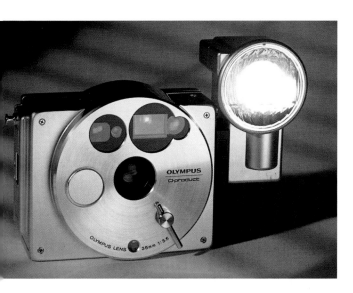

51

WATER STUDIO
Camera, *O-Product*
ALUMINIUM
Fully automatic focus,
exposure, detachable flash,
film loading, winding and
rewinding, 35 mm lens
Limited batch production
H 8.2 cm (3¼ in) W 9.9 cm (4 in)
D 4.5 cm (1¾ in)
Manufacturer: Olympus, Japan

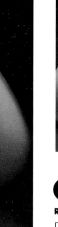

53

ROSS LOVEGROVE
Disc camera
ABS, LEATHER, GOLD-PLATED
BEZEL
Based on the Kodak disc
camera system, the film
cassette snaps on to the
back of the camera, the
large aperture on the front
contains the flash and the
smaller one the lens, and the
viewfinder is at the top
corner
Prototype
H 7.5 cm (3 in) W 2 cm (¾ in)
L 13.5 cm (5⅖ in)
Manufacturer: Ross Lovegrove, UK

52

SONY CORPORATION
8 mm camcorder,
Handycam CCP TR55
ABS
Lightweight, 790 g
H 10.7 cm (4⅓ in) W 10.6 cm
(4¼ in) L 17.6 cm (6⅞ in)
Manufacturer: Sony, Japan

MATSUSHITA SEIKO DESIGN
Electric fan
INJECTION MOULDED ABS, PAINTED
Controlled by microcomputer
H 76-90 cm (30-35⅜ in)
W 38 cm (15 in) D 34 cm (13⅜ in)
Manufacturer: Matsushita Seiko, Japan

In the year when diaries evolved into personal organizers and stored information went electronic, on disc, it is interesting to find the traditional ledger system applied to a new diary, on a ring binder. Heinz Waibl's *Ring* is subdivided into several sections which can be tailored to personal needs with a special data-to-file system. It opens upwards, complete with pen and envelopes. Files stored in the box can be reinserted in the diary when necessary. Information is printed in six languages: English, French, Italian, German, Spanish and Japanese.

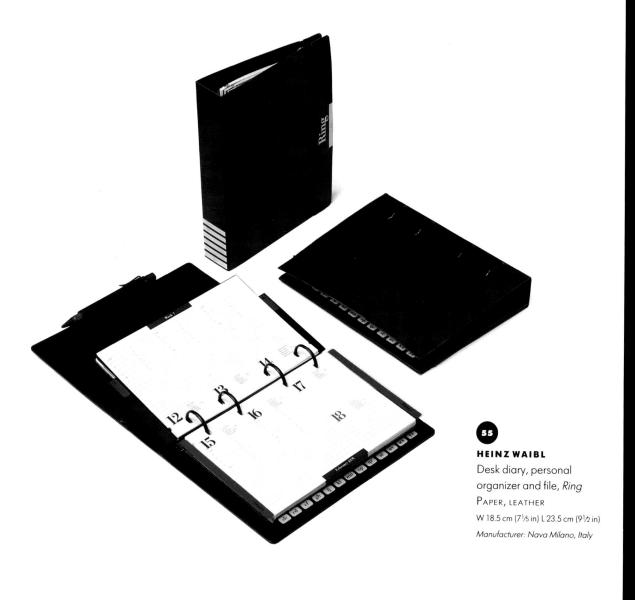

HEINZ WAIBL
Desk diary, personal organizer and file, *Ring*
PAPER, LEATHER
W 18.5 cm (7⅕ in) L 23.5 cm (9½ in)
Manufacturer: Nava Milano, Italy

56

GUNTER HORNTRICH

Ballpoint pens, *Design 3*
ABS
Part of a series of writing
utensils
L 14 cm (5½ in) Di 1 cm (⅖ in)
*Manufacturer: Pelikan/Kreuzer, West
Germany*

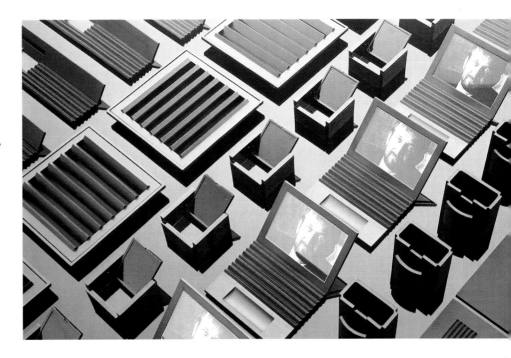

58

**MICHELE DE LUCCHI AND
TADAO TAKAICHI**

Desk accessories, *Segmenti*
THERMOPLASTIC
TECHNOPOLYMER, RUBBER
Left to right:
Desk-set H 4 cm (1½ in)
W 10.5 cm (4⅛ in) L 60 cm (23½ in)
Table ashtray H 3.4 cm (1⅗ in)
W 24 cm (9⅜ in) D 24 cm (9⅜ in)
Ashtray with top H 5 cm (2 in)
W 10 cm (4 in) L 10 cm (4 in)
Photo and pencil case H 12 cm
(4¾ in) W 18 cm (7 in) L 24 cm (9⅜ in)
Paper and pencil case H 9 cm (3½ in)
W 7.5 cm (3 in) L 10 cm (4 in)
Desk pad W 35.5 cm (14 in)
L 60 cm (23½ in) *Manufacturer:
Kartell, Italy*

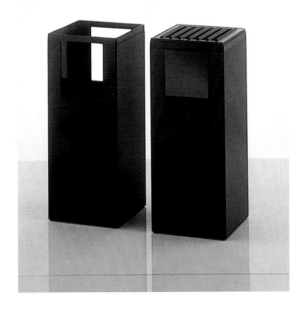

57

**MICHELE DE LUCCHI AND
TADAO TAKAICHI**

Multi-purpose containers,
Segmenti
THERMOPLASTIC
TECHNOPOLYMER
Various functions: umbrella
stand, waste-paper basket,
waste-paper basket with
integrated ashtray/top
W 25 cm (9⅞ in) L 25 cm (9⅞ in)
Umbrella stand H 60 cm (23½ in)
Basket/ashtray H 61 cm (24 in)
Manufacturer: Kartell, Italy

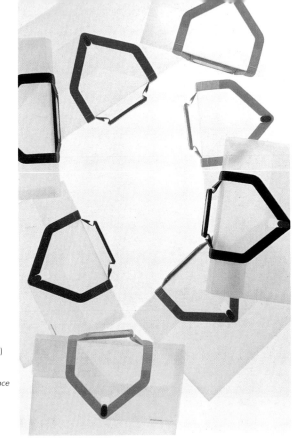

59

VITRAC DESIGN
Document holder,
Module Case
POLYPROPYLENE
Portable file with a
retractable handle
W 25 cm (9⅞ in) L 32 cm (12½ in)
D 2.5 cm (1 in)
Manufacturer: Mecanorma, France

60

JORGE PENSI
Desk accessories, *Calenda*
ANODIZED ALUMINIUM,
PLEXIGLASS
Clockwise from back left:
Letter tray H 7 cm (2¾ in)
W 25 cm (9⅞ in) D 35 cm (13¾ in)
Rubber seal holder H 7 cm (2¾ in)
W 20 cm (7⅞ in) D 8 cm (3⅛ in)
Desk case (large) H 7 cm (2¾ in)
W 11 cm (4⅜ in) L 30 cm (12 in)
Memo holder H 3.5 cm (1⅗ in)
W 17 cm (6⅝ in) D 12 cm (4¾ in)
Vertical sorter H 8.5 cm (3⅜ in)
W 20 cm (7⅞ in) D 8.5 cm (3⅜ in)
Ashtray H 7 cm (2¾ in) Di 5 cm (2 in)
Pencil pot H 11 cm (4⅜ in)
Di 7 cm (2¾ in)
Tape dispenser H 5 cm (2 in)
W 8 cm (3⅛ in) L 14 cm (5½ in)
Manufacturer: Sabat Selección, Spain

62

TOSHIYUKI KITA
Desk accessories, *Repro*
ALUMINIUM, RUBBER
Wall clock Di 18 cm (7 in)
H 3.5 cm (1⅜ in)
Ash tray Di 14 cm (5½ in)
H 3 cm (1⅓ in)
Pen stand H 9.5 cm (3¾ in)
W 8.5 cm (3⅜ in) D 4.5 cm (1¾ in)
Pen tray H 2 cm (¾ in)
W 6.5 cm (2½ in) L 22 cm (8⅔ in)
Table clock H 12 cm (4¾ in)
Di 10 cm (4 in) D 6 cm (2⅜ in)
Manufacturer: IDK, Japan

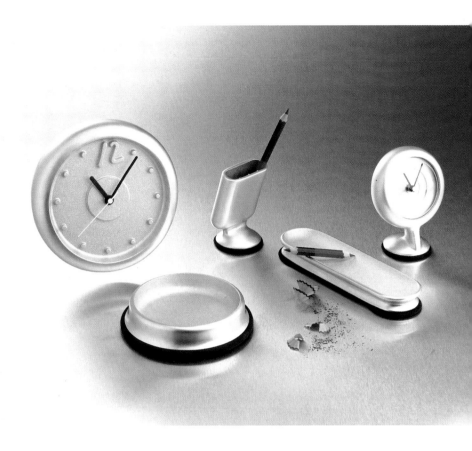

61

VINACCIA DESIGN
Telefax machine
NEOPRENE, ABS
Prototype
H 6.5 cm (2½ in) W 29 cm (11⅜ in)
L 28 cm (11 in)
Manufacturer: Vinaccia Design, Italy

63

**PLUS CORPORATION
DESIGN TEAM**
Scissors
HIGH-CARBON STAINLESS
STEEL, ELASTOMAR
POLYPROPYLENE GRIP
W 6.2 cm (2⅜ in) L 16.5 cm (6½ in)
D 0.7 cm (⅕ in)
*Manufacturer: Plus Corporation,
Japan*

64

GIULIO CONFALONIERI
Roller Pad
ABS, PAPER
200 sheet notepad with
sliding accessory tray
H 3 cm (1⅓ in) W 22 cm (8⅔ in)
L 31 cm (12¼ in)
Manufacturer: Nava Milano, Italy

65

FUMIO ENOMOTO
Ashtray
STAINLESS STEEL
A weighted head allows it to
tilt when used
Prototype
H 12 cm (4¾ in) W 7 cm (2¾ in)
L 30 cm (11⅞ in)
Manufacturer: Ishimaru, Japan

SHOEI YOH
Calendar,
Programming Schedule
Steel or aluminium
Coloured marker pins
indicate special days
H 16 cm (6¼ in) W 16 cm (6¼ in)
Manufacturer: Wakita Hi-Tecs, Japan

BIOGRAPHIES

Every effort has been made to obtain details about each designer whose work is represented in this book, but in some cases information was not available. The figures following each entry refer to the illustrations in which the designer's work is represented (the number before the full point indicates the chapter number).

A & E Design was founded by Tom Ahlström and Hans Ehrich in Stockholm in 1968. They have received numerous national and international design awards for their work, including the Industrial Designer of the Year award in 1987. 2. 25

Helle Abild was born in Denmark in 1965. Since graduating in textile design in 1989, she has worked with fabrics for fashion shows, experimenting with new techniques and materials. 4. 1

Lodovico Acerbis was born in Bergamo in 1939 and graduated in Economics and Business Studies. He founded and is currently president of Acerbis International SpA. He has served on several committees, including as European President of the Young Furniture Industrialists in 1976. Since 1977 he has worked as a designer in collaboration with Giotto Stoppino. 1. 110

Atelier Alchimia is a design group based in Milan. It includes among its designers Bruno and Giorgio Gregori, Adriana and Alessandro Guerriero and Alessandro Mendini. 1. 87, 88

Emilio Ambasz gained a Master's degree in Architecture at Princeton University, where he was subsequently a professor. While still in his twenties he helped to found New York's Institute of Architecture and Urban Studies, and served as Curator of Design at the Museum of Modern Art. He has won international recognition and several awards for his work as architect, interior and industrial designer, as well as for his lectures and writings on design. Among his buildings the Museum of American Folk Art and Houston Center Plaza are especially well known. 4. 18

Mikhail Anikst was born in Moscow in 1938. After training at the Moscow Architectural Institute, he worked for a time as an architect before designing books and stage sets. One of the most noted graphic designers in the Soviet Union, his many international and Soviet awards include Best Book in the World at the Leipzig Book Fair. He is a member of the Soviet Union of Artists, and since 1976 has been a chief art director of the publishing house Soviet Artist. 1. 148

Georg Appeltshauser was born in Coburg, Germany, in 1949. He studied at the Academy of Art in Stuttgart under Professor Lehmann from 1973 to 1978. Since then he has been working as a freelance designer and engineer. 1. 14

Ron Arad was born in 1951 in Tel Aviv, Israel. He studied at the Jerusalem Academy of Art and at the Architectural Association, London, graduating in 1979. After working for a firm of London architects, he founded the design company One-Off Ltd in 1981. He has exhibited widely and designs furniture, products and interiors. 1. 34, 35, 136

Junichi Arai, born in 1932 in Gunma Prefecture, Japan, is a textile designer and manufacturer specializing in sculptural, heavily textured fabrics. He has supplied Issey Miyake and Comme des Garçons, among other leading Japanese designers. In 1987 he was made an Honorary Member of the Faculty of Royal Designers for Industry. He has exhibited in Japan and the USA and his work can also be found in the permanent collections of the Victoria & Albert Museum, London, and the Cooper-Hewitt Museum, New York. 4. 7–13

Ramon Arbos is a Spanish industrial designer, born in 1938, whose work has won several awards and been exhibited in Barcelona. 1. 11

Danilo Aroldi, born 1925, **Corrado,** born 1936, and **Maurizio,** born 1954, are a design team working in Milan. They have exhibited work all over the world from Beirut to Cologne and in Ljubljana and Budapest in 1988. They were selected for the Compasso d'Oro in 1979 and a lamp, *Periscopio,* is in the design collection of the Museum of Modern Art in New York. 2. 41

Ennio Arosio, born in 1943, set up the design partnership Studio il Punto with Silvano Mariani, working initially with exhibits and renovations of furniture showrooms. He has acted as consultant for numerous furnishing firms and has worked on a wide range of projects, from residential interiors to the design of equipment for medical laboratories. 1. 71

Pietro Arosio is an Italian designer, born in Lissone in 1946. He gained a diploma from the Institute of Applied Art in Monza in 1966 and since 1972 has worked independently as an industrial designer for various companies. He won the Casaviva d'Oro in 1983 for his kitchen, *Agrodolce.* In 1982 his *Arco* desk, produced for Ciatti, was selected by the Victoria & Albert Museum, London. 1. 75, 76

Sigeaki Asahara is a native of Tokyo. From 1967 to 1971 he studied in Turin before starting as a freelance designer in Tokyo. Since 1979 he has divided his time between Japan and Italy, exhibiting at the Compasso d'Oro regularly as well as at exhibitions in Japan, West Germany and the USA. In 1989 he received the Japanese Good Design prize. 2. 27

Sergio Asti is an Italian architect who has lectured and exhibited extensively, and has sat on a number of award juries since he completed his studies at the Milan Polytechnic in 1953. In the mid-Sixties he studied glass techniques in Murano, Italy. His designs have won many awards and have been displayed in several Venice Biennale exhibitions as well as permanent museum collections. 3. 49

Rushton Aust gained a Master's degree from the Royal College of Art, London, in 1981. He has exhibited at various centres including the *Style '86* exhibition at Olympia in 1985, the Crafts and Folk Art Museum in Los Angeles and the Contemporary Applied Arts Christmas shows of 1987 and 1988 in London. Commissions include a one-off furnishing fabric for Habitat Ltd in 1980 and costume fabrics for the English National Opera also in 1980. 4. 29

Hiroshi Awatsuji, a textile designer, was born in Kyoto in 1929 and graduated from the Kyoto Municipal College of Fine Arts, establishing his own design studio in 1958. Since 1964 he has collaborated with the Fujie Textile Company. His principal commissions in Japan include textiles for the government pavilion at Expo 70, and tapestries for the Keio Plaza and Ginza Tokyu hotels. He exhibited at the Victoria & Albert Museum's *Japan Style* exhibition in 1980, and at the *Design since 1945* exhibition in Philadelphia. 3. 54–58; 4. 2, 6

Florin Baeriswyl is a Swiss designer who graduated from the Zurich School of Commercial and Industrial Arts. He has worked freelance on exhibitions with Edgard Reinhard in Zurich and on furniture design with Nick Roericht in Ulm, West Germany. In 1987 he set up Dai-Design with fellow student Christof Wüthrich. 1. 74

Adriano Baldanzi was born in Livorno in 1955 and graduated from the School of Industrial Design in Florence in 1979. Shortly after this he formed his own studio with Alessandro Novelli, working on a variety of projects for manufacturers such as Ciatti, Bieffe and Frezza. 1. 9

Michela Baldessari studied at the European Institute of Design in Milan and, between 1980 and 1982, worked on several designs for Isao Hosoe. Since 1983 she has been associated with the architecture and design studio of Baldessari & Baldessari in the fields of product, interior, environmental and visual design. 1. 113

Enrico Baleri studied in Milan and since then has been involved with a number of companies, including Pluri and Alias, where he held the position of art director until 1983. He then set up Baleri Italia, a firm which has commissioned work from, among others, Philippe Starck and Alessandro Mendini. 1. 73

Stephen Balser, having initially studied forestry, became an interior designer and formed the company Adirondak in 1980 with his wife, Shelby. They concentrated on wall plastering and restoration work, developing new techniques with tinted plaster and novel finish-coat mixtures. In 1983 the company was renamed Art In Construction and they now receive commissions from a wide range of industrial, corporate and private clients. 4. 25

Manuel Baño was born in Valencia in 1959. He obtained an arts degree from the University of Valencia and in 1984 founded the design studio Baño & Asociados. He currently lectures at the Valencia College of Arts and has received grants for his work from the Valencia Chamber of Commerce and the British Council. 1. 70

Carlo Bartoli was born in Milan in 1931, where he studied and began his professional career. He worked initially as an architect and subsequently on industrial and interior design, producing furniture and consumer goods for companies such as Antonangeli, Arflex and Kartell. Since 1988 he has been teaching advanced industrial design in Rome. 1. 28

Aldo Bartolomeo, born in 1933 in Formia, is an Italian furniture designer working particularly with metal and wood. His first major design was a chair, in 1956, made of tube and pierced sheet metal. In 1968 he designed the room-divider *Unigramma* with Giorgio De Ferrari, following this with a series of office cabinets, *Unigramma Ufficio,* in 1970. In 1986 he began *Alluminati,* a series of furniture pieces in metal or metal and wood combined. 1. 78

Roger Bateman, a British designer, was born in 1965. He graduated from the Ravensbourne College of Art and Design in 1987 and then took a Master's degree at the Royal College of Art. His work was exhibited at the Business Design Centre and Olympia, London, in 1987 and at the Designers' Saturday at the Sunar Hauseman showroom, London, in 1988. Since completing his course at the RCA in 1989, he has set up a design partnership with fellow-student Alison Crowther, designing and making individual, hand-made furniture and accessories. 1. 172

Anne Beetz was born in Brussels in 1939. She is self-taught, having worked for a Belgian weaving company, designing linen in the 1960s. Since 1972 she has been producing her own interior fabrics, as well as working with a number of manufacturers, including Knoll International. She received the Signe d'Or in Belgium in 1980. 4. 14, 16

Gretchen Bellinger, the American textile designer, was educated at the MacDuffie School in Massachusetts, Sophia University, Tokyo, Skidmore College, New York, and Cranbrook Academy of Art, Michigan. She worked for a number of textile manufacturers, including Skidmore, Owings and Merill, Knoll International, and V'Soske Incorporated, before setting up her own group in New York in 1976. 4. 28

Giandomenico Belotti was born in Bergamo in 1922 and studied in Milan and Venice. He practised as an architect and interior designer on several private and public projects. In 1979 he began an association with Alias designing furniture and in 1983 two of his designs, the *Spaghetti Chair* and the *Spaghetti Stool,* were included in the permanent collection of the Museum of Modern Art, New York. Recently he has developed an interest in urban projects and industrial design as well as extending his interests in the fields of architecture and restoration. 1. .126

Joaquín Berao, born in Madrid in 1945, has been exhibiting jewellery and sculpture since 1972. He opened his own studio in 1982 in Madrid which has expanded into a chain of shops in several major Spanish cities. In 1985 he won first prize in the FAD competition for his showroom in Barcelona. 2. 47; 5. 6

Guen Bertheau-Suzuki was born in Paris in 1956 and has a diploma from the Institute of Architecture in Tournai, Belgium, and a Master's degree from Tokyo University. An industrial and graphic designer, Bertheau-Suzuki has worked in architectural offices in Paris, Brussels and Tokyo, where he currently lives. 1. 6; 2. 6; 5. 3

Ramon Bigas was born in Barcelona where he studied technology. He followed a career as a designer for various firms and as a freelance, publishing several articles on design in many specialized magazines. With Pep Sant he formed the design group Associate Designers. 2. 50

Tord Björklund, a Swedish designer, was born in 1939 and studied at the Indendor Architectural Academy in Copenhagen. He received his practical training with the architect Gunnar Waldermark and, since then, has worked on projects in the USA and India. He has been employed as a designer by Ikea since 1980. 1. 27

Marilena Boccato studied architecture at Venice University, before setting up a design partnership with Gian Nicola Gigante and Antonio Zambusi in Padua and then Treviso. Their designs have won several prizes, including the Macef Prize in 1966 and the Palladio Prize in 1969. She and her associates practise both as architects and interior and industrial designers. 1. 125

Cini Boeri graduated from Milan Polytechnic in 1950, where she subsequently taught during the early 1980s. She began her independent professional career in 1963, after collaborating with Marco Zanuso for several years, applying herself to civil and interior architecture and industrial design. Her book *The*

Human Dimensions of the House was published in 1980. She has lectured at many universities and colleges in Europe and the Americas and her projects can be seen at various international exhibitions and permanent collections. 1. 111

Ricardo Bofill, born in Barcelona in 1939, studied at the School of Architecture in Geneva. In 1963 he set up his own design company, which was to become Taller de Arquitectura. He has worked on a number of important architectural projects, including Petite Cathedrale and Les Halles in Paris and several housing projects in France and Spain. Taller has now grown to incorporate a number of offices and associated architects throughout the world. Ricardo Bofill lives and works primarily in Paris. 1. 65

Oriol Bohigas, a Spanish designer, works with Lluis Pau, Josep Martorell and David Mackay. 1. 72

Jonas Bohlin, a Swedish designer living in Stockholm, was born in 1953 and graduated as an architect in 1981. He works mainly in the fields of interior architecture, stage and exhibition design and furniture. His work has been exhibited in the National Museum of Art, Stockholm, and the Rhosska Museum of Artcrafts, Gothenburg. He has also exhibited at the ASF Gallery and Queens Museum, New York. 1. 124

Enrico Bona graduated from the Milan School of Architecture in 1965. He has offices in Milan and Genoa and works as an architect, architectural restorer and industrial designer, as well as teaching at the University of Genoa. In the 1970s he was editor in chief of *Casabella* and has written articles and reviews in several major publications. 1. 26

Pep Bonet was born in Barcelona in 1941. He graduated from the School of Architecture there in 1965 and, together with Cristian Cirici, Oscar Tusquets Blanca and Lluís Clotet he founded the firm of Studio Per. Since 1972 they have been involved in the production of furniture and building components. He taught at the School of Architecture in Barcelona between 1975 and 1978, and in the Washington School of Architecture, St Louis, Missouri in 1981. 5. 9, 45

Karel Boonzaaijer was born in The Netherlands in 1948 and studied at the Academy of Modern Art in Utrecht. In 1979 he went into partnership with Pierre Mazairac and they now have their own studio specializing in product development and interior architecture. 2. 12

Bruno Borrione, born in 1961, is an interior architect and, between 1985 and 1988, he collaborated with Philippe Starck on various projects including furniture for the Ministry of Culture in Paris and the design of the Royalton Hotel, New York. He now works independently on architectural and design projects and has exhibited at the Designer's Saturday in Paris in 1987 and the Salon du Meuble in 1988 and 1989. He works in collaboration with Bruno Lefebvre. 1. 13, 25

Sara Bossaert was born in 1964 in Ghent, Belgium, where she studied at the Hoger Architectuur Institut, graduating in 1987. Since then she has worked with Cristian Cirici at Studio Per. 5. 10

Mario Botta was born in 1943 in Mendrisio, Switzerland. He attended the Academy of Fine Arts in Milan, then graduated in architecture from the University of Venice. He gained practical experience in Le Corbusier's studio, establishing his own architectural practice in Lugano in 1969. Since 1982 he has been designing furniture for Alias. Two of his chairs are in the

study collection of the Museum of Modern Art, New York. 1. 79; 5. 14

Constantin Boym was born in Moscow in 1955. He attended the Moscow Architectural Institute and in 1981 emigrated to the USA. In 1984-5 he attended the Domus Academy in Milan, returning to New York to set up Red Square Design the following year. He works primarily in furniture, products, interiors and graphics. 5. 15

Jacob Brahe-Pedersen, a Danish designer, was born in Washington DC in 1950. He gained a Master's degree from the Royal Academy of Arts, Copenhagen, in 1977. Since then he has worked on a wide range of projects from products and furniture to shop design. In 1987 he joined Dansk Ingenior System, a consulting firm of designers and engineers working in industrial design. 5. 42

Andrea Branzi, born and educated in Florence, is educational director of the Domus Academy. He has consistently been a representative of the radical tendency in Italian design and until 1974 was with Archizoom Associati, the first avant-garde Italian group. He was involved in the establishment of Studio Alchimia, the Milan-based group which has created pieces closer to art than to conventional design, and with Memphis, collaborating with Ettore Sottsass. His work was awarded the Compasso d'Oro in 1987. 1. 120, 153, 154

Boris Brochard was born in Yugoslavia in 1958. He formed the design group Brand in 1983 with Rudolf Weber, creating avant-garde furniture and functional art pieces for the interior. The group's work has been exhibited in Austria, where they are based, and in West Germany. 2. 30

Manlio Brusatin, born in 1943, lives in Asolo, Veneto. He graduated in architecture in Venice, studying under Carlo Scarpa, and then worked with him for several years. Later he collaborated with Aldo Rossi on research into town-architecture. He now teaches in the Department of the History of Art and Art Criticism at the University of Venice. 2. 13

Colin Burns was born in Scotland and joined the US design group ID Two in 1988. He studied in Edinburgh and the Royal College of Art, London, gaining the Design Travel Award from the Royal Society of Arts in 1984 and the Bugatti Award from the Royal College of Arts in 1987. His work has been mainly in the field of computer products and communications. 5. 25

Jordi Busquets was born in Barcelona in 1965 and studied at Milan Polytechnic. He has collaborated with the Milano-Los Angeles studio and with the Allied International Designers group in London. He now runs the marketing and design studio FLO in Barcelona. 2. 42

Luigi Caccia Dominioni, the Italian architect, is known internationally for his work and has influenced several generations of architects in Milan and the rest of Italy with his distinctive style. 5. 44

Gaspare Cairoli is an Italian designer who was born in Meda in 1952. After graduating, he worked for Cassina and B & B Italia. In 1983 he started his own studio with Elisabetta Donzelli, specializing in furniture design and advertising. His chair, *Terna,* was included in the CooperHewitt Museum collection in 1986. He has been selected for the Compasso d'Oro twice, in 1987 and 1989. 1. 91

Santiago Calatrava was born in 1951 in Valencia, Spain. He studied art and architecture in Valencia and Paris, and took an engineering course at the Zurich Federal Institute of Technology. After teaching there for three years, he opened his own office and since then has worked on industrial buildings, engineering structures and, more recently, furniture. 2. 16

Mauro Canfori is an Italian designer living in Vicenza. 1. 2

Canon Design Team is based in Tokyo, Japan. 5. 50

Alain Carré was born in France in 1945, and, after graduating from the Art School of Tours, went on to study design at the National School of Applied Art. In 1970 he founded his own studio while working for Pierre Cardin as Chief of Construction Design. He became director of the French Designers Industry Union (UFDI) in 1984. 3. 47

Ronald Carter studied interior design in Birmingham and furniture design at the Royal College of Art, London. He won an RCA silver medal and a scholarship to study in the USA, where he started his career, before setting up his own design consultancy in the UK. His work ranges from the mass-produced to private commissions. He has considerable experience as a teacher, an external examiner, and as a judge of both British and international competitions. 1. 58

Lola Castelló Colomer was born in Valencia, where she studied interior design at the School of Art. She began her professional career in 1971. She has exhibited at the Milan, Cologne, Paris and Valencia design fairs. Currently she designs for En Canya and Punt Mobles. 1. 18, 19

Achille Castiglioni was born in Milan in 1918. He began his work as a designer in partnership with his brothers, Livio and Pier Giacomo, specializing in interiors, furniture and lights. He is particularly well known for the latter. Castiglioni is one of the foremost talents in Italian design, and has been honoured seven times with the Compasso d'Oro, as well as having six of his pieces selected for exhibition at the Museum of Modern Art, New York. 1. 105, 107, 116; 2. 19; 5. 13

Giorgio Cazzaniga, born in Lissone in 1946, studied design and applied art at Milan Polytechnic, before working for several furniture companies. He became an associate of A & D where he met Luigi Massoni, collaborating with him on several design projects for Matteograssi. 1. 115

Jeannot Cerruti was born in Casablanca and now lives in Turin. He has been collaborating with Toni Cordero since 1973 on a number of interior design projects in Europe and the USA. He also works on the restoration and rehabilitation of old buildings, notably the restructuring of the former Banco Mediceo in Milan and the restoration of the Israelite Synagogue in Turin. 1. 86

Cristian Cirici was born in 1941 in Barcelona where he studied at the Higher Technical School of Architecture, graduating in 1965. Subsequently he worked for Correa & Mila and, in 1962, for the London firm James Cubitt & Partners. He was a founding member of Studio Per and also of Bd Ediciones de diseño in 1972. From 1980 to 1982 he was president of ADI/ FAD and has been awarded several prizes, including the National Restoration Prize in 1972. 5. 7

Antonio Citterio was born in Italy in 1950. He studied at Milan Polytechnic, and has been involved in industrial and furniture design since 1967. He opened a studio with Paolo Nava in 1973. Jointly and individually they have worked for B & B Italia, Flexform and others. In 1979 they were awarded the Compasso d'Oro. 1. 83, 133

Giovanni Colantonio, an Italian designer, is a founding member of Speradisole, a cultural meeting centre that promotes and organizes exhibitions, debates and publications on design and fine art themes. He works as an architect and designer in collaboration with Stefano Contini, Andrea Mazzoli, Vanda Orlando and Giancarlo Stella. 1. 8

John Coleman was born in London in 1953 and studied furniture design at Kingston Polytechnic and the Royal College of Art. In 1981 he established his own company, specializing in limited editions retailed through outlets such as The Conran Shop and one-off commissioned pieces. 1. 82

Giulio Confalonieri was born in Milan in 1932. He is a member of various organizations and teaches image coordination at Milan Polytechnic. He has won several awards, including gold medals at the 11th and 15th Milan Triennali in 1957 and 1973. His work is in the permanent collections of the Museum of Modern Art, New York, and the Museum of Modern Art, Paris. 5. 64

Gigi Conti is an Italian designer working with Roberto Marcatti. 2. 21

Stefano Contini, an Italian designer, is a member of Speradisole and works in collaboration with Giovanni Colantonio. 1. 8

Stephan Copeland was born in Montreal in 1960 and now lives and works in California. He spent six years as a merchant seaman before commencing a career as an industrial designer. He has produced lamps for the US manufacturer Atelier International and for Arteluce. 2. 36, 37

Corporate Industrial Design (CID) is the design team for the multi-national electronics organization Philips. Headed by R. Blaich, the managing director, CID consists of 115 designers based in Philips' Eindhoven headquarters in The Netherlands, as well as an additional 110 designers worldwide. 3. 41

Riccardo Dalisi was born in Potenza, Italy, in 1931. Since 1962 he has been conducting experiments in architectural form using light and geometry, and taking part in various competitions connected with building construction at an academic level. He has written a number of books and teaches at the University of Naples. He is credited with revitalizing research into design in southern Italy and has been described by Alessandro Mendini as "the brains behind design in the South". 1. 49, 156

Robin Day was born in High Wycombe, England, and studied at the Royal College of Art, graduating in 1939. His work has included interior and exhibition design as well as graphics and products, and he was responsible for the seating installations of the Royal Festival Hall and the Barbican Arts Centre in London. He has won awards from the Milan Triennale, the Design Centre and Royal Designers for Industry. In 1983 he received the Order of the British Empire (OBE). 1. 57

Tom Deacon graduated in architecture from the University of Toronto in 1982, winning the RAIC medal. In 1984 he established the design group AREA to produce designs for seating and tables. His work has been published and exhibited in Canada and the USA and was included in *Time* magazine's "Best of '87" design review. He is currently developing furniture projects for several American companies. 1. 33

Michele De Lucchi was born in Ferrara, Italy, in 1951. He studied first in Padua and then at Florence University, graduating in 1975 and subsequently teaching there. In 1978 he began a close collaboration with Ettore Sottsass. He worked and designed with Alchimia until the establishment of Memphis in 1981, for whom he created some of their best-known products. In 1979 he became a consultant for Olivetti in Ivrea; under the supervision of Sottsass he designed their Icarus office furniture. Currently he is designing for a wide range of furniture manufacturers. 1. 98; 5. 57, 58

Jonathan De Pas was born in Milan where he studied and where he still works. In 1966 he set up the studio De Pas, D'Urbino and Lomazzi with Donato D'Urbino and Paolo Lomazzi. There work is on show in the design collections of the major museums of New York, London, Paris, Zurich, Munich and Jerusalem. They have won many awards, including the Compasso d'Oro in 1979, and they have taken part in many exhibitions, notably *Italy: The New Domestic Landscape* at the Museum of Modern Art, New York. 1. 10; 2. 31, 32

Jane Dillon was born in the UK in 1943. She trained in interior design in Manchester, and then in furniture design at the Royal College of Art, London. After graduating in 1968, she worked for Knoll International and for Olivetti under Ettore Sottsass. She has been a design consultant for many major companies and currently works with Floris van den Broecke and Peter Wheeler in London. 1. 101

Nanna Ditzel, a Danish designer, has created several advanced designs for factories in Denmark and other European countries, and a range of jewellery for Georg Jensen/Royal Copenhagen. Her versatility also extends to the design of furnishing fabrics and tableware. In 1956 she and her husband, Jorgen, were awarded the Lunning Prize and in 1960 they were presented with a Gold Medal at the Milan Triennale. Her designs are now represented in several museums. 1. 1

Douglas Doolittle was born in Canada in 1952. He graduated in graphic design from Sheridan College of Arts, Mississauga, Ontario. After working for a design firm in Toronto, he travelled to Europe and then Japan where he joined G.K. Industrial Design Associates as a graphic designer. In 1979 he established his own office in Tokyo, concentrating on corporate identity projects, while retaining clients in Canada, The Netherlands, Hong Kong and Taiwan. 3. 52

Sylvain Dubuisson, a French designer, began his career in the architectural practice of Ove Arup in London in 1973. After 1980 he worked independently on a wide range of projects. His work has been included in various exhibitions, notably *Art et Industrie* at the Musée National des Monuments Français in 1986 and an exhibition at the Musée des Arts Décoratifs, Paris in 1989. He was named Designer of the Year for 1990 at the Salon International du Meuble, Paris. 3. 12

Donato D'Urbino is an Italian designer working with the studio De Pas, D'Urbino and Lomazzi. 1. 10; 2. 31, 32

Charles Eames, the American designer and architect, was born in St Louis, Missouri, in 1907. He studied architecture at Washington University from 1924 to 1926, before setting up his own practice in 1930. In 1941 he married Ray Kaiser and collaborated with her on a number of design projects, experimenting with new techniques and materials. Their work brought numerous awards, including the President's Medal of Honour from the Art Directors' Club, New York, in 1965 and the Architectural Award Grand Prix from the American Institute of Architects, Los Angeles, in 1967, as well as several honorary doctorates. Charles Eames was noted as a director of documentary films on a variety of subjects, including his own work. He died in 1979. 1. 135

Erwin Ebenberger was born in Millstatt-am-See in Austria in 1957. He is a self-taught designer and his work has been seen in many exhibitions in Austria, notably *Living Style – a study in wood* at Millstatt in 1980, the *Unique Items* exhibition in Vienna in 1987 and the Vienna Furniture Fair in 1989. He founded his own studio, Ebenberger GmbH, in 1986. 1. 89

Siegfried Ebner was born in Graz, Austria, in 1954 and attended the Arts and Crafts School there before going on to study in Linz. In 1979 he joined Porsche Design. 5. 2

Fumio Enomoto, born in Tokyo in 1957, graduated from Tokyo University of Art and Design in 1979. Between 1980 and 1986 he worked for the Kuramata Design Office, before setting up his own studio, Fumio Enomoto Atelier. In 1988 his work was exhibited in a one-man show for Axis, Tokyo. 1. 3; 5. 65

Hans Es comes from West Germany, where he studied classics before serving as an officer in the Bundeswehr for four years. He then joined the glass and porcelain manufacturer, Rosenthal, rising steadily through the firm to become manager of the Rosenthal Studien Haus in Amsterdam at the age of 26. After four years he left to set up his own company, remaining in The Netherlands and concentrating on industrial and interior design. 2. 28

Thomas Exner was born in Salzburg, Austria, in 1963 and studied at the Vienna Academy of Applied Art. He has worked with a number of design studios, including Ellmecker & Reuter and Boris Podrecca, as well as Ebenberger. He has won several awards for his work, including a competition to refurbish the Operngasse branch of the chain-store Palmers of Vienna in 1988, a commission he shared with fellow-designer Stefan Zinell. His work was also shown at the Vienna Furniture Fair in 1989. 1. 121

David Ferrer is a Spanish designer working in Barcelona. 2. 11

Marco Ferreri, an Italian, was born in 1958. He graduated in architecture from Milan Polytechnic and worked as an architect for Manfiaroti, Zanuso & Munari until 1984, when he established his own office. He has worked since then for Milan City Council, Olivetti, IBM, Fontana Arte and others. 2. 2

Uwe Fischer lives in Frankfurt and is part of the design team Ginbande with Klaus-Achim Heine. 1. 132

Carlo Forcolini was born in Como, Italy, in 1947 and studied at the Brera Academy, Milan. In the 1970s he worked with various designers, including Vico Magistretti, before moving to London in 1978. In 1979 he helped found the design group Alias. His work has been included in the permanent collections of the Musée des Arts Décoratifs, Paris, and the Cooper-Hewitt Museum, New York. He now lives and works in Milan. 1. 66

Marianne Forrest graduated from the Royal College of Art, London, in 1983 and set up her own studio. She works as a designer-silversmith specializing in clocks and watches. She has won several prizes and has exhibited in various locations, including the International Contemporary Furniture Fair in New York in 1989 and *Dazzle* at the Royal Festival Hall, London, in 1990. 3. 45

Josep Fort was born in Manlleu, Barcelona, in 1958. He studied at the Higher Technical School of Architecture in Barcelona, graduating in 1986. He works with the Garces & Soria professional practice and at Studio Per and was director of the Department of Projects at the Town Hall of Vilanova i la Geltru between 1988 and 1989. He has recently set up a studio with fellow-designer Pau Batlle. 5. 10

Sam Francis, Abstract Expressionist painter, was born in San Mateo, California, in 1923. He studied medicine in the early 1940s and painting and art history under Mark Rothko from 1948 to 1950. Important exhibitions include those at Los Angeles County Museum of Art; Whitney Museum of American Art, New York; Louisiana Museum, Copenhagen/Humblebaek and the Musée National d'Art Moderne, Paris. 4. 41

Simon Fraser was born in Hamilton, New Zealand, in 1951 and studied at the School of Fine Arts in the University of Auckland. In 1979 he joined Porsche Design, working on a range of their products. 3. 42; 5. 16, 18

Jorge Armando Garcia Garay was born in Buenos Aires, Argentina, and has been working in Barcelona since 1979 where he heads Garcia Garay Design. He now works almost exclusively on lighting. In 1989 his ceiling lamp, *Fenix,* and floor lamp, *Enterprise,* were chosen for exhibition in the London Design Museum. 2. 23

Ignazio Gardella was born in Milan, Italy, in 1905. He graduated from the Milan Polytechnic in 1931. From 1949 to 1975 he taught at the Institute of Architecture in Venice and in 1955 won the Olivetti National Award for Architecture. 1. 50

Gian Nicola Gigante is an Italian designer working in collaboration with Marilena Boccato. 1. 125

Milton Glaser, the graphic designer and illustrator, was born in 1929 in New York, where he now lives. He studied at the Cooper Union Art School and later in Italy. He has worked on numerous book illustrations and magazine designs, including *New York Magazine* and *Paris Match.* He was responsible for the graphical concept of the recently renovated Rainbow Room in New York's Rockefeller Center and has also designed an international symbol for the fight against Aids. 4. 39, 42, 43, 57, 58

Michael Graves, the Princeton architect famed for his Post-Modern classicism, was born in 1934. His work, which has received numerous awards, includes the Newark Museum, the Whitney Museum, a library in San Juan Capistrano, the Humana Headquarters in Louisville and a winery in California's Napa Valley. His paintings and murals are in several major museums and he has designed furniture for Memphis and Sawaya & Moroni, and products for Alessi and Swid Powell. 1. 7; 3. 53

Zaha Hadid was born in Baghdad, Iraq, in 1950. She graduated from the Architectural Association,

London, in 1977 and in the same year joined the Office of Metropolitan Architecture. In 1982 she was awarded a gold medal in the *Architectural Digest* British architecture awards and in 1983 won first prize in the Peak International Competition, Hong Kong. Her work is published worldwide and is frequently exhibited. She lives in London. 4. 47–49

Carlos Hahn was born in Buenos Aires in 1961. He studied art in Hamburg and then set up his own design studio, Satō. Since 1988 he has been involved in lighting and furniture design. 2. 14, 15

Gorm Harkær was born in Odense, Denmark, in 1951 where he studied at the Academy of Fine Art, graduating in 1970. He then studied furniture design at The School of Arts, Crafts and Design and the Royal Danish Academy of Fine Art in Copenhagen. He has had his own studio since 1979 and has been a member of the Danish Furniture Group since 1983. He has also been working on a biography of the Danish architect Kaare Klint with the help of a scholarship from the Royal Danish Academy of Fine Arts. 1. 138

Klaus-Achim Heine, born in 1955 in Bischofsheim, West Germany, now lives and works in Frankfurt. He is part of the design team Ginbande with Uwe Fischer. 1. 132

Matthew Hilton, born in the UK in 1957, studied furniture design at Kingston Polytechnic and then worked with the product design consultancy CAPA for five years on a variety of high-technology products. He became an independent furniture and interior designer in 1984, producing lights as well as furniture. In 1986 he designed a range of furniture for Sheridan Coakley which was shown in Milan. He now has his own company, designing and manufacturing furniture and cast metal objects. 3. 36, 38, 39

David Hockney, painter, was born in Bradford, England, in 1937 and now lives in California. He studied at Bradford College from 1953 to 1957 and then at the Royal College of Art, London, graduating in 1962. He is an exponent of the English variation of Pop Art, his work being divided into painting, stage design and photography. In 1988 a large retrospective exhibition was held in the Los Angeles County Museum of Art, the Metropolitan Museum of Art, New York and the Tate Gallery, London. 4. 45, 56

Geoff Hollington studied industrial design at the Central School, London, and environmental design at the Royal College of Art, graduating in 1974. He established Hollington Associates in 1980 to work on industrial design projects for a number of major manufacturers around the world. 5. 28

Gunter Horntrich, an industrial designer, worked on the basic research for the Bosch car security system. In 1973 he set up his own group, Team-Industrieform, designing a wide range of items from typewriters and offices to dentistry. Since 1985 he has been working with Yellow Design, while lecturing in Schwabisch-Gmund and Offenbach. 5. 56

Isao Hosoe was born in Tokyo in 1942. His initial interests lay in science, and he took a Master's degree in aerospace engineering at the Nihon University of Tokyo. From 1967 to 1974 he collaborated with the architect Alberto Rosselli, becoming a member of the Italian Association of Industrial Designers, the Japan Design Committee and the Italian Society of Ergonomics. In 1985 he founded his own design company. He has won many awards for designs covering a wide variety of projects and his work has been shown in many exhibitions in Japan, Europe and America. Following a period as visiting professor to the Domus Academy in Milan from 1984 to 1987, he now teaches there full time. 1. 99, 100; 5. 48

Max Huber was born in Baar, Switzerland, in 1919 and studied at the Zurich Kunstgewerbeschule under Willimann. In 1940 he moved to Milan and worked in the Boggeri Studio, attending evening classes at the Brera Academy. He returned to Switzerland in 1942 and became a member of Allianz, the association of modern Swiss artists. He currently teaches graphic design at the CSIA in Lugano. He has received several awards, including a gold medal at the Eighth Milan Triennale and the Compasso d'Oro in 1954. 5. 13

Idée Original is the design team working for the Japanese manufacturer Idée. 1. 38

Takenobu Igarashi was born in Hokkaido, Japan, in 1944 and graduated from Tama Art University in 1968, where he is currently professor. He took a Master's degree at the University of California at Los Angeles in 1969 and then set up his own design studio working on corporate identity projects, exhibition posters and product design. His work is in the permanent collection of the Museum of Modern Art in New York. As well as his post at the Tama Art University, he is a visiting professor at the University of California at Los Angeles and has lectured at the Smithsonian Institution, Stanford University and Aspen Design Conference. 3. 32–35; 5. 49

Massimo Iosa Ghini is an Italian designer working on furniture, textiles, fashion and advertising. Born in 1959 in Borgo Tossignano, he studied in Florence and graduated in architecture from Milan Poytechnic. In 1981 he joined the group Zak-Ark, and from 1984 has collaborated with the firm AGO. Since 1982 he has worked on a number of discotheques, video projects and magazines. In 1986 he took part in the Memphis group's 12 New Collection. 1. 96, 97; 3. 13, 46

Arata Isozaki was born in Kyushu in 1931 and obtained his diploma at the University of Tokyo. He founded his own studio in 1963 and continued to collaborate with other architects and studios. Among his most famous projects are the Gunma Prefectural Museum of Modern Art at Takasaki (1971-2), the Kitakyshu City Museum of Art (1972-4), the Shukosha Building at Fukoka (1975), the new City Hall, Tokyo, and the Museum of Contemporary Art in Los Angeles (both 1986). 4. 52

Dakota Jackson was, in his early twenties, a professional magician. His sense of mystery and illusion was invested in early pieces of one-off furniture, expressed in moving parts and hidden compartments. He works in his own studio in New York and is the recipient of a National Endowment for the Arts Design Fellowship. He has lectured at universities and industry events. 1. 32

Elizabeth Browning Jackson, the American artist and designer, was born in 1948 and educated at San Francisco Art Academy, the University of New Mexico and Capella Gardin, Sweden. Her work has been shown at the Gallery of Applied Arts, San Francisco; Art et Industrie, New York; Arqitectonica, Miami; Grace Designs, Dallas, and Axis, Tokyo. 4. 64, 67

Ehlén Johanssen was born in Sweden in 1958 and studied at Gothenburg University between 1979 and 1984. Since 1985 she has been working for Ikea, designing furniture and interior products. 1. 12

Carsten Jørgensen was born in 1948 in Denmark. He graduated from the School of Arts and Crafts, Copenhagen, in 1973 and has been art director of the Bodum design workshop since 1978, working as an industrial designer on a range of household goods. 3. 31

Angel Jové is a Spanish painter and art teacher. He has been an actor, art director and scenic designer for the theatre, as well as a designer of textiles and lights. 4. 22

Kazuo Kawasaki was born in Fukui City, Japan, in 1949. After graduating from Kanazawa University of Arts, he joined Toshiba and worked on the development of hi-fi audio products. Subsequently he has worked independently as an industrial designer, moving his studio back to Fukui in 1980. He has won several awards for his work including Design Forum Silver Prize and the Small and Medium Enterprise Agency Prize. He currently teaches part time at Kanazawa and Fukui Universities. 1. 56; 5. 29, 30

Miles Keller was born in Canada in 1959 and graduated from the Ontario College of Art in 1988. He works as an industrial designer with the design group 20/20 in Toronto and also in partnership with Helen Kerr in Kerr.Keller Design. His work has won awards from Virtu (Canadian Residential Furniture Company) in 1987 and 1988 and was chosen for ID Magazine's annual design selection in 1988. 5. 40

Rodney Kinsman was born in London in 1943 where he studied furniture design at the Central School of Art. In 1966 he founded OMK Design to produce and promote his own work and the company now has licensing and marketing links worldwide. He is also chief design consultant of Kinsman Associates, specializing in design work commissioned internationally from independent companies. In 1983 he received a Fellowship from the Society of Industrial Artists and Designers (now the Chartered Society of Designers). 1. 59

Toshiyuki Kita was born in 1942 in Osaka, Japan, and graduated in industrial design in 1964. Since 1969 he has divided his time between Osaka and Milan where he has worked on furniture and accessories for many major manufacturers. He has received the Japan Interior Design Award, the Kitaro Kunii Industrial Design Award and the Mainichi Design Award. The *Wink* armchair and *Kick* table which he designed for Cassina are in the permanent collection of the Museum of Modern Art, New York. 1. 4, 5; 5. 62

Komplot Design is based in Copenhagen, Denmark, and comprises the Soviet-born designer Boris Berlin and two Danes, Lars Mathiesen and Poul Christiansen. The last two trained as architects at the Royal Academy of Fine Arts in Copenhagen, while Berlin, an industrial and graphic designer, graduated from the Institute of Applied Arts and Design in Leningrad, his home town. They set up Komplot Design in 1987 to work on industrial design projects for a number of clients, including Copenhagen Airport and Thonet, USA. 5. 20

Joseph Kosuth, the American artist, was born in Toledo, Ohio. His work represents the analytical

stream-of-conscience movement in art, using the printed word and textual quotations and consolidating these ideas with numerous writings. He is represented in many of the world's galleries and museums. Recent exhibitions include Leo Castelli, New York, in 1988 and the Museo di Capodimonte, Naples, in 1989. 1. 161

Minako Kubota was born in Tokyo in 1959 and graduated from Tama Art University in 1981. Since then he has been working in the product development department of the Sasaki Glass Co. In 1989 he received the prize for excellence at the Japan Craft Exhibition. 3. 17

Shiro Kuramata was born in Tokyo in 1934. He started an independent practice as a furniture designer in 1965, having served an apprenticeship in cabinetmaking. Apart from his celebrated glass armchair of 1976, and a number of other equally elegant but quirky pieces of furniture, Kuramata has designed interiors for the fashion designer Issey Miyake and for Siebu stores. In 1981 he received the Japan Cultural Design Prize. 1. 52, 53

Masayuki Kurokawa was born in Nagoya, Japan, in 1937. He graduated in architecture from the Nagoya Institute of Technology in 1961 and completed his training at the Graduate School of Architecture, Waseda University, in 1967. That same year he established Masayuki Kurokawa Architects and Associates. He has been accorded numerous prizes for his work, including six IF prizes for his designs of tables and lighting fixtures. 1. 127

Danny Lane was born in 1955 in the USA. He moved to Britain in 1975 to work with the stained-glass artist Patrick Reyntiens, and then studied painting at the Central School of Art, London, until 1980. The following year he set up his first studio in London's East End. Then in 1983 he established Glassworks, using glass in unfamiliar and challenging ways in one-off pieces, furniture and interiors. In 1986 his studio was equipped to handle large-scale architectural installations. 1. 170, 171

Wolfgang Laubersheimer, born in 1955 in Bad Kreuznach, West Germany, studied metal sculpture at the Academy of Art and Design, Cologne. In 1982 he co-founded the company Unikate and then in 1985 set up the design group and gallery Pentagon. He has exhibited work at various shows and museums, including the Biennale at São Paolo, Brazil, the Gallery Nolte, New York, and *Art '88* in Basel, Switzerland. In 1989 he exhibited architectural projects on the German stand at the World Design Exhibition in Nagoya, Japan. 1. 16

Roberto Lazzeroni is an Italian designer, born in Pisa where he lives and works. He studied art and architecture in Florence and is now involved in a number of industrial and interior design projects. 1. 84, 85

Jack Lenor Larsen, the American textile designer, was born in 1927. He trained at the University of Washington, Seattle, and at the Cranbrook Academy of Art, Michigan, graduating in 1951. In the following year he opened a studio in New York. Larsen Carpet and Larsen Leather were established in 1973 and Larsen Furniture in 1976. He has received numerous honours and awards including a gold medal at the 1964 Milan Triennale and a nomination as Royal Designer for Industry in the UK in 1982. 4. 63

Jennifer Lee was born in 1956 in Aberdeenshire, Scotland. She studied at the Edinburgh College of Art and at the Royal College of Art, London. In 1979-80 she was awarded an Andrew Grant Travelling Scholarship to the USA. Her hand-built pots have been exhibited in the UK, USA and throughout Europe and are in the collections of the Victoria & Albert Museum, London; the Royal Scottish Museum, Edinburgh, and the Los Angeles County Museum of Art. 3. 18, 19

Bruno Lefebvre, a French designer, was born in 1963. From 1985 to 1986 he collaborated with Philippe Starck and is now an industrial designer for a number of companies, including Allibert Habitat, Acova and Odo. He works closely with the designer Bruno Borrione on a number of architectural projects primarily in France; their work has been exhibited in France, Italy and the USA. 1. 13, 25

Robert Le Héros is a design studio set up in Paris in 1986 by four French designers — Christelle Le Déan, Blandine Lelong, Isabelle Rodier and Corinne Helein — all of whom studied at the Ecole Nationale Supérieure des Arts Décoratifs in the early 1980s. The studio designs textiles for several manufacturers and stores, chiefly Nobilis Fontan. 4. 24

Christian Leprette was born in Berlin in 1953 and studied architecture at the Ecole Nationale Supérieure des Beaux-Arts, Paris, and Harvard University, USA. He has been involved in several architectural projects, including designs for bank agencies and private residences in Paris. Since 1988 he has been teaching architecture at the University of Geneva. 1. 39

Max Leser, a Canadian designer, was born in London. He studied ceramics at the Banff School of Fine Arts, Alberta, and glass-working at Georgian College, Barrie, Ontario, the Sheridan School of Design, Missassauga, Ontario, the Alberta College of Art and the Pilchuck Glass Center, Stanwood, Washington. His work has been exhibited worldwide and is in permanent collections in Canada and the USA. He currently lives in Toronto, where he is the president of Leser Design Inc. which specializes in the design and manufacture of modern glass products. 5. 47

Sol Le Witt was born in Hartford, USA, in 1928 and studied in Syracuse, New York, from 1945 to 1949. He worked as a teacher in New York while building up a corpus of artworks. These have been exhibited in several museums, notably the Whitney Biennial in the Whitney Museum, New York; the Institute of Contemporary Art, Boston; the Museum of Modern Art, New York; the Kunsthalle, Berne, and the Kestner-Gesellschaft, Hanover. 4. 59

Roy Lichtenstein, Pop Art painter, was born in New York in 1923. He will go down in the history of art as the man who brought Mickey Mouse and Donald Duck into galleries throughout the world. Between 1957 and 1963 he was lecturer at New York State University and Rutgers University. His work has been exhibited in the most important galleries in Europe, Japan and America. 4. 53

Alberto Liévore was born in Buenos Aires in 1948, where he studied architecture. He moved to Spain in 1977 and joined the Berenguer design group along with Jorge Pensi and others. Consequently he was involved in the creation of SIDI, the general forum for Spanish design. Since 1985 he has been director of Alberto Liévore and Associates, working on design and communications for private institutions and manufacturers such as Perobell, Indartu and Kron. 1. 20–22

Stefan Lindfors was born in Mariehamn, Finland, in 1962 and studied interior and furniture design at the University of Industrial Arts, Helsinki, from 1982 to 1988. His work has received many awards in Finland and Europe, including the silver medal at the 1986 Milan Triennale. Among recent projects are the studio and furniture for the Finnish Broadcasting Companys television evening news programme in 1988 and the interior and furniture for the café of the Museum of Industrial Arts in Helsinki in 1989. His design interests also extend to the stage. 1. 41

Josep Lluscá was born in Barcelona in 1948. He studied design at the Escola Eina, Barcelona, where he is now professor, and the Ecole des Arts et Métiers, Montreal. He was vice-president of ADI-FAD (Industrial Designers Association) from 1985 to 1987, and a member of the Design Council of the Catalonian government. He has won several awards and has taken part in international conferences and exhibitions. 1. 62–64; 2. 45–47; 5. 46

Paolo Lomazzi is an Italian designer working in Milan. He is part of the studio De Pas, D'Urbino and Lomazzi. 1. 10; 2. 31, 32

John Lonczak is a graduate of Syracuse University, New York, and began his career at Pulos Design Associates and Cousins Design. In 1985 he established his own company working on cosmetics, household goods, electronic and personal care products. He has received recognition from several major museums, including the Museum of Modern Art, New York, as well as a number of design publications. 5. 37, 38

Ross Lovegrove was born in Wales in 1959 and studied at Manchester Polytechnic and the Royal College of Art, London, from which he graduated in 1983. He worked for several design consultancies, including Allied International Designers and the West German group Frog Design. In 1984 he was a member of the Atelier de Nîmes with Jean Nouvel and Philippe Starck and in 1986 he co-formed Lovegrove & Brown in London. This was dissolved in 1990 when he set up his own studio, Lovegrove Design. 5. 53

David Mackay was born in Eastbourne, England, in 1933. He works in Barcelona with, Lluis Pau, Josep Martorell and Oriol Bohigas. 1. 72

Vico Magistretti was born in Milan in 1920. He took a degree in achitecture in 1945 and subsequently joined his fathers studio. Until 1960 he was mainly concerned with architecture, town planning and interiors. He began designing furniture and household articles for his buildings in the 1960s and collaborates closely with a number of manufacturers who produce his designs. He has participated in nearly all the Milan Triennali since 1948 and has won numerous awards. Fifteen pieces are in the collection of the Museum of Modern Art in New York. 1. 128–131

John Makepeace was born in the UK in 1939 and studied at Denstone College, Staffordshire. He began his professional training in a small workshop and his career has since been punctuated by study and worldwide consultancy projects. In 1976 he moved to Parnham in Dorset, setting up the Parnham Trust and School for Craftsmen in wood, which he directs. His work has been exhibited at the Victoria & Albert Museum, London; the Frankfurt Museum, and at Kortrijk, Belgium, among others. 1. 140

Angelo Mangiarotti was born in 1921 in Milan and educated there, graduating from the Polytechnic in 1948. He has worked as a designer in America and in Italy, as well as teaching at the Illinois Institute of Technologys design school. He has specialized in small sculptural objects, often intended for the table top, including a stainless steel clock for Portescap and other pieces for Knoll and Munari. 1. 139

Roberto Marcatti was born in 1960 in Milan and graduated in architecture at the Polytechnic. Since 1985 he has been a member of the Zeus group and collaborated for five years with Maurizio Peregalli at Studio Noto on a number of design projects. He teaches technology at the International College of Art in Milan and has recently opened his own studio. 2. 21

Enzo Mari is an Italian designer, born in 1932. He studied at the Brera Academy of Fine Art in Milan and taught design methods at Milan Polytechnic. In 1972 he participated in *Italy: the New Domestic Landscape* at the Museum of Modern Art, New York. Since the 1950s he has worked on the design of glass for Danese as well as on furniture for Driade and Gabbianelli. He has twice been awarded the Compasso d'Oro: in 1967 for his research, and in 1979 for his Delfina chair manufactured by Driade. 1. 90; 3. 11, 14, 37, 43

Silvano Mariani, an Italian designer born in 1943, works in collaboration with Ennio Arosio in the Studio il Punto. 1. 71

Javier Mariscal, a Spanish designer, was born in 1950. He trained as an artist and graphic designer and collaborated on the Memphis collection of 1981. He has designed lights with Pepe Cortes for the Barcelona firm Bd Ediciones de diseño, textiles for Marieta and carpets for Nani Marquina. 4. 23, 33

Nani Marquina was born in Barcelona in 1952. She studied design at the Escola Massana. She designs interiors and textiles and, with Pep Feliu, started her own company, based in Barcelona. Among the designers whose work she produces are Javier Mariscal, Patti Nuñez and Carlos Riart. 4. 60

Jesse Marsh was born in Washington DC in 1953. She graduated from Williams College, Williamstown, Massachusetts, in 1975 and the following year moved to Milan, where she now lives and works. Until 1982 she collaborated with Marco Zanuso on industrial design projects and then with the architecural firm Trabucco e Vecchi. In 1983 she set up her own studio. She is a member of the Association for Industrial Design. 1. 17

Vicent Martinez-Sancho is a Spanish designer, born in Valencia in 1949. He studied at the Escuela de Artes Aplicadas in Valencia and the Escola Massana in Barcelona. Having started a career as a graphic designer, he set up his own studio in 1972 specializing in industrial and furniture design. In 1980 he established the firm Punt Mobles. He has received several design awards and his work has been shown at many international events. 1. 106

Josep Martorell was born in Barcelona in 1925. He works as a designer with Lluis Pau, Oriol Bohigas and David Mackay. 1. 72

Josep Massana is a Spanish industrial designer born in 1947. Together with Josep Tremoleda he has worked on a number of projects, primarily for their own studio, Mobles 114, which was set up in 1981. 1. 61

Luigi Massoni, born in Milan in 1930, has worked as an architect, a journalist, a publicist and an editor. In 1959 he founded the studio Il Mobile Italiano with Carlo De Carli as a centre for the promotion of Italian design. He designed the *Esquire* collection and the bed *Menelao,* with Giorgio Cazzaniga, for Matteograssi. 1. 115

Matsushita Design is part of the Matsushita Seiko Co., Japan. 5. 54

Ingo Maurer was born in West Germany in 1932. After training as a typographer and graphic artist, he emigrated to America in 1960. He moved back to Europe in 1963 and started his own lighting design firm in 1966. He now designs furniture and his work has been collected by the Museum of Modern Art, New York, and Neue Sammlung, Munich. 2.48, 49

Pierre Mazairac was born in The Netherlands in 1943 and studied at the Academy of Modern Art in Utrecht. He worked as a designer for Pastoe, a furniture manufacturer, before setting up his own studio with Karel Boonzaaijer. 2. 12

Sergio Mazza was born in Milan in 1931, and has worked as an independent architect since 1955. In 1959 he helped set up Artemide, working as the company's art director until 1971, and until 1988 was director of the magazine *Ottagono*. He has collaborated on six Milan Triennali and was awarded the Compasso d'Oro in 1979. 2. 18

Alberto Meda was born in Como, Italy, in 1945 and studied at the Milan Polytechnic. In 1973 he assumed the technical direction of Kartell before setting up as a freelance designer in 1979. Since then he has worked for Fontana Arte, Alias, Luceplan, Mandarina Duck, Alfa Romeo and the communications company Italtel Telematica, and has lectured at the Domus Academy in Milan. 1. 15; 2. 34, 35

Luca Meda, born in 1936 in Chiavari, Italy, attended the Hochschule für Gestaltung in Ulm, West Germany. In 1961 he started a professional relationship with Aldo Rossi, working on a number of architectural projects in Italy as well as corporate image design, exhibitions and interior design. 1. 50, 146

Richard Meier was born in the USA in 1934. He founded Richard Meier and Partners Architects in New York in 1963. He has taught at the Cooper Union School of Art and Architecture, New York, and at Yale and Harvard universities. Recent works include the High Museum in Atlanta, the Museum for the Decorative Arts in Frankfurt, the J. Paul Getty Center in Los Angeles and a new city hall for The Hague in The Netherlands. He also designs ceramics and silverware for Swid Powell. 4. 44

Alessandro Mendini was born in Milan in 1931. He was a partner of Nizzoli Associates until 1970, and a founder-member of Global Tools. He then edited *Casabella* and *Mondo* and, until 1985, *Domus*. He has collaborated with a number of companies, has written widely and received the Compasso d'Oro in 1979. 1. 155

Serge Meppiel, born in 1957 in Mulhouse, France, attended the Ecole d'Architecture de Strasbourg until 1982. He followed a career as an architect and designer, producing several lighting designs for Lumen Center, Noto and Quattrifolio. Since 1985 he has been the architecture and design assistant at the Ecole d'Architecture de Strasbourg. He now designs and produces limited series. 2. 10

Makiko Minagawa graduated from Kyoto University, Japan, having specialized in dyeing. She has been working for Issey Miyake's design studio since then. 4. 3, 5

Minale, Tattersfield and Partners is a multi-disciplinary international organization based in London. It was founded in 1964 by the Italian designer Marcello Minale and his British counterpart Brian Tattersfield, both of whom still play a day-to-day role in the consultancy. 1. 60

Jordi Miralbell, born in 1953 in Barcelona, studied design at the Escuela Elisava in that city. He works in collaboration with Mariona Raventós on a wide range of projects including industrial design, interior decoration and advertising. 1. 68

Pedro Miralles is a Spanish architect, born in Valencia in 1955. He has participated in many exhibitions in Madrid and Valencia and in 1987 won the IMPIVA scholarship from the Domus Academy in Milan. He has worked for many major companies, including Punt Mobles, Arflex, Bd Ediciones de diseño, Santa & Cole, Akaba, Artespana and DeSedie. 5. 8

Mondo Design Team is part of Mondo Srl, an Italian company set up in 1987 by Giulio Cappellini, Paola Navone and Rodolfo Dordoni. 1. 93–95; 3. 21

Loyd Moore, an American designer, studied fine art at the University of Washington where he now runs design workshops. In 1982 he established the consultancy Technology Design which has offices in several US cities and works on various projects concerned with electronics and automation. Loyd Moore has served as a juror for the Industrial Designers Society of America and *ID Magazine,* from whom he has won numerous awards. 5. 24

Jasper Morrison is a British furniture designer, educated in New York, Frankfurt and England. He graduated from the Royal College of Art, London, in 1985 and since then has designed and made limited-batch production pieces. In 1986 he started in private practice and took part in Zeus's exhibition in Milan. He has also produced a number of projects for Sheridan Coakley, London; Idée, Japan, and Cappellini, Italy. His prototypes have been donated to the Vitra Museum in Weil am Rhein, Germany. 1. 134, 167–169

Pascal Mourgue began working as an interior designer at the end of the 1960s. Since 1982 he has been concentrating on furniture and carpet designs, tableware and even trimarans. He was named French Designer of the Year in 1984, and in 1986 won the Grand Prix de la Critique du Meuble Contemporain. He lives in Paris. 4. 34, 35

Karen Mückel was born in Hamburg in 1959 where she studied at the Muthesius School before graduating in furniture design at the Kunstakademie, Stuttgart, in 1985. She now works as a designer for the Berlin-based group Berliner Zimmer. 1. 147

Bruno Munari was born in Milan in 1907 and was active as a second-wave Futurist painter around 1930. After 1945 he was an Abstract painter and in 1948 a founder of the Movimento Arte Concreta. He has published much avant-garde theorizing on communication and design as well as being active as a designer. His cube ashtray for Danese was much admired, as were many lights and toys. He has won the Compasso d'Oro and has been honoured by the Academy of Science in New York and the Japan Design Foundation. 1. 158

Johann Munz is a Swiss designer working with the manufacturer Wogg in Baden, Switzerland. 1. 145

Eckart Muthesius was born in Berlin in 1904, the son of Hermann Muthesius, architect and founder of the Deutsche Werkbund, and could claim the Scottish painter Frank Newbery and the architect Charles Rennie Mackintosh for godfathers. He studied in Berlin-Charlottenburg and later in London where he gained his first practical experience as an architect, returning to Germany as apprentice in his father's office. He then set up his own offices in Berlin, receiving commissions from such notables as Carl August Von Gablenz, founder of Lufthansa, and the Maharajah of Indore. He died in 1989. 1. 103

Hilton MacConnico was born in Memphis, Tennessee, but has been living in Paris for 25 years. He worked as a fashion designer and was responsible for the decor in Jean-Jacques Beinex's films *Diva* and *La Lune dans le Caniveau.* He became a textile designer in 1985. 4. 36

Cordula Nies-Friedländer graduated in industrial design from the Royal College of Art, London, having trained initially at the Academy of Fine Arts, Stuttgart. In 1987 she joined the British firm Foster Associates as a furniture and industrial designer. She is also a member of the Uno Design Team and lectures at the Central School of Art and Design, London. 5. 33

Anne Nilsson, the Swedish designer, was born in 1953 and was educated at Dickenson College, Pennsylvania, The National College of Art and Design, Stockholm, and the California College of Arts and Crafts. Since 1980 she has worked for Hoganas Keramik and AB Orrefors and was distinguished in the "Excellent Swedish Design" competitions of 1985 and 1986. Her work is represented in the National Museum, Stockholm, and the Rohss Museum of Arts and Crafts, Gothenburg. 3. 15

Jean Nouvel, one of France's best-known contemporary architects, was born in 1945. His most celebrated project is the Institut du Monde Arab in Paris for which he won the Equerre d'Argent in 1987. In the same year the Salon International du Meuble nominated him Designer of the Year for his furniture. As well as architecture and furniture, Jean Nouvel has had a lifelong interest in theatre and set design. 1. 112; 4. 46

Alessandro Novelli was born in Florence in 1955 where he studied at the School of Industrial Design. With Adriano Baldanzi he formed the design studio Baldanzi & Novelli, producing designs for a number of major companies. 1. 9

Pati Núñez is a Spanish textile designer working for Nani Marquina. 4. 65

134 is a Danish design consultancy set up in 1989 by three graduates from the Royal Danish Academy of Fine Arts in Copenhagen: Bjorli Lundin, Flemming Steen Jensen and Erling Christoffersen. 1. 55

Mimmo Paladino was born in 1948 in Paduli, Italy, and is one of the foremost exponents of the Italian Transaavant-guardia school. His work is multi-disciplinary, combining painting with sculpture, drawing and monumental work. Exhibitions include the Kunsthalle, Basel; the Stedelijk Museum in Amsterdam; the Royal Academy's *Twentieth-Century Italian Art* in London in 1989, and the Lenbachhaus, Munich. 1. 159, 165; 4. 42, 50, 51

Paolo Pallucco is an Italian furniture designer, architect and manufacturer born in Rome in 1950. He established Pallucco Italia in 1980, producing new designs and re-editions of modern classics and putting his own creations into production. In 1984 he started Pallucco Design to work on projects independently of his other company. He works in conjunction with Mireille Rivier. 1. 142–144

David Palterer is an architect born in Haifa, Israel, in 1949. He graduated from the University of Florence in 1979 where he then taught and lectured. He has also taught at Syracuse University, Werk Bund at Stuttgart and the Bezalel Academy for Art and Crafts, Jerusalem. He has produced designs for many international companies, including Artemide, Swid Powell, Factotem Vistosi and Zanotta. Many of his designs have been exhibited worldwide and his work is in the permanent collections of the Vienna Kunstgeverbe Museum, the Prague Museum and the Israel Museum in Jerusalem. 3. 1,2

Lluis Pau, born in Girona, Spain, in 1950, is the leading architect of the studio IDP, comprising Josep Martorell, Oriol Bohigas and David Mackay. They have been responsible for a number of architectural projects in Spain and their work has been exhibited in Venice, Madrid, London and Barcelona. 1. 72

Jorge Pensi is a Spanish architect and industrial designer, born in 1946 in Buenos Aires, Argentina. In 1977 he formed Grupo Berenguer, Design, Form and Communication with Alberto Liévore, Norberto Chaves and Oriol Pibernat. Since 1979 he has been associated with Perobell, the SIDI group and the magazine *On Diseño*. His products have been shown in exhibitions in Barcelona, Valencia and Cataluna and he has been featured in many Spanish and international publications. 1. 102; 2. 51–53; 5. 60

Maurizio Peregalli, an Italian designer, was born in 1951 in Varese. He studied in Milan and, after graduating, started work on designing shops for Giorgio Armani. In 1984, along with five other designers, he established Zeus in Milan, a gallery showing avant-garde furniture, textiles, ceramics and glass. He is also a member of Noto, an interior design and manufacturing comapany. 2. 8

Nestor Perkal was born in Argentina and trained as an architect. He manages a gallery in Paris where he presents a selection of new design products. He is also involved in the interior design of apartments and offices as well as furniture and lighting design. 3. 27

Gaetano Pesce, artist and designer, was born in 1939 and trained as an architect at Venice University. He is constantly researching into the new materials made possible by technological advances. His works include the doughnut-like polyurethane foam *Up 1* armchair of 1969, and a cave-like commune for twelve people shown in 1972. His projects have been exhibited worldwide and many are in permanent collections. He has lectured extensively and in 1987 was a visiting professor at the School of Architecture in São Paolo, Brazil. 1. 92

Poul Petersen is a designer living and working in Copenhagen, Denmark. 1. 40

Renzo Piano was born in Genoa and now divides his time between that city and Paris. He graduated from the Milan Polytechnic in 1964 and then worked for his father and under Franco Albini in Italy and Lewis L. Kahn in Philadelphia, USA. In 1984 he was awarded the Commandeur des Arts et des Lettres and in 1985 the Legion d'Honneur for his work on the Centre

Georges Pompidou in Paris with architect Richard Rogers. He has taught at Columbia University, the University of Pennsylvania, Oslo School of Architecture and Central London Polytechnic. He was awarded the Compasso d'Oro in 1981 for his design work. 1. 123

Pirate Design Associates was set up in London in the early 1980s to work on projects related to industrial design. The four principal designers involved in the group are Michael Ganss, Matthew Archer, Martin Godward and Mark Walters, all of whom have considerable experience in industrial and design research. 5. 23, 32, 43

Michelangelo Pistoletto was born in 1933 in Turin, Italy, where he lives and works. His work as a painter is well-known and he has been long concerned with bringing art to the people, often quite literally, with experiments in "public" art and street theatre, particularly with the group Zoo established in 1967. His work was recently represented by a major retrospective at the Museum of Modern Art, New York, and an exhibition at the Staatlich Kunsthalle, Baden-Baden, West Germany. 1. 163

Christian Ploderer is an Austrian designer, born in 1956, who studied industrial design at the Hochschule für Angewandte Kunst, Vienna. From 1979 to 1985 he had his own design studio, Ploderer & Rollig, and since 1986 has been an independent designer and design consultant for lighting, furniture and interior decoration. In 1987 he received a National Award for Design. 2. 7

Plus Corporation is a design team based in Japan. 5. 63

Ferdinand Alexander Porsche was born in 1935 in Stuttgart, Germany, where he worked as an apprentice in the design office Bosch. In 1957 he attended the School of Design in Ulm and the following year joined the design consultancy Porsche AG, taking over as director in 1962. He has been responsible for the development of the Formula 1 racing car and the sports car models 904 and 911. In 1972 he founded Porsche Design in Stuttgart, moving the studio to Zell-am-See in 1975. 2. 40; 3. 42; 5. 2, 16, 18

Kuno Prey was born in 1958 in San Candido, Bolzano, Italy. He gained a diploma from the Istituto Statale d'Arte in Cortina Ampezzo and from 1983 to 1984 he attended the Domus Academy, Milan. Since 1980 he has been working as an independent designer for a number of companies specializing in product design, and has been awarded the Compasso d'Oro twice. In 1989 the *Penny Pack* was selected for *Form 89* in Frankfurt while his watches *Tino* and *Milo* were chosen for the permanent collection of the Museum für Angewandte Kunst, Munich. 5. 35

Product First was formed in 1987 by Graham Thomson, David Scothron and John Boult to combine design, engineering and marketing disciplines. It is based in Chiswick, London. 5. 19

Ritva Puotila, the Finnish textile designer, studied at the University of Industrial Art, Helsinki, before opening her own studio in 1960. She produces textiles for manufacturers on a mass-produced basis as well as limited edition art pieces. Since 1988 she has also been working in glass, particularly for Hadeland Glassverk, Norway. In 1960 she won a gold medal at the Milan Triennale and her work was recognized by the Finnish government in 1981 as well as by the Paritex 88 exhibition in Paris. 4. 61

Andrée Putman was born in Paris. She studied piano at the Paris Conservatoire under François Poulenc. After several years as a journalist she began

working as an industrial designer and was co-founder of Createurs et Industriels in the 1970s, bringing together designers such as Issey Miyake and Castelbajac to produce objects as well as fashion. In 1978 she founded Ecart International, specializing in re-editions, and began her own career as an interior designer. 4. 15, 17, 37, 38; 5. 4

Eric Raffy was born in 1951 in Bordeaux and trained as an architect, working for a number of agencies and practices. In 1984 he was contracted to advise on a number of interior design projects in Saudi Arabia such as furniture for the Saudi National Guard and a wide range of schools, libraries, mosques, clinics and commercial centres. Since then he has produced designs for manufacturers, chain stores and restaurants in France. He is also a lecturer at the Ecole d'Architecture de Bordeaux Talence. 1. 122

José Luis Ramon-Solans Prat, a Spanish architect, was born in 1951 in Zaragosa and graduated in 1977 in Madrid. His architectural projects include a private house in Madrid and a factory in the Philippines. He also designs furniture for many of his projects. He has exhibited in Valencia and Madrid. 4. 30, 31

Bruna Rapisarda was born in Milan in 1960. She studied design at the European Institute and then worked freelance as a designer and as a journalist for *Interni* from 1980. In 1986 she formed a partnership with Arturo Silva working on projects in the fields of industrial design, furniture, lighting and graphics. She was selected for the Compasso d'Oro in 1989. 5. 1

Prospero Rasulo is one half of the design partnership Oxido which was set up with Gianni Veneziano to create and show in their own gallery art pieces for the domestic environment. They have developed several collections and have also been involved in interior design and exhibition promotions, and are public image consultants for a number of companies. 1. 51

Red Square Design, established by the Soviet-born designers Constantin Boym and Lev Zeitlin in New York in 1986, is a multi-disciplinary design studio which provides professional services in the design of furniture, products, interiors and graphics as well as theatre design. The studio's work has been shown in several exhibitions in the USA, including Gallery 91, New York, and *Art in Exile* at the Nexus Gallery, Philadelphia. 2. 3–5

Carlos Riart was born in Barcelona in 1944 and studied design and industrial technology there. Since 1963 he has been involved in several interior decoration and design projects as well as designs for the cinema. He has also been awarded medals for his work by ADI-FAD, IBD and the Contemporary Resources Council, New York. 4. 66

Gerhard Richter, the painter, was born in Dresden, Germany, in 1932 and studied at the Dresden Art Academy between 1951 and 1956. He also graduated from the Düsseldorf Art Academy in 1963 and subsequently became Professor of free-style painting there. His work alternates between figurative and abstract painting. He has exhibited at the Centre Georges Pompidou in Paris; the Whitechapel Gallery, London; the Kunsthalle, Düsseldorf, and museums in Frankfurt and Krefeld. 4. 40

José Ripoll, born in Madrid in 1960, studied architecture at Barcelona and Madrid universities. He has been a set designer for the TV-3 Catalan channel

and for the theatre; he currently works in Madrid as an architect. 2. 9

Umberto Riva was born in Milan in 1928 and graduated in architecture from Venice University in 1959. From the 1960s onwards his projects have been published in the major specialized reviews and he has been involved in several important exhibitions. He lives and works in Milan. 1. 108, 119; 2. 1

Mireille Rivier was born in 1959 in Lyon, France. She graduated in architecture at the Polytechnic of Lausanne before moving to Rome where she works with Paolo Pallucco. 1. 142–144

Aldo Rossi was born in Milan in 1931. In 1956 he began his career working with Ignazio Gardella and later with Marco Zanuso. From 1955 to 1964 he was editor-in-chief of *Casabella-Continuità*. Since 1975 he has held the chair of Architectural Composition at Venice University. He has also taught at the Federal Polytechnic of Zurich and has collaborated with the principal American universities since 1976. In 1983 he was named director of the architecture sector of the Venice Biennale. He has designed many award-winning buildings. 1. 42, 43, 50

Michael Rowe was born in 1948 in High Wycombe, England. He graduated from the Royal College of Art, London, in 1972 and set up his own metal-working studio the same year. He became head of the Department of Metalwork and Jewellery at the RCA in 1984. Rowe's work is in the British Crafts Council; the municipal galleries of Birmingham and Leeds; the Victoria & Albert Museum, London; the Karlsruhe Museum, West Germany, and the Art Gallery of Western Australia. 3. 28–30

Mike Ryan was born in Long Beach, California, in 1961. He studied architecture in San Luis Obispo, spending his final year in Florence. In 1985 he joined Sottsass Associati in Milan, becoming a partner in 1989. 3. 44

Lino Sabattini is an Italian silversmith, born in 1925. His metalwork first attracted international attention in 1956 when it was exhibited in Paris at a show organized by the architect Giò Ponti. Since then Sabattini has continued to be closely associated with a simple, sculptural approach to metal and glassware, working for companies such as Rosenthal and Zani. He exhibits at the Milan Triennale and other major venues. In 1979 he was awarded the Compasso d'Oro. His work is in the permanent collections of the Museum of Modern Art and the Cooper-Hewitt Museum, New York, as well as the British Museum, London. 3. 22–25

Pete Sans is a Spanish designer, born in Barcelona in 1947. During 1962 and 1963 he worked in the studio of the architect José Pratmarso while he was studying for his baccalaureate. In 1971 he opened a studio in graphic design, directed the Galeria and the Escuela Nikon, and published the magazine *Papel Especial*. With the impetus of design awards in Spain and abroad, he turned to full-time industrial design. 2. 44

Pep Sant was born in Barcelona and studied physics at the University of Madrid. He works in Barcelona with Ramon Bigas. 2. 50

Santa & Cole Design Team is based in Barcelona, Spain. 1. 69

Denis Santachiara was born in Reggio-Emilia, Italy, but now lives and works in Milan. Since 1974 he has

been working as a designer, participating in several important international exhibitions such as the Milan Triennale and the Venice Biennale. He has organized shows at the Centre Georges Pompidou, Paris, The Museum of Modern Art, Tokyo, and at the Berlage Museum, Amsterdam. 1. 54

Richard Sapper was born in Munich in 1932. After studying at the University there, he joined Daimler-Benz's styling department in 1956. Two years later he moved to Italy, working initially with Giò Ponti and then in the design department of La Rinascente before joining Marco Zanuso. After establishing his own studio, Sapper designed the classic modern adjustable light, the *Tizio*, and the *Tantalo* clock, both produced by Artemide. In addition to furniture for Castelli, Molteni and Knoll, Sapper has designed tableware for Alessi. His numerous awards and distinctions include the Compasso d'Oro and the German Die Gute Industrieform prize. 1. 77

Toshimitsu Sasaki was born in Hita City, Oita Prefecture, Japan, in 1949 and graduated from the department of Telecommunications Engineering, Shibaura Institute of Technology, in 1973. In 1978 and 1980 he set up his own atelier and office, working on furniture and lighting designs for a number of Japanese manufacturers. 1. 67

Afra and Tobia Scarpa are an Italian husband-and-wife team who have worked together for more than 25 years. Tobia, born in 1935 in Venice, spent some time working in the glass industry before their collaboration. Afra, born in Montebelluna in 1937, graduated from the Architectural Institute, Venice. In 1958 they began working in glass with Venini at Murano. They occasionally work as architects as well as designers. Examples of their work can be seen in major museums all over the world and many have been chosen for international exhibitions. 1. 30

Carlo Scarpa, the Italian architect, was born in Venice in 1906, where he gained a diploma from the Academy of Fine Arts. Subsequently he was elected professor and director of the Faculty of Architecture of the University of Venice. His principal works include the restoration of the Castelvecchio Museum, Venice, the Olivetti shop, Venice, and the Carlo Felice Theatre, Genoa. He died in Kyoto, Japan, in 1978. 1. 104

Christian Schwamkrug was born in Düsseldorf, West Germany, in 1957 and graduated in Industrial Design at Wuppertal. In 1987 he joined Porsche Design. 2. 40

Barbara Seidenath was born in Munich, West Germany, in 1960. She studied at the Staatliche Fachschule für Glas und Schmuck Neugablonz and the Akademie der biedenden Kunste, Munich, from which she graduated in 1989. 3. 50

Peter Shire was born in Los Angeles, California, in 1947. He has a degree in ceramics from Chouinard Institute of Art. In 1972 he opened his own studio and held his first solo show in a Hollywood gallery in 1975. His sculptural furniture designs attracted the attention of Ettore Sottsass and he consequently produced furniture designs for the Memphis group until its demise in 1989. 3. 26

Takenao Shishikura, a Japanese designer, was born in 1963. He is a recent graduate of the Faculty of Engineering, Chiba University, and has been working for the Asahi Pentax Optical Co. on a number of their binocular designs. 5. 34

Dieter Sieger was born in Munster, Germany, in 1938 and graduated from the Arts and Crafts School in

Dortmund in 1964. He set up his own architectural office in the following year, designing a number of family houses in Greece, Spain, France, the USA and Saudi Arabia. Between 1976 and 1982 he was also involved in the design of yacht interiors. He now lives and works in the Schloss Harkotten in Sassenberg, Westphalia. 4. 26

Arturo Silva was born in Mexico City in 1954 where he studied industrial design. He worked in the USA and Mexico before moving to Italy to study at the European Institute of Design in Milan. In 1986 he set up a studio with Bruna Rapisarda. 2. 39

Danilo Silvestrin is a German designer working for the Draenert Studio in Munich. 1. 24

Bořek Šípek was born in Prague in 1949. He studied furniture design in Prague, architecture in Hamburg and philosophy at Stuttgart University. His works are included in the collections of the Museum of Modern Art, New York; the Museum of Decorative Arts, Prague, and museums in Düsseldorf and The Hague. He has a studio in Amsterdam, designing for Sawaya & Moroni, Driade, Vitra and Cleto Munari as well as for the Dutch company, Alterego. In 1990 he accepted the position of professor at the Academy of Decorative Arts in Prague. 3. 1–9

Site is a firm founded in New York in 1970 to develop architectural and design projects for a number of companies in the USA and abroad. Their work has been exhibited in fifty museums and galleries worldwide. 1. 46; 3. 10

Finn Sködt was born in 1944 in Aarhus, Denmark, and studied at the Jutland Academy of Art and the Graphic College of Denmark in Copenhagen. He has worked in Italy and the USA as well as his native country. His collaboration with the Danish textile company Kvadrat began in 1977. 4. 20, 21

Susana Solano was born in Barcelona in 1946, where she lives and works. She is a sculptor working primarily in iron, lead and galvanized metal. Pieces by her have been shown in several of the major museums of Europe. She exhibited on the Spanish stand at the 1988 Venice Biennale and in the same year won the prize of Spanish Sculptor '88. 1. 160

Sony Design Team is based in Tokyo. 5. 22, 52

Ettore Sottsass was born in Innsbruck, Austria, in 1917. He graduated as an architect from Turin Polytechnic in 1939, and opened an office in Milan in 1946. Since 1958 he has been a design consultant for Olivetti but is also active in fields as various as ceramics, jewellery, decorations, lithographs and drawing. He has taught and exhibited widely. In 1980 he established Sottsass Associati with other architects, and has designed many pieces of furniture that were part of the Memphis collection. 1. 48, 157; 2. 20; 4. 27

Vic Stannard, born in Kingston-upon-Thames, England, in 1960, is a graduate in classics from the University of London. Between 1985 and 1988 he studied at Camberwell School of Arts and Crafts, London. His work includes pieces of sculpture and sculptural design. 3. 20

Philippe Starck was born in Paris in 1949 and works as a product, furniture and interior designer. In Paris he was commissioned by President Mitterand to give a new look to part of the Elysée Palace and designed the Café Costes, together with a number of fashion shops. In New York he remodelled the interior of the Royalton Hotel, and in Tokyo he has designed two restaurants and is currently working on a number of other buildings. His furniture design includes projects for Disform, Driade, Baleri and Idée. Among his industrial design projects are cutlery for Sasaki, clocks for Spirale and mineral water bottles for Vittel. 1. 36, 37, 149–152

Christian Steiner was born in Eisenstadt, Austria, in 1961. He studied at the Viennese Academy of Applied Arts. He has participated in various exhibitions, including the 1989 Furniture Fair in Vienna. He has collaborated with Thomas Exner on several projects. 1. 121

Giancarlo Stella is a member of Speradisole; *see* Giovanni Colantonio. 1. 8

Marianne Stokholm is a Danish architect, born in 1946 in Copenhagen. She studied at the School of Architecture, Aarhus, graduating in 1974. In 1983 she formed a design consultancy with Gad Zorea to work primarily in the field of industrial and product design. 5. 27

Carouschka Streijffert was born in Stockholm in 1955 and educated at the National College of Art, Craft and Design there. She works as a textile designer producing one-off and limited batch pieces for manufacturers worldwide. She has exhibited in Sweden regularly since 1978. 4. 32

Franz Alban Stützer is a German product designer working in the Rowenta design studio. 5. 39

Taru Syrjänen, a Finnish glass designer, was born in 1953 and studied at the University of Tampere and the University of Helsinki as well as the West Surrey College of Art and Design in England. He has produced designs for several of the major Finnish glass manufacturers and has exhibited in Finland, Frankfurt, Moscow and at the Hermitage in Leningrad. 3. 16

Mario Talli Nencioni, an Italian textile designer, studied at the Textile School of Bergamo, Italy, and at the Bocconi University, Milan. He has been Art Director of his own manufacturing company Telene SpA for twenty years. 4. 4

Gerard Taylor was born in Glasgow, Scotland, in 1955. He studied design at Glasgow School of Art and then the Royal College of Art, London, from which he graduated in 1981. After working for BBC TV in London he moved to Milan, joining Sottsass Associati in 1982. As well as working on furniture and retail design projects, he also exhibited with the Memphis design group both in Europe and the USA. In 1985 he established a design partnership in London with Daniel Weil. 1. 47

Gabriel Teixido, a Spanish designer, was born in 1947 and studied at the School of Applied Arts in Barcelona, graduating in 1969. He has worked as a furniture and lighting designer, collaborating with a number of Spanish companies in this field. He was awarded two SIDI prizes, in 1986 and 1987, as well as the Nuevo Estilo prize in 1987 for his sofa *Calando*. 1. 114; 2. 33

Benjamin Thut, a young Swiss designer, served an apprenticeship with Reishauer in Zurich before taking a diploma at the Kunstgewerbeschule, from which he graduated in 1989. He has worked for a number of design consultancies, mostly in the areas of interior and industrial design. He has also worked as an exhibition designer on motor shows for manufacturers such as BMW. 2. 26

Shozo Toyohisa was born in Fukuoko Prefecture, Japan, in 1960. He graduated from the Toyohashi

University of Technology in 1984 and in the same year established the Deco Design section at the Koyo Sangyo Co., Ltd. He spent some years working in the USA where he won "The most creative use of design" prize from *Accent on Design,* New York, for his *Deco Tools* in 1985. In 1987 he founded Nobile Produzione in Tokyo to promote arts and crafts. 3. 48

Jaime Tresserra Clapés was born in Barcelona in 1943. He began studying law but switched to the arts, where he pursued an interest in jewellery making. For fifteen years he worked in interior design and architecture and then moved into furniture design. He won the 1986 Casa Viva award for best design at the Mogar fair in Madrid and then established his own company. He has recently designed packaging for the Olympic Games to be held in Barcelona in 1992 and is currently working on designs for furniture, lamps and carpets. 1. 80, 81

Oscar Tusquets Blanca was born in Barcelona in 1941. He attended the Escuela Tecnica Superior de Arquitectura, Barcelona, and in 1964 established Studio PER with Lluis Clotet, collaborating on nearly all their projects until 1984. He has been a guest professor and lecturer at universities in Germany, France and the USA, and his work has been exhibited worldwide. Both his architecture and his design projects have received many awards. 1. 118, 137, 141; 2. 29; 4. 19; 5. 5

Shigeru Uchida was born in Yokohama, Japan, in 1943 and graduated from Kuwasawa Design School in 1966. In 1981 he established Studio 80 with his wife Ikuyo Mitsuhashi and fellow-designer Toru Nishioka. In the same year he received the Japan Interior Designers Association Award and in 1987 the Mainichi Design Award. He has lectured at Columbia University, the University of Washington and Tokyo University of Art and Design. Studio 80 has been a principal participant in the interior decoration of the hotel Il Palazzo in Fukuoka, Japan, for which this clock was designed. 5. 12

Masahiko Uchiyama, a Japanese designer, was born in 1956. He worked in the design laboratory of Hitachi, and then studied at Chiba University, Japan, from 1980 to 1984. Subsequently he joined GK Industrial Design and in 1987 established his own studio, Step Design. 5. 11

Masanori Umeda was born in Kawagawa, Japan, in 1941 and graduated from the Kuwasawa Design School in Tokyo in 1962. Between 1967 and 1979 he worked in Italy for the Castiglioni studio and, later, for Olivetti. In 1979 he set up Umeda Design Studio in Tokyo, renaming it U-MetaDesign Inc. in 1986. Among the awards he has won are the Braun Prize in 1968, the design prize of the Japan Commercial Designers Association in 1984 and the If '87 in West Germany in 1987. 3. 51

Oswald Mathias Ungers was born in 1926 in Kaisersesch/Eifel in Germany. He studied under Egon Eiermann in Karlsruhe and has worked as a freelance architect since 1950. He taught at the Technical University, Berlin, and later at Cornell University, Ithaca, before returning to West Germany in 1970. Among his pricipal works are the German Architectural Museum in Frankfurt, the Galleria and Gatehouse at the Frankfurt Trade Fair in 1985 and the IBA apartment complex in Berlin in 1989. 1. 44, 45; 4. 54, 55

Floris Van Den Broecke was born in Harlingen, The Netherlands, in 1945. He studied fine art in Arnhem and furniture design at the Royal College of Art, London. In 1969 he established a design studio and now works in collaboration with Jane Dillon and Peter Wheeler. He has been Professor of Furniture Design at the Royal College of Art since 1985. 1. 101

Jan Van Lierde was born in Beveren, Belgium in 1954. He studied architecture at the Academy of Ghent, graduating in 1978, and set up his first studio in Beveren working mainly on architectural projects in the Middle East and Europe. In 1982 he established Kreon which has since become primarily a lighting manufacturer. In 1984 he moved the company to Antwerp where he now lives. 2. 38

Francesco Venezia was born in Lauro, Italy, in 1944. He trained as an architect and is now Professor of Architectonic Design at Genoa University. His work ranges from town planning to the design of museums. 1. 117

Bill Verplank, an American industrial designer, has worked for a variety of electronics companies developing both computer hardware and software. From 1971 to 1975 he was Assistant Professor at Stanford University, where he also gained his Bachelor's degree, and has given seminars on interaction design for a number of manufacturers and societies. He has also been involved in projects for NASA and has carried out graduate research at the Massachusetts Institute of Technology. In 1986 he joined the American product design consultancy ID Two. 5. 25

Lella and Massimo Vignelli are a husband-and-wife team. They studied in Venice and in 1960 established the Vignelli Office of Design and Architecture in Milan, working with graphics, products, furniture and interiors. In 1965 they founded Unimark International Corporation and, in 1971, Vignelli Associates, with an office in New York and liaison offices in Paris and Milan. They have received awards and honorary doctorates for their work. 1. 29, 31; 2. 24

Mario Villa was born in Nicaragua and now lives in New Orleans, USA. He has a degree in architecture from Tulane University and in 1981 formed Graphic Editions, retailing as well as publishing fine art editions. He designed his first collection of furniture in 1984. He is now head designer and president of Mario Villa Inc. and consultant for a number of other projects. In 1987 he launched a furniture collection at the Gallery of Applied Arts, New York. 2. 43

Vinaccia Design is an Italian design team consisting of two brothers, Giulio and Valerio Vinaccia. They work primarily in the field of product design and have offices in Milan and Rome. 5. 61

Vitrac Design was founded by Jean Pierre Vitrac in 1974 and is based in Paris. The studio works on a wide range of product designs for a number of international manufacturers. 5. 59

Heinz Waibl was born in Verona in 1931 and received a diploma from the Liceo Artistico in Milan. He worked as an assistant to Max Huber between 1950 and 1954 and with the design group Unimark until

1971. Since then he has been Professor of Visual Design at Milan Polytechnic. Waibl is a member of the Alliance Graphique Internationale and the Associazione Disegno Industriale. 5. 55

Morten V. Warren, a British designer, studied general art and design at Barnet College and later at Kingston Polytechnic. Since graduating in 1988 he has worked for B & W Loudspeakers on the aesthetic styling of their products. 5. 21

Water Studio was established in 1973 to work on new product concepts based on fashion trends. They are involved in a wide range of projects from cars to corporate identity packages and even food products. Their clients are among the largest product manufacturers in the world, including Seiko, Nissan and Olympus Optical. 5. 51

Rudolf Weber was born in Austria in 1955. He founded the design group Brand with Boris Brochard in 1983. 2. 30

Daniel Weil was born in Buenos Aires in 1953 where he studied architecture at the university. In 1977 he went to study at the Royal College of Art, London, and then started his own manufacturing company, Parenthesis, to produce electronic products. From 1983 to 1985 he was a unit master at the Architectural Association in London and then set up a design partnership with Gerard Taylor to work on a variety of projects for companies such as Driade, French Connection, Alessi and Anthologie Quartett. 1. 47

Lawrence Weiner, the artist, was born in 1940 in New York. He deals with a variety of media including the written word and film. His most recent exhibitions were at the Stedelijk Museum, Amsterdam, and Le Magazin in Grenoble, France, both in 1988. 1. 164

John Werner graduated from the London College of Furniture in 1986. He then worked for Sheridan Coakley (SCP) while still designing and producing limited batches of furniture by himself. His work has been marketed by Portfolio Furniture (Martin Ryan) and, since 1988, Viaduct where he is now also employed as general manager. 1. 23

Franz West was born in 1947 in Vienna where he attended the Academy of Fine Art, exhibiting in his first solo show in 1970. He works primarily as a sculptor, experimenting with ideas of mass and space as well as colour. 1. 162, 166

Peter Wheeler was born in Bruck-an-dem-Mur, Austria, in 1947. He studied industrial design at the Central School of Art and Design in London, and furniture design at the Royal College of Art. He has received a number of awards in Britain and America, notably two gold medals from IBD in 1983. Since 1986 he has been collaborating with Jane Dillon and Floris Van Den Broecke on numerous furniture projects for Spanish and Italian companies. 1. 101

Wogg Design is based in Baden, Switzerland. 1. 145

Jack Woolley, a British designer, was educated at the University of Edinburgh and the Royal College of Art, London. Since 1987 he has worked as a senior designer at Isis (UK) Ltd, while also acting as a freelance on a number of other projects for Toucan, Lagoon, Little Acorn, and King's College Hospital, all in London. 2. 22

Christof Wüthrich comes from Bern, Switzerland, and studied at the Zurich School of Commercial and Industrial Arts, where he met Florin Baeriswyl. With the latter he set up the design group Dai-Design in 1987. 1. 74

Komin Yamada is a Japanese product designer working in Tokyo. 5. 41

Yamaha Corporation Design is based in Hamamatsu, Japan. 5. 17

Helen Yardley, a British textile designer, studied at Plymouth and Manchester polytechnics and received an MA in textile design from the Royal College of Art, London, in 1978. Her work has been exhibited throughout the UK and in Germany and Czechoslovakia and her first solo exhibition was held in 1989 at the New York Furniture Fair. 4. 62

Shoei Yoh was born in Kumamoto, Japan, in 1940. He studied economics at Keio University and then fine and applied arts at Wittenberg, West Germany, until 1963. In 1970 he established Yoh Design, producing furniture and lighting, and working in interior design and architecture. He has won a number of awards including the Japan Architectural Institute Award for 1989. 5. 66

Antonio Zambusi studied at Venice University before setting up a design partnership with Marilena Boccato and Gian Nicola Gigante. 1. 125

Marco Zanini was born in Trento, Italy, in 1954. He graduated from Florence University and, after some years working in the USA, settled in Milan in 1977. He collaborated with Ettore Sottsass and eventually became managing director of Sottsass Associati. In 1980 he was involved in the creation of Memphis for which he designed a number of pieces until 1989. 2. 17

Ziba Design was established in Oregon, USA, in 1982 by the Iranian-born Sohrab Vossoughi and now employs a number of designers, including Christopher Alviar, Paul Furner, David Knaub and Henry Chin. Their work ranges from furniture to computers, from fitness equipment to household appliances, and from consumer electronics to office systems. 5. 26, 31, 36

Gad Zorea was born in 1953 in Israel and studied at the Academy of Fine Arts, Tel Aviv, graduating in 1979. He now lives and works in Aarhus, Denmark, collaborating with Marianne Stokholm in a design partnership. 5. 27

SUPPLIERS

Fullest possible details are given of suppliers of the designs featured here; the activities of some outlets and manufacturers, however, are limited solely to the place of origin of their work.

A

Helle Abild
Ole Suhrs Gade 21, 1 TV, 1354 K, Copenhagen, Denmark.

A.B. Optimus
Industrivaegen 5, 171 48 Solna, Sweden.

AGROB Wessel Servais AG
101 Münchener Strasse, Ismaning b. Munich 8045, West Germany.

Airon
Via Don Sturzo 10, 20050 Truggio, Milan, Italy. *Outlet* UK: H.N.B., 19-30 Alfred Place, London WC1E 7EA.

Alcatel Kirk
21 Ane Stauningsvej, Horsens 8700, Denmark. *Outlets* Finland: Alcatel SEP, P.O. Box 53, Helsinki 00381. France: Telic Alcatel 54 avenue Jean Jaures, Colombes 92700. Italy: Industri Face Standard, 33 Via Luigi Bodio, Milan 20158. Japan: Alcatel North Asia Pacific, P.O. Box 21, Shinjuku Sumitomo Bldg., Shinjuku-ku, Tokyo 163. The Netherlands: Alcatel Business Systems B.V., 10-12 Platinaweg (postbus 40660), The Hague 2504 LR. New Zealand: Alcatel STC, P.O. Box 40-140, Upper Hutt. Spain: Alcatel Standard Electica SA, 7-13 Paseo Martiricos, Malaga 9. West Germany: Alcatel SEL, Postfach 400749, 7000 Stuttgart 40.

Alchimia Trade Srl
14 Via Cappuccio, Milan 20123, Italy. *Outlets* Belgium: Artiscope N.V., 35 Blvd St Michel, Brussels 1040. The Netherlands: Interhal Select B.V., P.O. Box 1008, Zwijndrecht 3330 CA. UK: The Ikon Corporation, B5L Metropolitan Wharf, Wapping Wall, London E1 9SS. West Germany: Designer's Agency, 7 Prinzregentenstr., Rosenheim 8200.

Aleph
see Driade.

Alessi SpA
Via Privata Alessi 6, 28023 Crusinallo, Novara, Italy. *Outlets* Denmark: Gense A/S, 17 Maglebjergvej, 2800 Lyngby. Finland: Casabella OY, 24 Yliopistonakatu, 20100 Turku. France: Société Metallurgique Lagostina, 62 rue Blaise Pascal, 93600 Aulnay-sous-Bois. Japan: Italia Shoji Co Ltd, 5-4 Kojimachi, 1-Chome, Chiyoda-ku, Tokyo 102. The Netherlands: Interhal BV, 8 Zoutverkoperstraat, 3330 CA Zwijndrecht. Sweden: Espresso Import, 10E Furasen, 42177 V, Frolunda. Switzerland: Guido Mayer SA, 9 rue du Port Franc, 1003 Lausanne. UK: Penhallow Marketing Ltd, 3 Vicarage Road, Sheffield S9 3RH. USA: The Markuse Corporation, 10 Wheeling Avenue, Woburn, MA 01801. West Germany: Van Der Borg GmbH, 6 Sandbahn, 4240 Emmerich.

Algorithme
79 rue Melingue, 75079 Paris, France. *Outlets* Austria: Officina, 18-20 Pangl Gasse, Vienna 1040. Japan: Eternal Inc., 3F Nakajima Bld, 3-17-15 Nishiazabu, Minato-ku, Tokyo. The Netherlands: Wilhelm Broekelmann 23-25, Groot Nieuwland Et Alkmaar 1811. Spain: Bd Ediciones de diseño, 291 Mallorca, 08037 Barcelona. Sweden: Asplund, 26 Nybrogatan,

Stockholm 11439. West Germany: Best Form, 40 Weibelsheidestrasse, Arnsberg-1 5760.

Alias Srl
Via Respighi 2, 20122 Milan, Italy. *Outlets* France: Roger van Bary, 18 rue Lafitte, 75009 Paris. Japan: Casatec Ltd, 2-9-6 Higashi, Shibuya-ku, Tokyo 150. The Netherlands: Kreymborg, 63 Minervaalan, 1077 Amsterdam, Sweden: Design Distribution, 38a/1 Dobelnstan, 113 52 Stockholm. Switzerland: Renato Stauffacher, 2 Capelli, 6900 Lugano. UK: Artemide GB Ltd, 17-19 Neal Street, London WC2H 9PU. USA: International Contract Furniture, 305 East 63rd Street, New York, NY 10021. West Germany: Peter Pfeifer Focus, 87 Leopoldstrasse, 40 Munich 8.

Alterego
3 Jennerstraat, Amsterdam 1016 UJ, The Netherlands. *Outlet* UK: The Ikon Corporation, B5L Metropolitan Wharf, Wapping Wall, London E1 9SS.

Anthologie Quartett
Schloss Huennefeld, Haus Sorgenfrei, 4515 Bad Essen, West Germany. *Outlets* Belgium: Surplus, 9 Zwarte Zusterstraat, 9000 Ghent. France: Altras, 24 rue Lafitte, 75009 Paris. Hong Kong: Le Cadre Gallery, 8 Sunning Road g/f, Causeway Bay. Italy: Via R. Drengot 36, 81031 Aversa. Lebanon: Intermeuble Sarl, Boite Postale 316, Beirut. The Netherlands: Binnen, 82 Kaisergracht, 1015 Amsterdam. Switzerland: Andome, 75 Schaffhauserstrasse, 8302 Kloten.

Antonangeli
Via de Amilis 42, Cinsello Balsamo, Milan 20092, Italy.

AREA Group Inc.
334 King Street East, Toronto M5A 1K8, Ontario, Canada. *Outlet* UK: The Ikon Corporation, B5L Metropolitan Wharf, Wapping Wall, London E1 9SS.

Arflex SpA
Via Monte Rosa 27, 29951 Limbiate, Milan, Italy. *Outlets* Argentina: Colleccion SACIF, Florida 890, 1er Piso, 1005 Buenos Aires. Brazil: Arflex do Brazil, Rua Libero Badaro 377, 20 Andar CJ., 2004 São Paulo. Japan: Arflex Japan Ltd, 2-9-8 Higashi Shibuya-ku, Tokyo 150.

Artemide SpA
Via Brughiera, 20010 Pregnana Milanese, Milan, Italy. *Outlets* Australia: Artemide Pty Ltd, 69-71 Edward Street, Pyrmont, NSW 2009. Belgium: Horas SA, 25 Beemdstraat, 1610 Ruisbroek-Brussels. Canada: 354 Davenport Road, Designers Walk, 3rd Floor, Toronto M15 RK5. Denmark: Renzo D'Este, 1A Brodrevej, 2860 Soborg-Copenhagen. France: Artemide Sarl, 4 rue Paul Cezanne, 75008 Paris. Japan: Artemide Inc., 1-5-10 Sotokanda Chiyodaku, Tokyo 101. Spain: Artemide SA, 12-18 C/o Vico, Barcelona 21. UK: Artemide GB Ltd, 17-19 Neal Street, London WC2H 9PU. USA: Artemide Inc., 528 Center One, 30-30 Thomson Ave, New York, NY 11101. West Germany: Artemide GmbH, 60 Konigsallee, 4000 Düsseldorf 1.

Art-In Construction
205 Plymouth Street, Brooklyn, New York, NY 11201, USA.

Asahi Optical Co. Ltd
2-36-9 Maenocho, Itabashiku, Tokyo 134, Japan.

Atelier International Inc.
30-20 Thomson Ave, Center 2, Long Island City, NY 11101, USA.

Rushton Aust
21 Iliffe Yard, Kennington, London SE17 3QA, UK.

Outlets UK: Contemporary Applied Arts, 43 Earlham Street, London WC2H 9LD; Wilson & Gough, 106 Draycott Ave, London SW3.
Hiroshi Awatsuji Design Studio 1-21-1 Jingumae Shibuya-ku, Tokyo, Japan.

A-Z Studios
3-5 Hardwidge Street, London SE1 3SY, UK.

Baleri Italia
Via San Bernardino 39, Lallio 24040, Bergamo, Italy. *Outlets* Australia: Artedomus, Rokeby Road, Subiaco, Western Australia. Belgium: Kreyborg, 66 Avenue Molière, Brussels 1180. France: Christian Denis, 41 rue du Colisée, Paris 75008. Japan: Casatec Ltd, 9-6 Higashi, 2-Chome Shibuya-Ku, Tokyo 150. The Netherlands: Domani Designs, 90 Singel, Amsterdam 1015 AD. UK: Liberty Plc, Regent Street, London W1R 6AH. USA: I.C.F. Inc., 305 East 63rd Street, New York, NY 10021. West Germany: Walter Schiedermeier, Marienbergerweg 12, 5000 Cologne.

Roger Bateman
219 Algernon Road, Ladywell, London SE13 7AG, UK.

Barazzoni SpA
46 Via Cesare Battisti, Invorio 28045, Italy.

B & B Italia
SPA Strade Provinciale, 22060 Novedrate, Como, Italy. *Outlets* Denmark: Renzo D'Este, 1A Brodrevej, 2860 Soborg, Copenhagen. France: Helven Francis, 52 rue de Lille, 59130 Lambersart. Japan: B & B Japan Ltd, 8F Book Center Building, 2-5-23 Kaigan, Minato-ku, Tokyo 105. The Netherlands: Wanno Carolo, 14 Houtkoperstraat, 3330 Swijndrecht. UK: Keith de la Plain, 5 Sayers Lane, Tenterden, Kent TN30 6BW. West Germany: Klaus Wasche, 266 Bachemer Strasse, 5000 Cologne 41; Bernd Schmidt, 25 Tannenweg, 8000 Munich 50.

Bd. Ediciones de diseño
291 Mallorca, 08037 Barcelona, Spain. *Outlets* Belgium: Quattro, Centre Le Bosquet, Jodoigne-Geldenaken 5900. Canada: Triedei, 460 McGill, Montreal, Quebec H2Y 2H2. France: Nestor Perkal, 8 rue des Quatre Fils, 75003 Paris. Hong Kong: Le Cadre Gallery, 8 Sunning road G/F. Italy: Bd. Italia, Piazza San Marco 1, 20100 Milan. Japan: Gendai Kikakushitsu, Koshin Bldg., 302-2-2-5 Sarugaku-cho, Chiyoda-ku, Tokyo. Switzerland: IMD Inter-Marketing Distribution AG, Eerburnestrasse 26, Hausen (AG) 5212. UK: The Ikon Corporation, B5L Metropolitan Wharf, Wapping Wall, London E1 9SS. USA: Manifesto, 200 West Superior Street, Chicago, Illinois; Lymnn, 457 Pacific Avenue, San Francisco 94133. West Germany: IMD Inter-Marketing Distribution AG, Flothbruchstrasse 11, 4156 Willich 2, Anrath.

Becker Designed Inc.
8950 Brookville Road, Silver Spring, Maryland 20910, USA.

Gretchen Bellinger Inc.
IDCNY Center II, Suite 706, 30-20 Thomson Avenue, Long Island City, New York, USA; 330 East 59 Street, New York, NY 10022 1599, USA.

Belux AG
Bremgarterstrasse 109, Wohlen 5610, Aargau, Switzerland. *Outlets* Denmark: Osterby Chr./ Schuricht, Birkewaenget 21, 3520 Farum. France:

Nourissat Pierre, 33 avenue des Champs-Elysées, 75008 Paris. Italy: TWIN di Mascherpa Massimiliano, II Strade Torre 3, 20090 S. Felice Segrate-Milano. Japan: Hybec Corporation, Miyakawa Bldg, 1-17 Tsukiji 2-chome, Chuo Sku, Tokyo 104. The Netherlands: Interlinea BV, Weeresteinstraat 49, 2182 GR Hillegom. UK: Light Projects Ltd, 32 Jacob Street, London SE1 2BG. USA: Lee's Studio Inc., 220 West 57th Street, New York, NY 10019. West Germany: Nils Holger Moormann, Statt 1, 8201 Frasdorf.

Belysia AB
566 00 Habo, Sweden. *Outlets* Finland: Kone-Tukku OY, Valaisinosasto, 00211 Helsinki. The Netherlands: Fagerhult-Lyktan BV, Lage Dijk 27, 5700 AH Helmond. Norway: Fagerhult-Lyktan A/S, Sinsenveien 47 B, (0513 Oslo 5. West Germany: Fagerhult-Lyktan GmbH, Borsteller Chaussee 85-99A, Gebaude C, Haus 12.2, Stock, 2000 Hamburg 61.

Berliner Zimmer Design-Agentur GmbH,
Clausewitzstrasse 1, 1000 Berlin 12, West Germany.

G.B. Bernini SpA
Via Fiume 17, 20048 Carate Brianza, Milan, Italy.

Bigelli Marmi
Via Arceviese 26, 60019 Senigallia (AN), Italy.

Blauet SA
Aragon 333, 08009 Barcelona, Spain.

B-Lux Herriola SCL
Avda. de Xemein 19, P.O. Box 4, 48270 Markina-Bizkaiá, Spain.

Bodum (Schweiz) AG
Kantonsstrasse, 6234 Triengen, Lucerne, Switzerland. *Outlets* Denmark: Peter Bodum AS, 18 Nglegaardsvej, 3540 Lynge. France: Martin SA, 82-84 rue de Dessous-des-Berges, 75013 Paris. Italy: Italtrade SA, 10-17 Piazza della Vittoria, 16121 Genoa. Japan: Zojirushi Vacuum Bottle Co., 20-5 Tenma, 1-Chome, Kita-ku, Osaka 350. The Netherlands: Mepal BV, 1 Kwinkweerd, 7241 CW Lochem. UK: Bodum (UK) Ltd, 7 Neal Street, London WC2H 9PU. USA: Rosti (USA) Inc., 18 Sydney Cirlce, New Jersey 07033. West Germany: Peter Bodum, 6 Bochstrasse, 2358 Kaltenkirchen.

Bros's SrL
1 Via Sotto Rive, S. Giovanni al Matisone 33048, Udine, Italy. *Outlets* Austria: Otto Silhavicek, Nussdorfestrasse 36, 1060 Vienna. Belgium: Horas International, 22 rue Copernic, Brussels 1180. France: Horas International, 136-50 rue Championet, 75918 Paris. Greece: J. Deloudes AE, Kiffissias 217 ET, Parnassouz Amaroussion, 15124 Athens. The Netherlands: Horas International, Zonnebos 29, NN Vught 5263. Sweden: Swedia, P.O. Box 138, Lammhult 376030. Switzerland: O. Daehnel, Zollierstrasse 28, Zollikon, Zurich. UK: Interior Marketing, 36 Stansted Road, Hockerill, Bishop's Stortford, Hertfordshire CM23 2DY. USA: Cy Man Design Ltd, 150 Fulron Ave, Garden City Park, New York, NY 11140. West Germany: Sedia GmbH. Zoppenbroich 1, 4050 Mönchengladbach 2.

B & W Loudspeakers
Meadow Road, Worthing, West Sussex BN11 2RS, UK. *Outlets* Canada: B & W Loudspeakers of America, 104 Carnforth Road, Toronto, Ontario M4A 2KY. France: Marantz France SA, 4 rue Bernard Palissy, 92600 Asnières. Italy: Audiogamma SRL, Via Pietro Calvi 16, 20129 Milan. Japan: Nakamichi Corp., Shinjuku Daiichi Seimei Bldg 11F, 2-7-1 Nishishinjuku, Shinjuku-ku, Tokyo 160. The Netherlands: Audioscript BV, P.O.

Box 213, 3760 AE Soest. Spain: Musicon SA, Apartado de Correos No 252, 08190 Sant Cugat del Valles, Barcelon. Sweden: ARD AB, Linkopingskontoret, P.O. Box 3041, 580 03 Linkoping. Switzerland: B & W AG, Malzstrasse 11, 8045 Zurich. West Germany: B & W Loudspeakers Vertrieb GmbH, Westrasse 85, 4802 Halle, Westphalia.

Cadet Manufacturing
P.O. Box 1675, Vancouver, Washington 98668, USA.

Campeggi Srl
Via Cavolto 8, 22040 Anzano del Parco, Como, Italy.

Canon Inc.
P.O. Box 55050, Shinjuku Dai-Ichi Seimei Bldg, Tokyo 160, Japan. *Outlets* Austria: Canon, Modecenterstrasse 22 A-2, 1030 Vienna. Belgium: Canon Copiers Belgium NVISA, Luidlaam 33-Bus 6, 100 Brussels. Canada: Canon Canada Inc., 3245 American Drive, Mississauga, Ontario L4V 1N4. Denmark: Christian Bruhn AS, Vasekaer 12, 2729 Herlev, France: Canon France SA, P.O. Box 40, 93151 Le Blanc Mesnil. Italy: Canon Italia SPA, Centro Direzionale, Palazzo Verocchio, 20090 Milan 2-Segrate MI. The Netherlands: Canon Verkooporganisatie Nederland BV, Cruquiusweg 29, 2102 LS Heemstede, Amsterdam. Norway: Noiseless AS, Tventenveien 30B, Oslo 6. Spain: Canon Copiardoras de Espana SA, Avd. Menendez Pelayo, 57 Torre del Retiro, Madrid. Sweden: Canon Svenska AB, Box 2084, Stensatrava gen 13, 12702 Skarholmen. Switzerland: Canon SA, 1 rue de Hesse, 1204 Geneva. UK: Canon UK Ltd, Canon House, Manor Road, Wallington, Surrey SM6 0AJ. USA: Canon USA Inc., One Canon Plaza, Lake Success, New York, NY 11042-9979. West Germany: Canon Copylux GmbH, Leurriper Strasse 1-13, 4050 Mönchengladbach.

Cappellini International Interiors
Via Marconi 35, 20060 Arosio, Italy.

Carpyen SA
Duran y Borrell 29, 08023 Barcelona, Spain.

Casamania
see Frezza.

Casas SL
40 C. Milagro, 08028 Barcelona, Spain. *Outlets* Belgium: Quattro, 25 rue de la Régence, Brussels. France: Casas SL, 27 rue des Tournelles, 75004 Paris. Spain: Casas SL, 15 Rodriguez de San Pedro, Madrid. Switzerland: Gatto Diffusion, 30 rue des Chavannes, 2016 Cortaillod. UK: Architectural Trading Company, 219-29 Shaftesbury Avenue, London WC2H 8AR. USA: International Contract Furnishings, 305 East 63rd Street, New York, NY 10021.

Casigliani Srl
Via P. Barsanti 4, Ospeddaletto-Pisa 56014, Italy. *Outlets* France: Dominique Devoto, 47 rue Henri Barbusse, 75224 Paris Cedex 05. Japan: Ambiente International Inc., 3-1-30 Sumimoto Seimei Bldg, Minamiaoyama Minato-ku, Tokyo 10700. Netherlands: Andrea Kok, 4 Pilatus, Amstelveen EK 1186. Switzerland: Domani AG, 231 Seefeldstrasse, Zurich 8008. UK: Paul Beauchamp, 36 Stansted Road, Hockerill, Bishop's Stortford, Herts. CM23 2DY.

Cassina SpA
Via Luigi Busnelli 1, Meda Milano 20036, Italy. *Outlets* Argentina: Interieur Forma SA, 545-55 Paraguay, 1057

Buenos Aires. Australia: Artes Studio – Arredorama, 1 Ross Street, Glebe, NSW 2037. Belgium: Mobica, 50 Gossetlaan, 1720 Groot Bijgaarden. Brazil: Probjeto SA, 8400 Rue Vergueiro, 04272 São Paulo. Japan: Cassina Japan Inc., 2-9-6 Higashi, Shibuya-ku, Tokyo 105. The Netherlands: Mobica, 31 Middenweg, 3401 (MB Ijsselstein. Spain: Mobilplast SL, 40 Calle Milagro. 08028 Barcelona. USA: Atelier International Inc., The International Design Center, 30-20 Thomson Avenue, Long Island City, NY 11101. Venezuela: Capuy, 69 Chacaito-Apdo, Caracas 106.

Ceccotti Aviero SpA
P.O. Box 77, Viale Sicilia 4, 56021 Cascina Pisa, Italy.

Ceramica Mauri SpA
Via Brennero 43, Desio 20033, Milan, Italy.

Chairs
4F Axis Bldg, 5-17-1 Roppongi, Minato-ku, Tokyo 106, Japan.

Cidue
32 Via San Lorenzo, 36010 Carre, Vicenza, Italy. *Outlets* France: Jacques Dollard, 32 Bis rue des Jardiniers, Nancy 54000. Hong Kong: Executive Design, 53 Wong Nei Chong. Japan: Italcomm Ltd, Likura Comfy Bldg B 101, 4-4 Azabudai 3 Chome, Minato-ku, Tokyo. The Netherlands: Espaces et Lignes. P.O. Box 406, 2040 Zandvoort. Spain: Xarma SL, C/ San
Martin 57-3, San Sebastian 20007. Sweden: Inside AB, P.O. Box 7689, Stockholm 10395. UK: Atrium, 113 St Peter, St Albans, Herts AL1 3ET. USA: Niels Olehansen Inc., 1129 Magnolia Avenue, Larkspur 94939. West Germany: Cidue Service Buero, Fliegenstrasse 8, 8000 Munich 2.

Colur SA
55-57 C. Formiga, Banyoles 17820, Girona, Spain.

Creative Agent
31 boulevard Malesherbes, Paris 75008, France.

Bruno Danese SNC
Piazza San Fedele 2, Milan 20121, Italy. *Outlets* Belgium: Kreymborg Belgie NV, Avenue Molière Laan 66, 1180 Brussels. Canada: Triede Design Inc., 460 McGill, Montreal, Quebec H2Y 2H2. Denmark: Interstudio Aps, Ludersvej 4, Frihavnen, 2100 Copenhagen. France: Danese France SARL, 174 boulevard Voltaire, 75011 Paris. Japan: OUN Corporation, Seventh Minami Aoyama Bldg, 7-12-14 Minami Aoyama, Minato-ku, Tokyo 107. The Netherlands: Kreymborg BV, Minervalaan 63, 1077 Amsterdam. Portugal: Equipamento e Design de Interiors LDA, Rue da Rosa 241, 1200 Lisbon. Spain: Arflex & Martinez-Medina, Isla Cabrera 36, 46026 Valencia. Switzerland: Jean-Pierre Goumaz, 29-31 rue Centrale, 1003 Lausanne. UK: Objects by Environment, The Studio, 120 High Street, South Milford, Leeds LS25 5AQ.

Design Gallery Milano
Via Manzoni 46, 20121 Milan, Italy.

Design M Ingo Maurer GmbH
47 Kaiserstrasse, 8000 Munich 40, West Germany. *Outlets* Denmark: Finn Sloth, 1 Heilsmindevej, 2920 Charlottenlund. France: Altras, 18 rue Lafitte, 75009 Paris. Italy: Daverio SRL, Via Canova 37, 20145 Milan. The Netherlands: P.A. Hesselmans, 24 Korfgraaf, 4714 GM Hellouw. Sweden: Sandklef, P.O. Box 4112, 421 04 V. Frolunda.

Disform
63 Rda. Gral. Mitre, 08017 Barcelona, Spain. *Outlets* France: Edifice, 27 bis boulevard Raspail, 75007 Paris. Italy: Design and Design, 5 Via F. Witgens, 20123 Milan. Japan: Eishin Trading Co. Ltd, 6-5 Morishita Chome-3, Koto-ku, 135 Tokyo. The Netherlands: AMDA Frans Stroosnijder, 37 Oosterhoutlaan, 1181 Al Anstelveen. Sweden: Design (J.J. Lassagne), Dobelnsgatan 38A 1TR, 11352 Stockholm. UK: Maison Designs (Retail) Ltd, 917-19 Fulham Road, London SW6 5HU. USA: EDEAS, 1 West 64 Street, New York, NY 10023. West Germany: ALTECO, Postfach 56, 8021 Schaftlarn.

Draenert-Studio GmbH
Steigwiesen 3, 7997 Immenstaad-Bodensee, West Germany.

Driade SpA
Via Padane Inferiore 12, Fossadello di Caorso 29012, Piacenza, Italy. *Outlets* Belgium: Espace et Lignes, 55 rue Ulens, Brussels 1080. France: Arturo del Punta, 7 rue Simon Lefranc, 75004 Paris. Japan: Ambiente, Sumimoto Seimei Bldg 3-1-30, Minami Aoyama, Minato-ku, Tokyo. Spain: Sellex, 53A PCD de Mandas Torre Atocha 1, San Sebastian. Sweden: Design Distribution, Doebelnsg 38A1, Stockholm 11352. Switzerland: Peter Frischknecht, 31A Feldlistrasse, St Gallen 9000. UK: The Ikon Corporation, B5L Metropolitan Wharf, Wapping Wall, London E1 9SS. USA: Tonia Pozzoli, Primalinea, 30 Gustafson CT 94974, Novato CA. West Germany: Stefan Mueller, 18 Maximiliansplatz, Munich 8000.

Ebenberger GmbH
1 Volkergasse, Vienna 1150, Austria.

Edizioni de Padova
Corso Venezia 14, Milan 20121, Italy. *Outlets* Denmark: Paustian, 2 Kalkbraenderjiloebskay, Copenhagen 2100. France: Galeries Agora, 16 rue de la Grange Batelière, Paris 75009. Japan: Casatec Ltd, 9-6 Higashi Hsiboya-ku, Tokyo 150. The Netherlands: Koos Rijkse, Pr. Christinelaan, 7437 X2 Bathmen. Spain: Idea Mueble, 185 Augusta, Barcelona 08021. Switzerland: Formatera, 54 Stockerstrasse, 8002 Zurich. USA: ICF, 33 Kings Highway, Orangenburg, New York, NY 10962. West Germany: Habit, 44 Surderstrasse, 509 Leverkusen 22.

Effetto Luce
Via L. Manara 14, San Pietro all'Ormo, 20010 Milan, Italy.

Elam
Via Molino 27, 20036 Meda, Milan, Italy.

Emerald Computers
7324 SW Durham Road, Portland, Oregon 97224, USA.

Emmebi
Monteverdi 28, Cesano Maderno 20031, Milan, Italy.

En Canya CV
Partida del Tossal S/N, 46850 L'Olleria, Valencia, Spain.

ENEA
Poligono Industrial S/N, Legorreta, Gipuzkoa, Spain. *Outlets* France: BBL Diffusion, 6 Place Maréchal Leclerc, 35400 St Malo. Sweden: Claes Bauer, P.O. Box 30545,

20062 Malmo. West Germany: Flototto Handels, Ringstrasse 38-40, 4835 Rietberg 2.

Escofet
Ronda Universidad 20, 08007 Barcelona, Spain. *Outlet* France: M. Madjar, 1 bis rue Albert 1er, 92600 Asnières.

Christian Farjon
P.O. Box 21, 23 200 Aubusson, France.

Fiam Italia SpA
Via Ancona 1/13, 61010 Tavullia, PS, Italy. *Outlet* UK: Casa Bianchi, Roslyn House, Sun Street, Hitchin, Herts. SG5 1AE.

Flos SpA
Via Moretti 58, 25121 Brescia BS, Italy. *Outlets* Belgium: Flos SA, Gossetlaan 50, 1720 Groot-Bijgaarden. France: Flos SARL, 23 rue de Bourgogne, 75007 Paris. Japan: Flos Co. Ltd, Dowa Bldg 4F, 18-18 Roppongi 5-Chome, Minato-ku, Tokyo. Spain: Flos SA, c/Bovedillas 16, San Just Desvern, 08960 Barcelona. Switzerland: Flos SA, 36 Place du Bourg de Four, 1204 Geneva. UK: Flos Ltd, The Studio, 120 High Street, South Milford, Leeds LS25 5AQ. USA: Flos Inc., 200 McKay Road, Huntingdon Station, New York, NY 11746. West Germany: Flos GmbH, Am Probsthof 94, 5300 Bonn 1.

Fontana Arte SpA
Alzaia Trieste 49, 20094 Corsico, Italy. *Outlets* Austria: Einrichtungs-Verkaufs GmbH Co KG, 27 Hagenstrasse, 4020 Linz. Belgium: M. Frank PVBA, 25 Wijngaardstraat, 2000 Antwerp. Canada: Angle International, 296 St Paul West, Montreal, Quebec. France: Giuseppe Cerutti, 1 Loc Grand Chemin, 11020 Aosta, Italy. The Netherlands: Silvera BV, Postbus 163, 1250 AD Laren. Switzerland: Formatera AG, 54 Stockerstrasse, 8022 Zurich. USA: Interna Design Ltd, The Merchandising Mart, Space 6-168, Chicago, Illinois 60654. West Germany: Fr. Van Der Beck, 52 Bahnhofstrasse, 3472 Beverungen 1.

Form Farm Inc.
45 West 18th Street, 7th Floor, New York, NY 10011, USA.

Marianne Forrest
376 St John Street, London EC1V 4NN, UK.

Frezza Srl
Via Ferret 11/9, 31020 Vidor TV, Italy. *Outlets* France: Frezza France, avenue Henri Barbusse 163, 92700 Colombes. The Netherlands: Fagel New Line, Prinses Irenelaan 80, Egmond An Den Hoff 1934. Spain: Frezza Iberica SA, Calle Urgel 259, 08036 Barcelona. UK: Laytrad Ltd, 30 Harmsworth Way, London N20 8JU. West Germany: Ital-Creativ Mkt, Imgattberg 13, 4613 Belm.

Fujie Textile Co. Ltd
4-7-12 Sendagaya Sibuya-ku, Tokyo 151, Japan. *Outlets* Hong Kong: C.E.T.E.C. Ltd, 29 Wellington, Yuen Yick Bldg. USA: Fabriyaz, 41 Madison Avenue, New York, NY 10010. West Germany: Fuggerhaus Stoffe Fuer Den Modernen Raum GmbH & Co., 8900 Augsburg.

Galleria Fulvio Ferrari
Via Cavour 24, Turin 10123, Italy.

Garcia Garay SA
13 San Antonio, Sta Coloma de Gramanet 08923, Barcelona, Spain. *Outlets* Austria: Plan Licht, 187A Vomperbach, Schwaz 6130. The Netherlands: Frantzen BV, 49-51 Dr. Schaepmanstraat, AD Weert 6.004. UK: Opus Lighting, 58 Mount Ephrain, Tunbridge Wells, Kent TN4 8BB. West Germany: Mega Light, 4 Tilsiter strasse, Frankfurt 6000.

Richard Ginori SpA
Via Pio La Torre 4-C, 20090 Vimodrone, Milan, Italy. *Outlet* UK: ICTC, Unit 2, Worton Industrial Estate, Flemming Way, Isleworth, Middlesex.

Glass Design
1 Macherio, Milan, Italy.

Grundig Elektrogerate GmbH
Kurgatenstrasse 37, 8510 Furth, Bavaria, West Germany. *Outlets* France: Grundig France SA, 33-35 boulevard de la Paix, 78104 St Germain-en-Laye. Italy: Melchioni SpA, Via P. Colletta 37, 20135 Milan. The Netherlands: Grundig Nederland BV, Ind. Gebiet Amstel, Joan Muyskenweg 22, 1007 AB Amsterdam. Norway: Scan Electgro AS, Knud Bryns Vei 10, 0581 Oslo 5. Spain: Inter Grundig Commercial SA, Traversa de las Corts 312-314, Barcelona 14. UK: Grundig International Ltd, Millroad, Rugby, Warwickshire CV2 1FR.

Hanco Inc.
P.O. Box 1256, Lake Oswego, Oregon 97035, USA.

Matthew Hilton
Unit D16, Metropolitan Workshops, Enfield Road, London N1 5AZ. *Outlets* Japan: Kiya Gallery, 9-2 Sarugaku-Cho, Shibuya-ku, Tokyo. UK: SCP Ltd, 135-39 Curtain Road, London EC2A 3BX.

Hofstatter & Ebbesen AS
17 Bredgade, Copenhagen 1260, Denmark.

I.B. Office SpA
Via Treviso 99, Scorze Venezia 30037, Italy.

IBRA
237 Kalundborgvej, Holbaek 4300, Denmark. *Outlets* France: Inge With International, 25 Osterbrogade, Copenhagen 2100, Denmark. Italy: Inge With International, 25 Osterbrogade, Copenhagen 2100, Denmark. Sweden: Jan Dam, 14 Norrovagen, Akersberga 184 42. West Germany: Ole Cpion, 41 Hostrupvej, Langa 8870, Denmark.

ICF SpA
280 Via Padana Superiore, Vimodrone 20090, Milan, Italy. *Outlets* France: Cadsana France SA, 205 boulevard Saint Germain, 75007 Paris. Japan: Epson Trading KK, 11F Shinjuku ns Bldg, 2-4-1 Nishishinjuku, Shinjuku-ku, Tokyo 163. Switzerland: Cadsana-Buromobel Vertriebs AG, 15 Giassenstrasse, Schlieren 8952. UK: Cadsana Ltd, The Stephen Building, 30 Gresse Street, London W1 1PN. USA: Cadsana Associates, East Middle Patent Road, Greenwich, Coonecticut 06831.

Idée
5-4-44 Minamiaoyama, Minato-ku, Tokyo 107, Japan. *Outlet* UK: The Ikon Corporation, B5L Metropolitan Wharf, Wapping Wall, London E1 9SS.

IDK Design Laboratory Ltd
TS Bldg 2F, 3-1-2 Tenma Kita-ku, Osaka City, Japan. *Outlets* Italy: Hi-Plan International, Via Spartaco 8, 20135 Milan. West Germany: Tecnolumen, 1-5 Neuenstrasse, Bremen 2800.

Iittala Glass OY
SF-14500 Iittala, Finland. *Outlets* France: AG Distribution SARL, 8 rue Martel, F-75010 Paris. Italy: Seambe Srl, Via Marchesi de Taddei 10, 1-20146 Milan. Japan: Matsuya Shoji Co. Ltd, 2-20 Akashi-Cho, Chuo-ku, Tokyo 104. The Netherlands: Indoor, Paulus Potterstraat 22-24, 1071 DA Amsterdam. Spain: Italcris, Serrano 93/3D, Madrid 28006. Sweden: Knut & Per-Ake Sarnwald AB, Kungsgatan 56, 41108 Gothenburg. UK: Storrington Trading Co. Ltd, Eastmead Industrial Estate, Midhurst Road, Lavant, Chichester, West Sussex PO18 0DE. USA: Iittala Inc., 175 Clearbrook Road, Elmsford, NY 10523. West Germany: B.T. Dibbern GmbH & Co. KG, Heinrich-Hertz-Strasse 1, 2072 Bargteheide.

Ikea of Sweden
34300 Almhult, Sweden.

Indartu Simeyco SAL
Ctra Goizueta s/n 20120, Hernani, Guipuzcoa, Spain.

Industrie Secco SpA
195 Via Terraglio, Preganziol 31022, Treviso 31100, Italy. *Outlets* Belgium: Trademart Brussels, Bus/Bte 653, 1020 Brussels. Canada: Claude Ganley, 4020 rue Dandurand, Montreal, Quebec H1X 1P9. France: Sedec, Centre Commercial de Ranguin, 06321 Cannes. Switzerland: Rohr AG, Industriesteingasse, Madiswil 4934. UK: Ideas For Living Ltd, 215-6 Business Design Centre, Upper Street, London N1 0QH. West Germany: Belform GmbH, 14 Kapellenfeldstrasse, 8000 Munich 90.

Intent
27 Llull, Barcelona 08005, Spain. *Outlets* France: B.B.L. Diffusion, 6 Place Maréchal Leclerc, Saint Malo 35400. Japan: Tanifuji Co. Ltd, 1-6-7 Shinyokohama-Cho, Kohoku-ku, Kanagawa-Ken 222. Sweden: Palk, 72A Drottninggatam, Helsingborg 25003. USA: Domus Massini Inc. 123 Townsend Street, Suite 470, San Francisco, CA 94107. West Germany: Kare, 10 Augustenstrasse, 8000 Munich.

Interflex SpA
Via Indipendenza 161-3, 20036 Meda Milan, Italy. *Outlets* Denmark: Interstudio, Luedersvej 4, Frihavnen, 2100 Copenhagen. Switzerland: Inter Marketing Distribution, Eebrunnestrasse 26, 5212 Hausen. UK: Neil Rogers Interiors, Unit 23, Abbeville Mews, 88 Clapham Park Road, London SW4 7BX.

Ishimaru Co. Ltd
202 Maison Akashi, 7-3-24 Roppongi, Minato-ku, Tokyo, Japan.

Dakota Jackson Inc.
306 East 61st Street, New York, NY 10021, USA.

Elizabeth Browning Jackson
P.O. Box 3001, Westport, Massachusetts 02790, USA.

Kai Corporation
3-9-3 Iwamoto-cho, Chiyoda-ku, Tokyo 101, Japan.
Outlets Italy; E. Levi & Co. SpA, Via Giambellino 11,
20146 Milan. UK: Intra Corporation Ltd, The Grand
Union Centre, 334A Ladbroke Grove, London W10
5AH. USA: Elika, 1108C West Washington Blvd,
Venice, CA 90291. West Germany: Kai Europe GmbH,
Sud 30, D-5650 Solingen 11.

Kallemo AB
P.O. Box 605, 331 01 Varnamo, Sweden.

Kartell SpA
Viale delle Industrie 1, 20082 Noviglio, Milan, Italy.
Outlets Australia: Plastex, 85 Fairbank Road, 3168
Clayton, Victoria. Austria: Eugen Leopold, 19
Grunauerstrasse, 4020 Linz. Belgium: Tradix SA, 104
Avenue Louis Lepoutre, 1060 Brussels. Denmark: John
Anker, 6 Esplanaden, 1263 Copenhagen. France:
Marais International Group, 5 rue de Faubourg St
Antoine, 75011 Paris. Japan: Kartell Japan Co. Ltd,
Dowa Bldg 4F, 18-18 Roppongi, 5-Chome, Minatoku,
Tokyo 106. The Netherlands: Modular Systems,
Assumburg 73-1, 1081 GB Amsterdam. Spain: Grupo
T SA, 37 Casanova, Barcelona 08011. Switzerland:
Piermilio Gatto, 3 Ch. des Graviers, 2016 Cortaillod.
UK: Ideas For Living, Lin Pac Mouldings, 5 Kensington
High Street, London W8 5NP. USA: Kartell USA, P.O.
Box 1000, Easley SC 29640.

Knoll Textiles
The Knoll Building, 655 Madison Avenue, New York,
NY 10021, USA.

Kokuyo Co. Ltd
6-1-1 Oimazato Minami, Higashinari-ku, Osaka,
Japan.

Koyo Sangyo Co. Ltd
9-9 Kaji-cho 1-Chome, chiyoda-ku, Tokyo 101, Japan.
Outlet USA: Eastern Accent, 237 Newbury Street,
Boston, Massachusetts 02116.

Kreon NV
126 Frankruklei, Antwerp B2000, Belgium. Outlets Italy:
Luce Plan, Via Bellinzona 48, 20155 Milan. Spain: Bd
Ediciones de diseño, 291 Mallorca, 08037 Barcelona.
UK: The Ikon Corporation, B5L Metropolitan Wharf,
Wapping Wall, London E1 9SS.

Kvadrat Boligtextiler AS
10 Lundbergsvej, Ebeltoft 8400, Denmark. Outlets
Iceland: Epal HF, Faxafen 7, 108 Reykjavik. Italy:
Rapsel SpA, Via Alessandro Volta 13, 20019 Settimo
Milanese. Japan: Euro Design Ltd, Onozuka Bldg 3F
10-4. Shiba Park 2-Chome, Minato-ku, Takyo 105. The
Netherlands: Danskina, Hettenheuvelweg 14, 1101 BN
Amsterdam 20. UK: Kvadrat Ltd, 62 Princedale Road,
London W11 4NL. USA: Rudd International, 13934-44
Park Center Road, Renaissance Park at Dulls, Hemden,
Virginia 22071.

Danny Lane
55-60 Metropolitan Works, Enfield Road, London N1
5AZ, UK.

Jennifer Lee
16 Talfourd Road, London SE15 5NY, UK.

Ligne Roset
FA BT9 Briord, 501470 Serrières de Briord, France.

Outlet UK: S.A.M. Creative, 12 Flitcroft Street, London
WC2H 8DJ.

Lilyriver KY
P.O. Box Lilyriver, 25460 Toija, Finland.

Gorm Lindum
4 Rytter Marken, Farum 3520, Denmark.

Luce Plan Srl
Via Bellinzona 48, 20155 Milan, Italy. Outlet UK:
Artemide GB Ltd, 17-19 Neal Street, London WC2H
9PU.

Luxo Italiana SpA
1 Via delle More, Presezzo 24030, Bergamo, Italy.
Outlets Denmark: Luxo Lamper, 27-29 Tempovej,
Ballerup 2750. France: Luxo France, 11 rue Auguste
Lacroix, Lyon 69003. The Netherlands: Ansems
Industrial Design, 10A Dorpsstraat, Ledeacker 5846
AA. Spain: Luxo Espanyola, 39-41 Sugranyes,
Barcelona 08028. Sweden: Luxo Sweden, 10A
Kraketerpsgatan, Molndal 431 33. UK: Thousand and
One Lamps, 4 Barmeston Road, London SE6 3BN.
West Germany: Mazda Licht, 19 Taunusstrasse, 6000
Frankfurt 1.

MA & MO Srl
358 Nuova Valassina, Lissone 20035, Italy.

John Makepeace
Parnham House, Beaminster, Dorset DT8 3NA, UK.
Outlet USA: Clifford Buisch, Genoa Gallery, Box 250
Academy Street, Genoa, New York 13071.

Marieta Textil SA
15 Ballester, 08023 Barcelona, Spain. Outlet UK:
Inhouse, 28 Howe Street, Edinburgh, Scotland.

Nani Marquina
3C Bonavista, 08012 Barcelona, Spain. Outlets France:
Marie Bacou, 200 rue La Fayette, 75010 Paris. Italy:
Tisca, Via Donizetti 6, 24050 Lurano, Bergamo.
Switzerland and West Germany: IMD, Franz Baars, 26
Eebrunnestrasse, 5212 Hausen AG, Switzerland.

Masterly Srl
Via Brianza 62, 20030 Lentate sul Seveso, Milan, Italy.

Matsushita Seiko Co. Ltd
6-2-61 Imafuku-Nishi, Joto, Osaka, Japan.

Matteo Grassi SpA
Via Sta Caterina da Siena 26, 22066 Mariano C.se
(CO), Italy.

Mecanorma
14 route de Houdan, Le Perray en Yvelines 78160,
France.

Metalarte SA
Avda de Barcelona 4, 08970 Saint Joan Despi,
Barcelona, Spain. Outlets France: Electoama, 11
boulevard Saint Germain, 75006 Paris. The
Netherlands: Hooge Products, 12 Bebers Pijken, 5221
ED Hertogenbosch. UK: Direct Light Ltd, 275 Fulham
Road, London SW10 9PZ. USA: California Artup
Corporation, 3000 Shanon, Santa Ana, CA 92704;
Hansen Lamps Inc., 121 East 24th Street, New York, NY
10010. West Germany: Altalinea, 6 Sandhof, 4040
Neuss 21 Norff.

Meta Memphis (Memphis Milano Srl)
9 Via Olivetti, Pregnana Milanese 20010, Italy. Outlets

Australia: Artemide Pty Ltd, 69 Edward Street, Pyrmont,
NSW 2009. Austria: Prodomo, 35-7 Flachgasse, 1150
Vienna. Belgium: Horas SA, 25 Beemstraat, 1610
Ruisbroek. Canada: Artemide Ltd, 354 Davenport
Road, Designers Walk, 3rd Floor, Toronto, M15 RK5.
Denmark: Renzo d'Este, 1A Brodrevej, 2860 Soborg,
Copenhagen. France: Roger Von Bary, 18 rue Lafitte,
75009 Paris. Hong Kong: Le Cadre Gallery, 8 Sunning
Road G/F, Causeway Bay. The Netherlands: Copi,
90A Prinsestraat, 2513 CG The Hague. Switzerland:
Bell'Arte C. Arquint, 13 Loostrasse, 6430 Schwyz. UK:
Artemide GB Ltd, 17-19 Neal Street, London WC2H
9PU. USA: Memphis Milano, International Design
Center, Center One, Space 525, 30-30 Thomson
Avenue, Long Island City, NY 11101. West Germany:
Agentur Brunnbauer, 51 Ehmckstrasse, 2800 Bremen
33.

Micrognosis Inc.
700 Gale Avenue, Campbell, CA 95008, USA.

Miles Carter Ltd
Millers Green, Wirksworth, Derbyshire DE4 4BG, UK.
Outlets Italy: Cherubini Arredamenti, Via Triumplina
10C, 25127 Brescia. USA: Interna Designs, 520 West
Erie Street, Chicago, Illinois 60610. West Germany:
Fred Winter, Hille Ergonom, Schuberstrasse 32,
Postfach 23, 6301 Fernwald 1.

Minerva Co. Ltd
1-10-7 Hiratsuka, Shinagawa-ku, Tokyo 142, Japan.

Mines & West Group Ltd
Downley, High Wycombe, Buckinghamshire HP13 5TX,
UK.

Misura Emme SAS
Via IV Novembre 72, Mariano Comense 22066, Italy.

Misura Emme SAS
Via IV Novembre 72, Mariano Comense 22066, Italy.

Miyashin
582-11 Kitanocho, Hachioti, Tokyo, Japan.

Miyatake
1 Madegawa Horikawa, Kamigyo-ku, Fyoto, Japan.

Mobles 114
Enric Granados 114, 08008 Barcelona, Spain.

Molteni & Co. SpA
Via Rossini 50, Giussano 20034, Milan, Italy. Outlets
France: Giorgio Corvaja, 1 rue de Lille, 75007 Paris.
Japan: Ambiente, Sumimoto Seimei Bldg 3-1-30,
Minami-Aoyama, Minato-ku, Tokyo. The Netherlands:
Beltane, Stratumsedijk 33, 5611 NB Eindhoven. Spain:
Atri, Balmes 0427, 08022 Barcelona. UK: Atrium Ltd,
22-24 St Giles High Street, London WC2H 8LN. West
Germany: Modern Line, Hungener Strasse 6-12, Block
C, 1-OG, Frankfurt.

Mondo Srl
Via Vittorio 25, 22060 Carugo, Italy. Outlets Austria:
Wolfgang Bischoff, Judenplatz 6, 1010 Vienna.
Belgium: Rika Andries, 144B Turnhoutsebaan,
Borgerhout 2200. France: Giuseppe Cerutti, Loc.
Grand Chemin 1, 11020 Saint Christophe. The
Netherlands: Koos Rijkse Agency, P.R. Christinalaan 1,
7437 XZ Bathmen. Spain: Jose Martinez Medina SA,
Camino del Bony S/N, Catarroja Valencia. Sweden:
Mobile Box AB, Hargs Saeteri, 19490 Upplands Vasby.
Switzerland: Yves Humbrecht Diffusion, Saleve 10,
1004 Lausanne. UK: Essential Business Contacts,
Lawnfield House, Westmorland Road, Maidenhead,

Berkshire SL6 4HB. West Germany: Novus, 26 Gartenstrasse, 7959 Achstetten 3.

Morimoto Hikawa
1393, Okutama-cho, Nishi Tama-Gun, Tokyo, Japan.

Morphos (Acerbis International SpA)
Via Brusaporto 31, Seriate 24068 BG, Italy. *Outlets* Australia: Arredorama International Pty Ltd, 1 Ross Street. Glebe, NSW 2037. Belgium: Artiscope SA, 35 boulevard St Michel, 1040 Brussels. Denmark: Interstudio APS, 6-8 Esplanade, 1263 Copenhagen. France: Agences Generales Reuter, D915 route de Paris, Domain de la Pissotte, 95640 Marines. Greece: J. Deloudis AE, 217 Kifisias/2 Parnassou, Amaroussion, Athens. Japan: Atic Trading Inc., 2-9-8 Higashi, Shibuya-ku, Tokyo. The Netherlands: Modular Sustem, 73 Assumburg, 1081 GB Amsterdam, Buitenveldert. Spain: Axa International SA, 13 5 KM, Llissa de Vall, Barcelona. Switzerland: Wohndesign AG, 123 Rychenbergstrasse, 8400 Winterhur. UK: Environment Communication, 15-17 Rosemont Road, London NW3 6NG. USA: Atelier International Ltd, 30-20 Thomson Avenue, Center 2, Long Island City, NY 11101.

Muebles Dul SA
Pol. Can Coll. Vial 2, Naves 2,4,6, 08185 Llissa de Vall, Barcelona, Spain.

Nava Milano SpA
Via Martin Lutero 5, Milan 20126, Italy. *Outlets* Canada: The Olann Corporation, 339 Lesmill Road, Don Mills, Ontario M3B 2V1. Finland: Motto Co., 10 Hietalahden Katu, Helsinki 00180. France: Telefrance International SA, 20 passage Alexandrine, Paris 75011. Japan: Christy Associates, Chez Azabu 1F 4-14-12 Ishiazabu, Minato-ku, Tokyo 106. Spain: Juan Antonio Garate-Batu, C/ Felipe II 28, 28009 Madrid. UK: Authentics, 42 Shelton Street, London WC2H 9HZ. USA: Nava US Inc., 50 Main Street, Suite 1000, White Plains, NY 10606. West Germany: Design Distribution, Oberstrasse 2, 3000 Hanover 1.

Nichii Department Stores
Daiichikango Bank Bldgs, 3-29 Chome, Kitakyutaro-machi, Higashi-ku, Osaka, Japan.

Nichinan
1599-10 Yoshioka, Ayase City, Kanagawa-ken 252, Japan.

Nobilis Fontan
38 rue Bonaparte, 75006 Paris, France. *Outlets* Italy: Nobilis Fontan, Largo Treves 5, 121 Milan. Spain: Arte 2000, Don Ramon de la Cruz 40, Madrid. UK: Nobilis Fontan 1-2 Cedar Studios, 45 Glebe Place, London SW3 5JE. West Germany: Nobilis Fontan, Hebwigstrasse 9, 8000 Munich.

Noto
Via Vigevano 8, 20144 Milan, Italy. *Outlets* Denmark: Decasa, Hyskenstraade 3, 2-1207 Copenhagen. France: Protis, 77-101 avenue du Vieux Chemin St Denis, 92230 Gennevilliers. Japan: Ambiente International Inc., Sumimoto Seimei Bldg 3-1-30, Minamiaoyama, Minato-ku, Tokyo 107. The Netherlands: Surplus PVBA, Zwarte Zusterstraat 9, 9000 Ghent. Spain: Casimiro Fernandez, Urbanizacion Soto de Llanera, Asturias. Switzerland: Schreinerei Anderegg AG, Olensbachstrasse 7, 9631 Ulisbach, Toggensburg. UK: Aram Designs Ltd, 3 Kean Street, London WC2B 4AT. USA: Modern Age Galleries Ltd, 795 Broadway, New York, NY 10003. West Germany:

Quartett GmbH, Haupsstrasse 95, 3004 Isernhagen F.B.

Novalia Srl
Zona Industriale, Via Cividale, Moimacco 33040, Udine, Italy. *Outlet* France: Nourissat Pierre, 33 avenue des Champes Elysees, 75008 Paris.

Nuno Corporation
Axis B1, 5-17-1 Roppongi, Minato-ku, Tokyo 106, Japan.

Olympus Optical Co. Ltd
1-22-2 Nishi-shinjuku, Tokyo, Japan. *Outlets* France: Son Cine Optique Photo SA, 27/33 rue d'Antoine, Silie L-165, 94533 Rungis-Cedex. Italy: Polyphoto SpA, Via dei Gracchi 8, 20146 Milan. The Netherlands: Olympus Nederland BV, Hoogstraat 43, 3001 Rotterdam. Spain: Commercial & Industrial Ros SA, Emilio Munoz 51, 28037 Madrid. Sweden: Olympus Optical AB, Industrigatan 14-18, 21214 Malmo. UK: Olympus Optical (UK) Ltd, 2-8 Honduras Street, London EC1Y 0TY. USA: Olympus Corporation, Crossway Park, West Woodbury, NY 11797. West Germany: Olympus Optical Co. (Europa) GmbH, Wendenstrasse 14-16, 2000 Hamburg 70.

OMK Design Ltd
30 Stephen Street, London W1P 1PN, UK. *Outlets* Austria: Pro Domo, Flachgasse 35-37, 1151 Vienna. Belgium: Ardeco International Belgium, avenue Général de Gaulle 47, 1050 Brussels. Canada: Italinteriors Ltd, 359 King Street East, Toronto, Ontario M5A 1L1. Finland: Funktio, Lonnrotinkatu 7, Helsinki. France: Protis, 67-101 avenue Vieux Chemin St Denis, 92230 Gennevilliers. Japan: Nova Oshima, 9-6-14 Akasaka, Minato-ku, Tokyo 107. The Netherlands: Interlinea, Weeresteinstraat 49, 2182 GR Hillegom. Norway: Italian House, Oeverland Garden, Ringeriksvelen 123, 1340 Bekkestua. Spain: Kaes Internacional SA, Nafarroa Kalea 24 Bajo, 20800 Zarauz (Guipuzcoa). South Africa: Innovation, PO Box 4621, Cape Town. Sweden: Inside AB, PO Box 7689, 10396 Stockholm. Switzerland: Design Agentur, Hafnerstrasse 47, 8005 Zurich. USA: Gullans International Inc., IDC 30-30 Thomson Avenue, Space 407, Long Island City, NY 11101. West Germany: Andreas Weber, Nymphenburger Strasse 79, 8000 Munich 19.

One Off Ltd
39 Shelton Street, London WC2, UK.

Orrefors Glasbruk
Box 8, 38040 Orrefors, Sweden. *Outlets* Argentina: Steinthal SAIC, Arengreen 1039/41, 1405 Buenos Aires. Australia: Orrefors Australia Pty Ltd, PO Box 701, Chatswood 2067. Austria: Criposi, Industriezentrum NO Sud, 2351 Vienna Neudorf. Belgium: Baeyens SA, rue de Laeken 162, 1000 Brussels. Denmark: Orrefors Sea Danmark A/S, Lyngbygardsvej 38, Lyngby, 8220 Brabrand. France: Armige, 30 avenue Amiral Lemonnier, 78160 Marly le Roi. Greece: Joanna Samaropoulos EE, Crustal Imports, Aristotelous Street 65, 15232 Athens. Hong Kong: MacNab Drummond Ltd, Unit D, 9/F Lladro Centre, 72-80 Hoi Yuen Road, Kwun Tong, Kowloon. Italy: Messulam SpA, Via Rovigno 13, 20125 Milan. Japan: J. Osawa & Co. Ltd, 2-8 Shibaura 4-Chome, Minato-ku, Tokyo 108. The Netherlands: Postava-Continent BV, Burg Van Baaklaan 21, 3648 XS Wilnis. New Zealand: Moore, Wheeler & Co., PO Box 527, Wellington 5. Norway:

Orrefors orge AS, Drammensvn 51, 0271 Oslo 2. Portugal: Carlos Figuerola, Avenue de Roma 12D, 1000 Lisbon. Singapore: Pacific Kigyo Enterprise Pte. Ltd, RM 01, 11th Floor, Far East Shopping Centre, 545 Orchard Road, Singapore 0923. Spain: Paulino SL, Plaza Mayor 24, Salamanca. Switzerland: Orrefors (Schweiz) AG, Postfach 200, 5034 Suhr. UK: Dexam International Ltd, Haslemere, Surrey GU27 3QP. USA: Orrefors Crystal Gallery, 58 East 57th Street, New York, NY 10022. West Germany: Orrefors Glasbruk GmbH, Elbestrasse 50, 4330 Mulheim-am-Ruhr.

Ospag AG
3 Goethegasse, Vienna 1015, Austria.

PAF Srl
Via Edison 118, 20019 Settimo Milanese, Italy.

Pallucco Srl
Via Salaria 1265, 00138 Rome, Italy. *Outlets* Belgium: Tradix, 104 avenue Louis Lepoutre, 1060 Brussels. France: Ready Made, 40 rue Jacob, 75006 Paris. Japan: Arc International Isugarucho, Kamanzadori Nakagyoku, Kyoto 604. The Netherlands: Hansje Kalff, 8 Puttensenstraat, 1118 JE Anstelveen. West Germany: Abitare, 3-5 Auf dem Berlich, 5000 Cologne 1.

Elio Palmisano
Edizioni Tessili, Via Stra Madonna C.P. 142, 21047 Saronno, Milan, Italy.

Pelikan AG
Kreuzer Postfach 103, 3000 Hanover 1, West Germany.

Perobell
Avenue Arraona 23, 08205 Sabadell, Barcelona, Spain.

Poul Petersen
Vesterbrogade 47, 1 sal, 1620 Copenhagen V, Denmark.

Philips NV
Building SX, P.O. Box 218, 5600 MD Eindhoven, The Netherlands. *Outlets* Austria: Osterreichische Philips Industrie GmbH, 64 Triester Strasse, 1100 Vienna. Belgium: NV Philips, 2 De Brouckereplein, PO Box 218, 1000 Brussels. Denmark: Philips Elapparat AS, 80 Pragsboulevard, 2300 Copenhagen. East Germany: Philips GmbH, Unternehmensbereich Haustechnik, 19 Kilianstrasse, 8500 Nurnberg. Finland: OY Philips AB, 8 Kaivokatu, Helsinki. France: SA Philips Industriale et Commerciale, 50 avenue ‹Montaigne, 75380 Paris. Italy: Philips Italia SA, Piazza IV Novembre 3, 20100 Milan. Japan: Philips Industrial Development and Consultants Co. Ltd, Shuwa, Shinagawa Building, 26-33 Takanawa 3-Chome, Minato-ku, Tokyo 108. Norway: Norsk AS Philips, PO Box 5040, 6 Soerkedaksveien, Oslo 3. Spain: Philips Iberica SAE, 2 Martinez Villergas, Apartado 2065, 28027 Madrid. Sweden: Philips Norden AB, 115 84 Stockholm. UK: Philips Electrical and Associated Industries Ltd, Arundel Great Court, 8 Arundel Street, London WC2 3DT. USA: North American Philips Corporation, 100 East 42nd Street, New York, NY 10017. West Germany: Allgemeine Deutsche Philips Ind. GmbH, 94 Steindamm, 2000 Hamburg.

Plus Corporation
1-20-11 Otawa, Bunkyo-ku, Tokyo, Japan.

Poggi SNC
Via Campania 5, 27100 Pavia, Italy.

Poltrona Frau SpA
SS77 KM 74, 500, 62029 Tolentino, Macerata, Italy. *Outlets* France : Poltrona Frau France Sarl, 242 bis boulevard St Germain, 75007 Paris. The Netherlands: Poltrona Frau Benelux, 9 Parkstraat, 4818 SJ Breda. Switzerland: Seleform AG, 8 G. Maurerstrasse, 8702 Zollikon. USA: Poltrona Frau USA Corp., 14 East 60th Street, New York, NY 10022. West Germany: Andreas Jaek, 3 Neuestrasse, 2900 Oldenburg.

Présence Paris
Viale della Repubblica 9B, 42019 Scandiano (RE), Italy.

Punt Mobles
Islas Baleares, 48 Pol, Ind. Fte del Jarro, 46980 Paterna, Valencia, Spain. *Outlets* Austria: Otto Dunkelblum, Herrengasse 6/7/3, 1010 Vienna. Denmark: Frank Rasmussen, Hummeltoften 49, 2830 Virum. France: Dominique Devoto, 47 rue Henri Barbusse, 75224 Paris Cedex 05. The Netherlands: AMDA, Oosternoutlaan 37, 1181 AL Amselveen. Sweden: Sten Bergstroem, Liljekovanjens Wag 9, 13200 Saltsjo-boo. Switzerland: Claudia Marlier-Pollo, Rebbergstrasse 40, 8102 Oberengstringen. UK: Maison Design Ltd, 917-19 Fulham Road, London SW6 5HU. USA: Susana Macarron Imports, 934 Grayson Street, Berkeley, CA 94710. West Germany: Traudel Comte, Alfred Drexel Strasse 1, 8000 Munich 50.

Ritva Puotila
Woodnotes, Westendintie 69, 02160 Espoo, Finland. *Outlet* Italy: Finn Form, Viale Montesanto 4, 20124 Milan.

Quattrifolio SpA
Via Anna Kuliscioff 36, Milan 20152, Italy. *Outlets* Austria: Watch Company, Nubdorferstrasse 46-48 1/29, 1090 Vienna. Belgium: Carla Doesburg PVBA, Rechtstraat 178, 9108 Lokeren Eksaarde. Canada: Les Importations Volt, 368 rue Guy, Montreal, Quebec H3J 1S6. Denmark: Plus Collection, Glasmestervej 33, 5772 Kvaerndrup. France: Affinitées, 17 rue de Miromesnil, Faubourg St Honore, 75008 Paris. Greece: Casa Oggi, 118 Tsimiski Street, 54621 Thessaloniki. Japan: Casa Luce Inc., 1-4-2 Minamiaoyama, Minato-ku, Tokyo 017. Spain: Kaes Internacional SA, Av. de Navarra, 24 Bajo, 20800 Zarauz, Guipuzcoa. Sweden: C & B Interiors, P.O. Box 26050, 10046 Stockholm. UK: GEC Lighting Ltd, Westminster Business Square, Durham Street, London SE11 5JA. West Germany: Wolfgang Schonhard, 11 Rathausstrasse, 2072 Bargteheide.

Red Square Design
150 West 11th Street, New York, NY 10011, USA.

Refim SpA
Via Maddalena 6, Paina di Giussano 20030, Milan, Italy.

Rica Basagoiti Alfombras SA
7 Nuñez de Balboa, Madrid 28001, Spain.

Ross Consumer Electronics
Silver Road, White City Industrial Estate, London W12 7SG, UK.

Michael Rowe
401½ Workshops, 401½ Wandsworth Road, London SW8, UK.

Rowenta-Werke GmbH
Waldstrasse 202-256, 06050 Offenbach AM, West Germany. *Outlets* France: Rowenta France SA, PO Box 3026, 25045 Besançon. Italy: Rowenta Italia SpA, Via Venini 23, 20127 Milan. Japan: SEB Japan Co. Ltd, T.O.C. Bldg, 7-22-17 Nishigotanda-Shinagawa, Ku-Tokyo 141. The Netherlands: Rowenta Nederland BV, Generatorstraat 6A, 3903 LJ Veenendaal. Spain: Rowenta España SA, 151 Valencia, 08011 Barcelona. UK: Rowenta UK Ltd, 9 The Street, Ashtead, Surrey KT21 2AD. USA: Rowenta Inc., 281 Albany Street, Cambridge, Massachusetts 02139.

Ruckstühl AG
4900 Langenthal, Switzerland. *Outlet* UK: Hometex Trade Ltd, Sedbergh Chambers, 5 Chantry Drive, Ilkley, West Yorks. LS29 9HU.

Ruko AS
20 Marielundvej, Herlev 2730, Denmark. *Outlets* Bahrain: Elames Builders Hardware, P.O. Box 26095, Manama. Finland: Assa OY, Riipilantie 1, 01730 Vantea. Iceland: Velar & Verkfari HF and Gudmunder Jonsson HF, Bolholt 6, IS-121 Reykjavik. Kuwait: Hamad & Muller Co., PO Box 26043, 13121 Safat. The Netherlands: Stenman Holland BV, Energiestraat 2, 3900 AA Veenendaal. Norway: Lexow AS, PO Box 55, Kverner, 0136 Oslo. Sweden: Assa AB, Kungsgatan 71, 63105 Eskilstuna. UK: Assa Ltd, 75 Sumner Road, Croydon, Surrey CR0 3LN. USA: Assa Inc., 1235 Naperville Drive, Romeoville, Illinois 60441. West Germany: Assa-Ruko GmbH, Vogelsanger Strasse 187, 5000 Cologne 30.

Sabat Selección SA
c/o IDPA Avda. Coll del Portell 96-100, Bajos 1, 08024 Barcelona, Spain.

Sabattini Argenteria SpA
Via Don Capiaghi 2, 22070 Bregnano, Como, Italy. *Outlets* Japan: New Robin Co. Ltd, 2-11-2 Chome, Kajimachi, Kokurakita-ku, 802 Kitakyushushi-Fukuoka. The Netherlands: Mobica PVBA, Gossetlaan 50, 1720 Groot, Bijaard. UK: Objects, 49 Parliament Street, Harrogate, North Yorks., HG1 2RG. USA: Italarte, 4203 West Alamos 106, Fresno, CA 93711. West Germany: Sabattini Deutschland, 50 Kennedyallee, Frankfurt.

Sanistyl
33 avenue du Maréchal de Lattre de Tassigny, 94127 Fontenay S/Bois, Cedex Paris, France.

Santa & Cole
Santisima Trinidad Del Monte 10, 08017 Barcelona, Spain. *Outlets* Austria: Ronni Kufferle, 7 Rennagasse, 1010 Vienna. Italy: Roberto Sorba, 29/5 Corso Chieri, Turin 10132. The Netherlands: Binnen, 82 Keizersgracht, 1015 CT Amsterdam. West Germany: Susanne Wirth, 168 Herbeusstraat, 6211RH Maastrich.

Sasaki Glass Co. Ltd
2-2-6 Nihonbashi-Bakurocho, Chuo-ku, Tokyo, Japan.

Satō
Designobjekt Eppendorfer, Landstrasse 120, 2000 Hamburg 20, West Germany.

Sawaya & Moroni SpA
Via Manzoni 11, 20121 Milan, Italy. *Outlet* UK: The Ikon Corporation, B5L Metropolitan Wharf, Wapping Wall, London E1 9SS.

Scan Light BV
30 Gorzen, 3831 GE Leusden, The Netherlands.

Sellex Innovator SA
Apartado 1366, San Sebastian, Spain.

SIG Workshop Inc.
3-4 Asahigaoka, Mattou-shi, Ishikawa-ken 924, Japan.

Sirrah SpA
Via Molino Rosso 8, 40026 Imola, Italy.

Skipper SpA
Via Serbelloni 1, 20122 Milan, Italy. *Outlets* Belgium: Skipper Benelux, 78 avenue Louise, 6069 Brussels. France: Gennaro Delisanti, 17 rue des Closeaux, 77240 Vert St Denis. The Netherlands: Koos Rijkse, Tr. Chirstinalaan 1, 7437 XZ Bathmen. UK: Atrium Ltd, 22-24 St Giles High Street, London WC2H 8LN. West Germany: Rohoff Edgar, Reinhard Hoppe Strasse 6-8, 6900 Heidelberg 25.

Skovgaard & Frydensberg
Lille Kirkestraede 3, 1072 Copenhagen K, Denmark.

Sony Corporation
6-7-35 Kitashinagawa, Shinagawa-ku, Tokyo 141, Japan.

Spend Co. Ltd
1-11-15 Shitaya, Taito-ku, Tokyo 110, Japan.

Vic Stannard
40 The Keep, Blackheath, London SE3 0AF, UK.

Stendig International
305 East 63rd Street, New York, NY 10021, USA.

Stildomus SpA
Via Laurentina 27, Pomezia 00040, Rome, Italy. *Outlet* Spain: Kaes SA, 24 Avenida de Navarra, Bajo-Zarautz 20800.

Stilnovo Srl
Via F. Borromini 12, Lainate 20020, Milan, Italy. *Outlets* France: Jean-Gabriel Robin, chemin des Sables, 69970 Chaponnay. Greece: Luce Design, 8-10B Bouboulinas Street, Callithea, 176-75 Athens. The Netherlands: Indoor BV, Paulus Potterstraat 22-24, 1071 DA Amsterdam. Switzerland: Guido Mayer, 1312 Eclepens-Gare VD, Case Postale. USA: Hampstead, 19772 MacArthur Blvd, Suite 203, Irvine, CA 92715. West Germany: Georg Hartl, Siedlungsweg 10, 8894 Hollenbach.

Synapse/Technology Design
10830 Main Street, Bellevue 98004, Washington, USA.

Tagono
Apdo. Coreos 382, 08190 San Cugat del Valles, Barcelona, Spain.

Takata Inc.
511 Hayakawa, Takaoka-shi, Toyama-ken 933, Japan.

Taller de Arquitectura
18 rue de l'Université, 75007 Paris, France.

Telene SpA
Strada Padana Superiore 53, Cernusco S/N, Milan 20063, Italy.

Thailand Carpet Manufacturing
Srivikorn Bldg, 18/8 Sukhumvitsoiqi, Bangkok, Thailand.

Gebruder Thonet GmbH
1 Michael Thonetstrasse, Frankenberg 3558, Hessen, West Germany.

Tonelli Srl
Via della Produzione 61, 61025 Montelabbate (PS), Italy.

Toucan
25 Balfour Road, London, UK. *Outlet* UK: Quip Lighting, Westbourne Grove, London W11.

Toulemonde Bochart
Z.I. de Villemilan, 14-16 boulevard Arago, 91320 Wissous, France.

Toyo Sash Co. Ltd
2-1-1 Oshima Koto-ku, Tokyo, Japan.

Transtam
63 Maria Cubi, 08006 Barcelona, Spain.

J. Tresserra Design SL
42 calle Freixa, Barcelona 08021, Spain. *Outlets* France: Biobject, 6 rue Domat, 75005 Paris. Japan: Akane International, 5-10-15 Higashinakano, Nakano-ku, Tokyo. UK: Mary Fox Linton Ltd, 249 Fulham Road, London SW3 6HY.

Umbra
2358 Midland Avenue, Scarborough, Ontario M1S 1P8, Canada. *Outlet* Umbra USA Inc., Gateway Metroport, Gate 1, 1951 Hamburg Turnpike, Lackawana, NY 14218.

Unifor SpA
Via Isonzo 1, 22078 Turate, Como, Italy.

Up & Up Srl
Via Acquale 3, 54100 Massa, Italy. *Outlets* Austria and Germany: Giovanni Marelli, Casella Postale 148, 20036 Meda Milan, Italy. Belgium: Trueno, 78 OL Vrouwstraat, 2800 Mechelen. Canada: Marble Trend, Unit 3, 2050 Steeles Avenue West, Dowsview, Ontario. France: Roger von Bary, 18 rue Lafitte, 75009 Paris; Studio Enea, 2 place St Sulpice, 75009 Paris. Japan: Everfast Ltd, Iwoki Bldg 9-6-12 Akasaka, Minato-ku, Tokyo; Joint Inc., Daikanyama-Parkside-Vill. 207-9-8, Sarugakucho, Shibuya-ku, Tokyo 150. USA: Inside, 715 5th Street, San Diego, CA 92101; Italdesign Center Inc., 8687 Melrose Avenue Suite 547, Los Angeles, CA 90069; Design Studio Inter Inc., 908 Linden Avenue, Winnekta, Illinois 60007; Frederick Williams, 200 Lexington Avenue, New York, NY 10016; Modern Living, 4063 Relwood Avenue, Los Angeles, CA 90066.

Vapor SA
Granada 30, 08005 Barcelona (Poble Nou), Spain.

Venini SpA
Fondamenta Vetrai 50, 30141 Murano, Venice, Italy. *Outlets* Denmark: Erik Rosendhal AS, Lundtoftevej 1/C, 2800 Lyngby, Copenhagen. France: Jean-Gabriel Robin, chemin des Sables, 69970 Chaponnay. The Netherlands: Kees Biermans, Parkstraat 9, 4818 SJ Breda. Switzerland: Guido Mayer SA, 9 route du Port Franc, 1003 Lausanne. USA: Hampstead Investments Inc., 19772 MacArthur Blvd, Suite 203, Irvine, CA 92715. West Germany: Graf Bethusy-Huc Vertriebs, Hans Sachs Strasse 1, 8033 Krailling.

Vereinigte Werkstätten AG
31 Ridler Strasse, 8000 Munich 12, West Germany. *Outlets* Austria: Hans Taus, Gordis Einrichtungen, 9 Porzellangasse, Vienna 1090. Denmark: Finn Sloth, 1 Heilsmindevej, Charlottenlund 2920. France: Claude Cenet, Hery sur Alby, Alby sur Cheran 74550. Italy: Imexa Italia SNC, Via Matteotti 40, Montagnan 35044, Padua. The Netherlands: Bob Smit, Design for Living, 52 Jasonstraat, Amsterdam KH 1007. Spain: Idea Mueble SA, 185 Via Augusta, Barcelona 21. USA: Lighting Association, 305 East 63rd Street, New York, NY 10002.

Vest Leuchten GmbH
Piaristengasse 21, Vienna 1080, Austria. *Outlets* Spain: Hustadt Iluminacion, C/Bolivia 340 Local 60, Barcelona 08019. Switzerland: Trend Design, Konsumstrasse 2, Ruti/ZH 8630. UK: Troika Ltd, Birmingham Road, Stratford-upon-Avon, Warwickshire CV37 0HU. West Germany: Handelsagentur Wolfgang Brunotte, Hohe Strasse 40, 6330 Wetzlar 13.

Mario Villa Inc.
3908 Magazine Street, New Orleans, LA 70115, USA.

Vitra International AG
Klunenfeldstrasse 20, Postfach 4127 Birsfelden, Switzerland. *Outlets* France: Vitra Sarl, 59 avenue d'Iena, 75116 Paris. The Netherlands: Vitra Nederland BV, 527 Strawinskylaan, 1077 XX Amsterdam. UK: Vitra Ltd, 13 Grosvenor Street, London W1X 9FB. USA: Vitra Seating Inc., c/o Stendig International Inc., 305 East 63rd Street, New York, NY 10021. West Germany: Vitra GmbH, 7858 Weil am Rhein.

Vorwerk & Co. Teppichwerke KG
Kuhlmannstrasse 11, 3250 Hameln 1, West Germany.

Wakita Hi-Tecs Inc.
3-3-46 Nishikimachi, Onojoshi, Fukuoka, Japan.

Franz Wittmann KG
3492 Etsdorf-am-Kamp, Austria. *Outlets* France: Horas International, 150 rue Championnet, 75018 Paris. Italy: Wittmann Italia Srl, Via E. Filiberto 10, 45011 Adria, RO. Japan: AIDEC, 28 Mori Bldg, 4-16-13 Nishiazabu, Minato-ku, Tokyo. The Netherlands: Art Collection BV, 63 Weijland, 2415 Nieuwerbrug. Sweden: Inside Galleria, 37 Hamnagatan, 11147 Stockholm. UK: MW United Ltd, 19 Dacre Street, London SW1 0DJ. USA: Stendig International, 410 East 62nd Street, New York, NY 10021. West Germany: Franz Wittmann KG, 20a Konigstrasse, 6729 Worth.

Wogg AG
im Grund 16, 5405 Baden-Dattwil, Switzerland. *Outlets* Japan: Nova Oshima, 9-6-14 Akasaka, Minato-ku, Tokyo 107. UK: HNB Systems, Whittington House, 19-30 Alfred Place, London WC1E 7EA. USA: Cumberland Furniture Corp., 36 36th Street, Long Island City, NY 11106.

Woka Lamps Vienna
16 Singerstrasse, 1010 Vienna, Austria. *Outlets* France: Altras, Roger von Bary, 18 rue Lafitte, 75009 Paris. Italy: Marina de Nardo, Via Lincoln 41, Milan. Sweden: Ide Individuell, 8 Norra Liden, 41118 Goteborg. UK: MW

United Ltd, 19 Dacre Street, London SW1 0DJ. USA: George Kovacs Inc., 24 West 40th Street, New York, NY 10018.

Yamada
3-16-12 Sotokanda Chyodaku, Tokyo 101, Japan.

Yamaha Corporation
10-1 Nakazawa-cho, Hamamatsu 430, Japan.

Yamasho Casting Co. Ltd
13 Imono-machi, Yamagata City, Yamagata 990-01, Japan.

Yoshikin
Sahara Heights 18-13, Natsumi 2-Chome, Funabashi, Chiba, Japan.

Zani & Zani SpA
Via del Porto 51-53, Toscolano Maderno 25088, Brescia, Italy.

Zanotta SpA
Via Vittorio Veneto 57, 20054 Nova Milanese, Italy. *Outlets* Australia: Arredorama International Pty Ltd, 1 Ross Street, Glebe, NSW ø2037. Austria: Prodomo, 35-37 Flachgasse, 1060 Vienna. Belgium: Zaira Mis, 35 bolevard Saint Michel, 1040 Brussels. Denmark: Paustian, 2 Kalkbraendrilbskaj, 2100 Copenhagen. France: Giuseppe Cerutti, 1 Località Grand Chemin, St Christophe 11020, AO Italy. Japan: Nova Oshima Co. Ltd, Sakakura Bldg, Akasaka, Minato-ku, Tokyo. The Netherlands: Hansje Kalff, 8 Puttensestraat, 1181 JE Amstelveen. Norway: Bente Holm, 64 Parkveien, Oslo 2. Spain: Bd Ediciones de diseño, 291 Mallorca, 08037 Barcelona. Sweden: Inside, 37 Hamngatan, 11147 Stockholm. Switzerland: Peter Kaufmann, 123 Rychenbergstrasse, 8400 Winterhur. UK: The Architectural Trading Co. Ltd, 219-29 Shaftesbury Avenue, London WC2H 8AR. USA: International Contract Furnishings, 305 East 63rd Street, New York, NY 10021. West Germany: Fulvio Folci, 14 Dahlienweg, 4000 Düsseldorf 30.

Alan Zoeftig & Co. Ltd
Bude, Cornwall EX23 8QN, UK. *Outlets* Australia: Minale, Tattersfield & Partners Pty Ltd, 212 Boundary street, Spring Hill, Brisbane QLD 4000. France: Design Strategy Sarl, Villa Souchet, 105 avenue Gambetta, 75020 Paris. Italy: Minale, Tattersfield & Partners, Via Petrarca 4, Milan 20123. Japan: Minale, Tattersfield & Partners, TCD Institute, 301 Tengyu Bldg, 5-14-7 Esaka-cho, Suita-shi, Osaka. Spain: Minale, Tattersfield & Partners, Garcia Ruescas Comunicacion, Gran Via 55-6 G, 28013 Madrid. UK: Minale, Tattersfield & Partners, The Courtyard, 37 Sheen Road, Richmond, Surrey TW9 1AJ. USA: Minale, Tattersfield & Partners, Cordis Inc., 12 Charles Lane, New York, NY 10014. West Germany: Minale, Tattersfield & Partners, Spriesterbach & Hild GmbH, Deutzer Freiheit 49, 5000 Cologne 21.

PUBLICATIONS

AUSTRALIA

Belle (bi-monthly) Showcase for contemporary Australian architecture and interior design, with a round-up that includes many imported influences.
Design World (quarterly) Technical and educational articles covering the design world in the Antipodes.
Interior Design (bi-monthly) Dedicated to decoration, with a mixture of articles on avant-garde designs and traditional interiors.
Vogue Living (ten issues a year) Lively, glossy lifestyle magazine on decoration and design.

CANADA

Canadian Interiors (eight issues a year) Quality magazine targeted at professionals with an interest in architecture and their environment. English text.
Contract Magazine (bi-monthly) Geared towards qualified designers, it deals with the planning and management of interiors for commercial establishments and public institutions. English text.
Décormag (monthly) Deals with interior decoration offering articles on different styles and editorials on specific rooms. French text.
Designs (quarterly) With a text in French and English this is the first and only bilingual trade magazine in Quebec. It deals with residential and commercial furniture, lighting, materials and interior decoration.

DENMARK

Arkitekten (23 issues a year) and **Arkitektur** (eight issues a year) Edited by the Danish Architectural Press for the professional federations of architects and building contractors.
Bo Bedre (monthly) Translates into English as "Live Better", precisely the editorial policy behind this consumer home-interest magazine.
Design from Scandinavia (annual) For the past 18 years a useful index of designers and manufacturers against a background of illustrated stories of architectural interest.
Fair Facts (quarterly) Published in Danish and English, the magazine deals with the major European furniture fairs and exhibitions.
Living Architecture (bi-annual) Scandinavia's best-looking glossy magazine on buildings and their interiors, by the celebrated photographer and architect Per Nagel. Published with English text.
Rum og Form (annual) "Space and Form", edited by the Danish Association of Furniture Designers and Interior Designers.
Tools (ten issues a year) Tabloid-format magazine in English produced by the Danish Design Council, with lively interpretations of product design worldwide.

FINLAND

Design in Finland (annual) Published by the Finnish Foreign Trade Association to promote the year's products abroad, with good-quality illustrations and an index of manufacturers and designers.
Form Function, Finland (quarterly) A magazine concerned with mass production and functional design in Finland, aimed at the export market, published by the Finnish Society of Craft and Design.

Muoto (monthly) Magazine on interior and industrial design, with articles on individual designers.
Space & Place (annual) Contract furniture collections presented by the Furniture Exporters' Association.

FRANCE

Architectural Digest (monthly) French version of the American magazine; see USA.
Art et Décoration (monthly) Concerned primarily with the plastic arts and interior decoration.
L'Atelier (ten issues a year) Specializes in objects, gadgets and daring designs.
BAT (monthly) Excellent coverage of design and advertising in fields as diverse as graphic design, videos and interiors.
Beaux Arts (monthly) This celebrated art and architectural magazine has recently included contemporary design articles.
Les Carnets du Design (irregular) Thematic presentation of various subjects concerned with design and interior decoration, such as chairs, tableware, sofas, etc.
City Magazine International (ten issues a year) Lifestyle magazine dealing with design, interiors and fashion for the upwardly mobile.
Créé (monthly) Leading professional design magazine with an architectural background.
Décoration Internationale (monthly, but erratic) Eclectic publication in its tenth year, covering houses, objects and painters in exotic locations.
Intramuros (monthly) Large-format black-and-white design and interiors magazine with in-depth interviews with people ahead of the pack. Technical information, freshly presented, is aimed at professionals, but the layout makes it generally appealing.
La Maison de Marie Claire (monthly) *Le style français* in a glossy magazine in which everything from plates to pastries is chic.
Maison et Jardin (monthly) High-life review of famous interiors and gardens with specific design articles included in most issues.
Maison Française (monthly) Covers furniture, interiors and architecture with special regional bias and promotional features.
Show Room (bi-monthly) A brand new publication started in 1990 containing useful information on design exhibitions and fairs for the professional market. Sold by subscription only.
Vogue Décoration (quarterly) Weighty and opulent interiors magazine with beautiful presentation and in-depth interviews.

ISRAEL

Binyan Diur (three issues a year) Design and interior architecture articles with interviews and special projects, aimed at the domestic market.

ITALY

Abitare (ten issues a year) English text published alongside the Italian in a heavily merchandized, up-to-the-minute round-up of new designs. Architects and interior designers look to its photographic stories for an international perspective. Some issues are devoted to a single country.
L'Arca (ten issues a year) Recently launched publication, dedicated to architecture, design and visual communication, with technical monographs.
AReA (bi-monthly) Design as art magazine.

concentrating on objects and decoration for the interior. Interviews with designers, artists, architects and students.
Casa Vogue (eleven issues a year) Definitive listing of new trends-in-the-making around the world in interiors, decoration, houses and furniture. An invaluable talent-spotters' magazine, famous for the inspired art direction of its merchandizing stories.
Disegno (quarterly) Technical, covering the tools, instruments and software needed for graphic and industrial design.
Domus (monthly) Giò Ponti founded this authoritative magazine on architecture, interiors, furniture and art; now Mario Bellini is its outspoken, informed editor. More textual than visual, it is consulted by architects and designers who submit schemes.
Gap Casa (monthly) Trade figures and commercial marketing strategies sit alongside the product lines in this stylish magazine aimed at retailers.
Gran Bazaar (monthly, but irregular) Environmental topics and architecture in a specialized formula, with monographs on general and philosophical themes, from the point of view of design, image or art.
In Design (bi-monthly) Bi-lingual (English/ Italian) review of architectural projects, design and interior design, aimed at a specialist market.
Interni (monthly) More than its name suggests, a round-up of products relating to external, as well as interior, design. Has interesting supplements, catalogues of addresses and international editions.
Modo (ten issues a year) Articles and opinions on design in depth, with a directory of products and producers, created by the omnipresent Alessandro Mendini. Regarded as the magazine of the avant garde in Italian design.
Ottagono (quarterly) A review of architecture, interior design, furniture and industrial design worldwide, published in Italian and English editions by eight Italian manufacturers – Arflex, Artemide, Bernini, Boffi, Cassina, Flos, ICF and Tecno. Leading writers contribute to this small-format publication.

JAPAN

A & U: Architecture and Urbanism (monthly) Highly professional, if conservative, coverage of international architecture. Aimed at professional architects and designers.
AXIS (bi-monthly) First-rate international publication with coverage of a wide variety of furniture, product and interior design projects, with a special interest in Italy. Some English summaries.
Design News (eight issues a year) Aimed at professionals and sold on subscription, this has a good coverage of Japanese design projects with an emphasis on industrial and product design.
FP: Fusion Planning (bi-monthly) Emphasis leans towards architecture and interior design in this well-produced and edited magazine with a good selection of international design projects.
GA: Global Architecture (irregular) Editor Yukio Futagawa established this as the première photo-essay magazine of architecture worldwide.
Icon (monthly) Targeted at architects and designers in Japanese and English, an iconoclastic review of architecture, design, interiors and art.
Picabia (bi-monthly) The most recent addition to the style magazine market in Japan. Excellent editorial content and superb graphic design. Bi-lingual.
Portfolio (bi-monthly) A less glossy, slightly down-market version of AXIS with more emphasis on quirky urban interiors and architecture.

SD: Space Design (monthly) Interior space – a thoroughly Japanese magazine concept – with a broad international coverage of projects which fits into theme-edited issues.

W.IN.D (quarterly) International coverage of interior design – shops, restaurants and commercial space – with frequent special issues on non-superstar designers. Japanese only.

MEXICO

Magenta (quarterly) Produced by a private foundation to promote design, this is proof of the need for private initiative.

THE NETHERLANDS

Avenue (monthly) Stylish photo-reportage of cars, products, travel, lighting and furniture alongside avant-garde fashion.

Industrieel Ontwerpen (bi-monthly) Eminently technical and professional publication covering industrial design and product development.

Interior View Magazine (annual) Retrospective view of design and architecture over the past twelve months, with forecasts for the home-furnishing and interior design industries.

Textile View Magazine (quarterly) Predominantly fabrics for home furnishing with styling forecasts and articles on lifestyle and consumer psychology.

NEW ZEALAND

New Zealand Home Journal (monthly) A home-interest magazine with interior design coverage.

NORWAY

Byggekunst (eight issues a year) Covers building, landscape architecture and interior design.

Hjem & Fritid/Bonytt (monthly) A consumer magazine on interior design, aimed primarily at the wealthy connoisseur rather than the professional.

Hus og Hem (quarterly) Glossy magazine on decoration and interiors.

Skala (monthly) Architecture and design from around the world.

SPAIN

Ardi (bi-monthly) Brilliantly art-directed publication introduces the best Spanish designers, architects, cartoonists and graphic artists to the world, alongside special reports on the international avant garde.

La Casa 16 de Marie Claire (monthly) Spanish edition of the French magazine, edited by Group 16.

Hogares (monthly) "Homes" is published in colour with photographic spreads on Spanish houses and interviews with Spanish designers.

De Diseño (monthly) Brainchild of Quim Larrea and Juli Capella, currently directors of Ardi. After a rigorous, risk-taking start, it later changed direction.

Futura (bi-annual) Covers art and design and is excellently printed in northern Spain.

I La Nave Va (fortnightly) Internationally published booklet in which the well-known Valencia group La Nave puts forth its latest multidisciplinary ideas. Private circulation only.

Nuevo Estilo (monthly) Major publication on design

and furniture, aimed at a wide public; not avant-garde, but the editing is exemplary.

ON Diseño (monthly) Pioneer in design, with articles on home-grown talent, and an international round-up of graphics and architecture.

SWEDEN

Arkitekten (monthly) A small, in-house official publication for the Federation of Architects and allied building trades in Sweden.

Arkitektur (ten issues a year) A round-up of architects' projects in Sweden, with plans and pictures.

Form (eight issues a year) The professional magazine for interior designers. Text in Swedish and English.

Kontur (monthly) Surveys industrial design with product information for the contract market.

Möbler & Miljö (ten issues a year) This specialist magazine, "Furniture and Environment", is read by the decision-makers who buy and make furnishings for interior designers.

Sköna Hem (quarterly) Sweden's showcase home-interest magazine with colourful photographic coverage of architecture and interior design.

SWITZERLAND

Textile Suisse (quarterly) Published by the Swiss Office for the Development of Trade, a review of the state of the textile business.

Werk, Bauen and Wohnen (monthly) Austere, sober publication on architecture and industrial design.

UK

Architects' Journal (weekly) The professional, opinionated and sometimes controversial magazine for British architects.

Architectural Review (monthly) A well-written and informed magazine which examines projects, with plans, worldwide.

Art and Design (monthly) Art, architecture, design, fashion, music, photography, news.

Blueprint (eleven issues a year) Fast-forward into what's being planned, built, assembled, launched or revived. Racy layouts in a large format, mostly black-and-white, with informed, hard-hitting comment.

Creative Review (monthly) Well-presented review of mainly graphic design, whether applied to computers, textiles or advertising.

Design (monthly) The official publication of the British Design Council, parochial and sometimes carping.

Design Week (weekly) Energetic design publication, highly agile in image and content with news and views on the industry.

Designers' Journal (ten issues a year) The enlightened companion to the *Architects' Journal*, aimed at a predominantly contract market with interviews covering all aspects of design from theatre to products.

Homes & Gardens (monthly) The home interest magazine equivalent to the high-street design shop, seen as inspirational by those who buy it.

House & Garden (monthly) Condé Nast's biggest-selling design and decoration magazine in the UK. Although the emphasis of the editorial is on interior decoration, the design and architectural information is strongly merchandized and it sponsors the annual competition "The New Designers".

Review (annual) Published by the Design Museum, this serves as an exhibition catalogue and a general

survey of new product design, with interviews with designers worldwide.

World of Interiors (eleven issues a year) *The* interiors magazine to be seen in, offering a voyeuristic tour around some of the world's most lavishly decorated homes, with international gallery listings that are wide-ranging and talent-spotting.

USA

Architectural Digest (six issues a year) An authoritative celebrity round-up of the lavish homes of the rich and famous, presented in a highly successful coffee-table format.

Architectural Record (monthly) A professional and trade-oriented architectural magazine.

HG (monthly) Ideas on decoration, design and architecture that follow fashion and the arts.

ID: International Design (bi-monthly) The industrial designers' product guide, with some coverage of the design industry, graphics and fashion.

Interiors (monthly) Rigorous and professional coverage of decoration for interior designers.

Metropolis (ten issues a year) The blueprint for Blueprint UK, this large-format tabloid with spirited news, views and ideas in the design world is creatively edited with a strong New York bias.

Metropolitan Home (monthly) An energetic trend-spotting magazine for the upwardly mobile, with fashions in furnishings and furniture presented by a young editorial team with a strong sense of direction. Plenty of consumer information.

Progressive Architecture (monthly) One of America's two heavyweight architectural journals, a forum for spirited debate.

Terrazzo (twice a year) Magazine dealing with architecture and design. Interviews and in-depth articles.

WEST GERMANY

Ambiente (bi-monthly) A consumer magazine on interior design.

Architektur und Wohnen (monthly) Interviews with the architects and owners of remarkable homes. It links professional and consumer interests, and contains exhaustively researched product reports.

Art Aurea (quarterly) Theme-related articles on art, design and fashion, published in German and English.

Design Report (bi-monthly) Factual magazine on the state of design in Germany, with reports, commentaries and interviews.

Form (quarterly) Lively articles discussing international design and the market-place.

Häuser (monthly) House case-histories, architectural portraits, design product round-ups and extensive floor plans. There is an English-language supplement.

MD Möbel Interior Design (monthly) Modest (black-and-white), interesting publication on furniture, with bold graphic covers.

Schöner Wohnen (monthly) The world of architecture and design in Germany, with reports from correspondents in all other major countries. Popular, informative and technical.

Select (quarterly) A photographic catalogue full of suggestive images, with special issues occasionally dedicated to particular cities.

Terrazzo (twice a year) German version of the Italian/US magazine.

Wolkenkratzer Art Journal (bi-monthly) Art design, image, architecture and music.

ACQUISITIONS

by Design Collections in 1989
Dates given in brackets refer to the dates of the designs
(from 1960 to the present day)

AUSTRIA

Austrian Museum of Applied Arts, Vienna
Eichinger Oder Knechtl: *Burning Table* (1989)
Manfred Nisslmüller: Set of Unwearable Jewellery (1987)
Ruudt Peters: bowl (1989)

DENMARK

Museum of Decorative Art, Copenhagen
Henning Andreasen: telephone, *danMark Classic* (1978)
Bang and Olufsen: *Pick-Up* (1980-82)
Bruel and Kjaer: studio microphones (1983-88)
L.M. Ericsson: telephone, *Ericofon* (1954 and 1976)
Knud Holscher: table lamp, *Stringline* (1976), service,
Manhattan (1985), sanitary fittings
Arne Jacobsen: sanitary fittings, *Vola*
T. Sarpaneva: dinner service, *More*
Sharp: radio/tape recorder (1980)
Siemens: mobile telephone, *NT 901-02*
Jan Tragardh: pick-up, *Concorde 20 Ortofon* (1979)

FRANCE

Musee des Arts Décoratifs, Paris
18 Août: under plate, *Chaud-froid* (1988).
Jean-Louis Barrault: fondu set, *Futura* (1986), manufactured
by Le Creuset, France
Mario Bellini: service, *Cupola* (1988), maufactured by
Rosenthal, West Germany
Andrea Branzi: silver jug (1988)
Zofia de Rostad: painted paper (1989), manufactured by
Essef, France
Guy de Rougemont: three plates (1988), manufactured by
Artcurial, France
Claude de Soria: pair of candlesticks (1989)
Sylvain Dubuisson: pair of candlesticks (1989),
manufactured by Creative Agents, France
August Fix: Appliqué in burnished steel (1970)
Kaj Frank: six drinking glasses (1960-74)
Elisabeth Garouste and Mattia Bonetti: chair, *Hiro-Hito* (1988)
Michaela Lange: breakfast service, *Fly High* (1988),
manufactured by Villeroy & Boch, West Germany
Jean and Jacqueline Lerat: two ceramic sculptures (1988)
Enzo Mari: cooking pot, *Mama* (1973), manufactured by Le
Creuset, France
Jean-Michel Meurice: service, *Tian* (1988), manufactured
by Artcurial, France
Kimpei Nakamura: tea pot (1985), manufactured by Sèvres,
France
Charlotte Perriand and Pierre Faucheux: bookshop stand
(1966)
James Pichette: plate (1988), manufactured by Multi
International, France
Editions Saluces: pair of door handles (1989)
Timo Sarpaneva: service, *Suomi* (1988), manufactured by
Rosenthal, West Germany
Max Sauze: table lamp (1970)
Richard Shaw: ceramic sculpture (1987), manufactured by
Sèvres, France
Betty Woodman: platter and vase (1987), manufactured by
Sèvres, France
Kansai Yamamoto: watch (1988)

JAPAN

There is no permanent design collection in Japan at the
present time, although there are a few private collections.

Several museums of modern art do have good examples of
contemporary, international design, but these almost
always have a practical purpose and are not part of their
displays. Temporary design exhibitions have been
increasing dramatically, however, and there is a very strong
possibility of a permanent design collection being formed.

THE NETHERLANDS

Museum Boymans-van Beuningen, Rotterdam
Willem Rietveld: *Pyramid Chairs* (1960), manufactured by
De Cirkel, Netherlands
Bořek Šípek: cheese dish, manufactured by Sussmuth
Glashutte, West Germany
Piet Stockmans: dinner service, *Fantasy* (1986),
manufactured by Mosa, Netherlands

SWEDEN

Nationalmuseum, Stockholm
Jonas Bohlin: cupboard, *Slottsbacken* (1987),
manufactured by Kallemo, Sweden
Torun Bulow-Hube: wrist-watch (1968), manufactured by
Georg Jensen, Denmark
Torun Bulow-Hube: table watch (1970), manufactured by
Georg Jensen, Denmark
Jan Dranger: chair, *Media* (1982), manufactured by Exellan
Produkter, Sweden
Stephan Gip: chair, *Blow Up* (1968), manufactured by
Hagaplast, Sweden
Yrjo Kukkapuro: armchair (1981-82), manufactured by
Avarte, Finland
Philippe Starck: armchair, *Wendy Wright* (1987),
manufactured by Disform, Spain

UK

Victoria and Albert Museum, London
Norbert Berghof, Michael Landes and Wolfgang Rank:
Frankfurt Cabinet (1985/6), manufactured by Draenert, West
Germany
Andre Dubreuil: *Spine Chair* (1988) and *Paris Chair* (1988),
manufactured by Andre Dubreuil, France
Norman Foster: table, *Nomos* (1986), manufactured by
Tecno, Italy
Shiro Kuramata: *Drawers in irregular form* (1970),
manufactured by Cappellini, Italy
Jasper Morrison: *Thinkingman's Chair* (1987),
manufactured by Aram Designs, UK

The Design Museum, London
Set up in the summer of 1989, the museum presents a series
of temporary exhibitions and collections following certain
themes. It also provides a study collection of about four
hundred objects, displayed and analysed in their social,
technological, commercial, aesthetic and economic
contexts. There is no permanent collection.

USA

The Art Institute of Chicago
Donald Judd: Library chair (1984), manufactured by Ichiro
Kato for Cooper Kato, Japan
Howard Meister: chair, *Learning her lie* (1982), USA
Forrest Myers: stool, *Brambler Seat* (1988), USA
Michele Oka Doner: table, *Terrible Table* (1988), USA
Peter Shire: table, *Rod and Transit* (1981), USA

Metropolitan Museum of Art, New York
Emilio Ambasz and Giancarlo Piretti: armchair, *Vertebra*
(1974-76), manufactured by Castelli, Italy
Masayuki Kurokawa: armchair, *Ingot Batta* (1975),
manufactured by Nippon Light Metal Co., Japan
Vico Magistretti: table, *Demetrio* (1966) and armchair,
Vicario (1971), manufactured by Artemide, Italy

Olivier Mourgue: chaise longue, *Djinn* (1965),
manufactured by Airborne, France

Museum of Modern Art, New York
Hedda Beese: portable solar lantern (1985), manufactured
by BP, UK
Mario Bellini: bench, *Forte Rosso* (1985)
Achille Castiglioni: floor lamp, *Arco* (1962), manufactured
by Flos, Italy
Luigi Colano: folding headphones (1986), manufactured by
Sony Corp., USA
Yasuhiro Kira: wind MIDI controller (1986), manufactured
by Yamaha, Japan
Shiro Kuramata: armchair, *How High the Moon* (1986),
manufactured by Vitra, Switzerland
NEC Design Center: audio teleconferencing unit,
VoicePoint (1988), manufactured by NEC Corp., Japan
Marcello Nizzoli: letter-opener (1960), manufactured by
Olivetti, Italy
Shuichi Obata: loudspeakers, *SST-1* (1988), manufactured
by Technics, USA
Ed Rossbach: *Paper Work* (1968); slip cover for a computer
(1969); raffia lace basket (1973); *Paper Work* (1974);
basket, *Gourd* (1986)
Asao Sakamoto: platters (1987 & 1989), manufactured by
Nakayamafuku Co., Japan
Timo Sarpaneva: casserole (1960), manufactured by W.
Rosenlew & Co., Finland
William N. Touzani: expandable containers (1987),
manufactured by Popeet Container Corp., USA

Philadelphia Museum of Art
Achille and Piergiacomo Castiglioni: lamp, *Arco* (1962),
manufactured by Flos, Italy
De Pas, D'Urbino and Lomazzi: clothes stand, *Sciangai*
(1974), manufactured by Zanotta, Italy
Yki Nummi: hanging lamp, *Ufo* (1960), manufactured by Oy
Stockmann, Sweden

WEST GERMANY

Kunstmuseum Düsseldorf
Susi and Ueli Berger: Tabouret and *Schubladenstapel* (1987/
1981), manufactured by Ernst Rothlisberger, West Germany
Mario Botta, Shoji Hayashi, Hans Hollein and Alessandro
Mendini: doorhandles (1986), manufactured by Franz
Schneider Brakel, West Germany
Kunstflug and Harald Hullman: glasses for sekt and schnaps
and cigarette case (1984), West Germany
Ettore Sottsass, Michael Graves and Aldo Rossi: products for
Alessi (1980s), manufactured by Alessi, Italy
Stiletto: table, *Sattelight* (1986/7)
Philippe Starck: vase, *Petite Etrangeté* (1989), manufactured
by Daum, France
Matteo Thun: tableware, manufactured by Porzellanfabrik
Arzberg, West Germany

Museum of Applied Arts, Munich
Yacoov Agam: watches, *Rainbow* collection, manufactured
by Watch Corporation, Switzerland
Bang and Olufsen: *Beo-Center 9000* (1988), Denmark
Alan Scharff: silver jug (1970), Denmark
Erich Slany Design Team: computer stand, manufactured
by Bosch/Philips, West Germany

Vitra Design Museum, Weil am Rhein
Over 1,200 designs have been collected to form this
museum, devoted primarily to the development of the chair
over the last 140 years. It was opened in November 1989
and is intended to serve as an exhibition space as well as a
permanent collection. Some major acquisitions are:
Ron Arad: all prototypes and complete interior of One Off
Studio, London
Shiro Kuramata: chair, *Miss Blanche* (1989), manufactured
by Kokuyo Co. Ltd, Japan
Jasper Morrison: all prototypes, UK
Philippe Starck: all prototypes (long-term loan), France